On the Wings of
MODERNISM

The United States
Air Force Academy

ROBERT ALLEN NAUMAN

University of Illinois Press • Urbana and Chicago

∞ This book is printed on acid-free paper.

Library of Congress Cataloging-in-Publication Data
Nauman, Robert Allen, 1948–
On the wings of modernism : the United States Air Force Academy /
Robert Allen Nauman.
p.   cm.
Includes bibliographical references and index.
ISBN 0-252-02891-0 (cloth : alk. paper)
1. United States Air Force Academy—Buildings.
2. Skidmore, Owings & Merrill—Criticism and interpretation.
3. Architecture—Colorado—Colorado Springs—20th century.
4. Colorado Springs (Colo.)—Buildings, structures, etc.
I. Title.
NA6610.C66U547   2004
727'.4358'0973—dc21   2003014286

Contents

Illustrations

Acknowledgments

This book began as a suggestion from Christopher Mead of the University of New Mexico. As my work developed, he offered continual encouragement, suggestions, and editorial comments. In the standards he set both as a scholar and a teacher, he has been an inspiration. Initial research support for the project was provided by the University of New Mexico, in the form of a Bainbridge Bunting Memorial Fellowship Award.

Since I began this project, the firm of Skidmore, Owings, and Merrill LLP and the people at the United States Air Force Academy have accommodated my endless requests with exemplary patience and kindness. Among those who warrant recognition are Alan Hinklin, director of Skidmore, Owings, and Merrill in Chicago, and Linda Marquardt and Patricia Gorman from the same office. Al Meadows, former warehouse supervisor for SOM, was an ever present help. At the Air Force Academy, Duane Reed, archivist and chief, Special Collections Branch, USAFA Library, and Duane Boyle, command architect, USAFA, offered continual help, insights, and support during this research. As the academy officials initiated new security standards following the events of September 11, 2001, they facilitated my entry onto the campus, allowing my final research to occur uninterrupted.

At the National Archives in Denver, Joel Barker, assistant regional administrator; Eileen Bolger, director of archival operations; and Joan Howard, archivist, provided assistance with the Academy Construction Agency documents. Walter Netsch cheerfully spent hours in person and on the phone with me recounting details of academy presentations, meetings, and construction. I owe a debt of gratitude to Robert Bruegmann and the others who graciously shared their research with me. Other readers who contributed invaluable comments as this book was being written include Thomas Barrow, David Craven, Vera Norwood, the anonymous readers solicited by the University of Illinois Press, and my copy editor, Carol Betts.

No acknowledgment would be complete without mentioning the friends and family who supported me during this project. The University of Colorado provided both financial and emotional support (special thanks to Joan Draper, Charles Moone, and Jerry Johnson). Many thanks also to Midge Korczak and Hal Osteen, Carl and Carla Hartman, Shaun and Trista Nauman, and my parents, Philip and Opal Nauman. Liz Goodman, friend and companion, provided constant support and help in both editing the text and correcting my computer malfunctions. To all those friends and colleagues who tolerated my obsessive behavior during this process, I offer my sincere thanks.

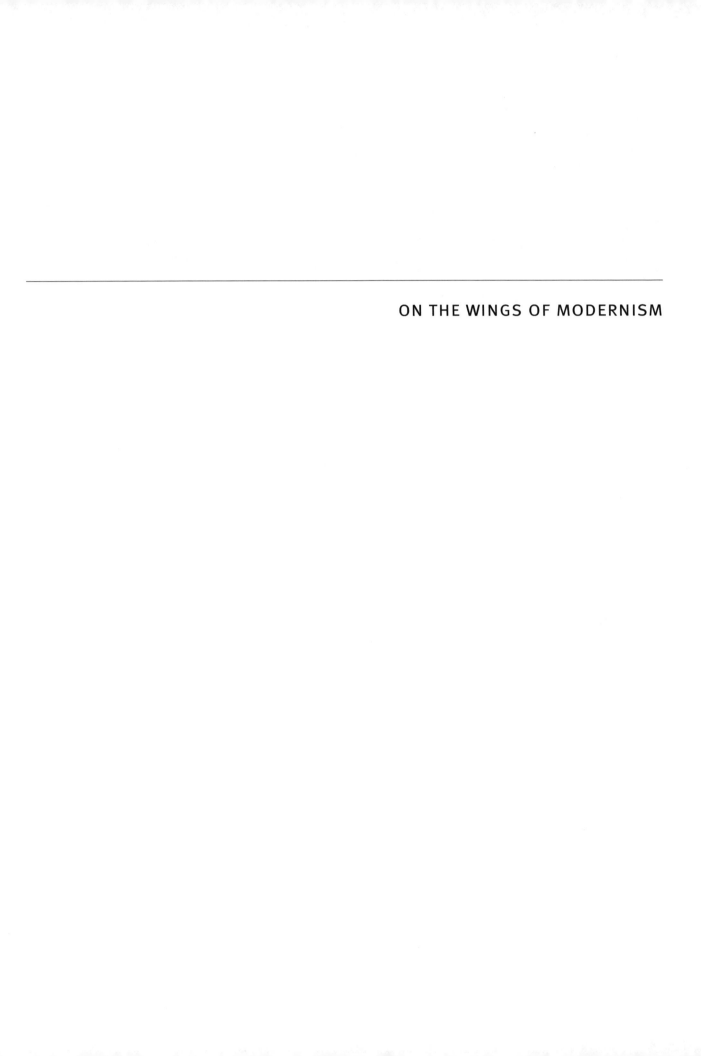

ON THE WINGS OF MODERNISM

Introduction

On July 23, 1954, the architectural firm of Skidmore, Owings, and Merrill (SOM) was awarded the contract to design and construct the United States Air Force Academy. Established during Dwight D. Eisenhower's presidency in response to the exigencies of the cold war, the Air Force Academy was intended to provide an education that would be equivalent to that of West Point or Annapolis. This study examines the history of that facility: its conception and the process of selecting its site and architect; the presentation of its initial design to Congress and the public; the reaction to that presentation and the ensuing discussion over its design; and its subsequent construction.

During its construction, the academy was defined by controversies that reflect the social and political complexities of the cold war era and reveal the problematic search for architectural meaning in the aftermath of World War II. The program of the Air Force Academy itself compounded those difficulties. Although it had to address the requirements for a university, the academy also served as a military institution. As the most recent addition to the military academies, it also had to assume the role of symbolically representing both the United States and the Air Force, as well as the philosophical and cultural agendas that defined this country during the cold war era. It was, at once, one of the largest single educational projects ever designed in this country and one of the largest government-funded projects of the time. The academy's degree of visibility in the United States and abroad made it the focus of debates within both political and public sectors. Discussions addressed pragmatic issues, such as functional requirements and cost effectiveness, and symbolic issues of meaning, including the appropriateness of the academy's modernist design vocabulary (figures 1 and 2).

From its inception, decisions affecting every aspect of the academy, from its location to its design and budget, were made within settings that were both bureaucratic and political.

Figure 1. United States Air Force Academy Cadet Area, c. 1962. Photograph by Cloyd Brunson. Stewarts Photographers and Custom Lab. Courtesy Pikes Peak Library District.

Figure 2. Cadet Area (showing retaining walls). To the left is the academic building; to the right are the cadet quarters. Photograph by Clarence Coil. Stewarts Photographers and Custom Lab. Courtesy Pikes Peak Library District.

The bureaucratic process, within the context of the academy project, refers to the formation of committees staffed by non-elected officials often associated with the military establishment. That process was employed in addressing issues such as the site selection and architect-engineer selection, and later extended into discussions about functional aspects and design. As Morris Janowitz observed at the time, military bureaucracies operated in much the same fashion as nonmilitary bureaucracies: "To analyze the contemporary military establishment as a social system, it is therefore necessary to assume that for some time it has tended to display more and more of the characteristics of any large-scale nonmilitary bureaucracy."[1] The bureaucratic process contrasted with the political process, of which Congress was a part. Congressional debates over the academy often centered around issues of funding, but the design itself also became a matter of heated discussion. Although the political processes were as hidden from the general public as the bureaucratic processes, taking place primarily in congressional subcommittee hearings, they were documented and are therefore more easily reconstructed. Operating within those bureaucratic and political parameters created problems of accountability for the architects. Congress would at times give SOM funding and permission to continue the project along certain guidelines, only to have them superseded or contradicted by military bureaucratic commissions. At other times, the reverse was true—it was the Air Force Academy Construction Agency that would authorize construction, only to be thwarted by congressional restraints. Nathaniel Owings, one of the founders of SOM, later criticized the system in his autobiography: "There was always a disturbing problem: just who was our client? By definition this at times could and did include every official with any opinion. On these terms our client's name was legion. There were the President of the United States, twelve to fourteen members of the cabinet, some ninety-six members of the Senate at the time, four hundred and thirty-five members of the House, the bureaucracy of the armed forces with special emphasis on the secretary of the air force, the undersecretary and the generals."[2]

Logically, many of those involved in the academy decisionmaking process looked to the United States Military Academy at West Point and the United States Naval Academy at Annapolis as models for both architectural form and functional requirements (figures 3 and 4). Members of the military hierarchy, Congress, and the press constantly compared the Air Force Academy to West Point and Annapolis. During the late nineteenth and early twentieth centuries, the other two academies

had undergone extensive rebuilding that employed vocabularies of historic architectural forms. West Point's rebuilding program included late nineteenth-century classical additions by Richard Morris Hunt and the firm of McKim, Mead, and White, and Gothic-style additions by the firm of Cram, Goodhue, and Ferguson, winners of the 1902 design competition for the academy. Annapolis, founded in 1845 on the site of Fort Severn, was redesigned by Ernest Flagg beginning in 1899 and was influenced by his Ecole des Beaux-Arts training.[3] In 1944, SOM architects entered a competition for additions to the West Point complex (which they failed to receive) and reached this conclusion: "After serious study of the past and present and looking into the future of West Point, it is firmly believed that the present character of architecture should be continued."[4] Ironically, SOM would later be forced to justify its modernist Air Force Academy design against the more traditional architectural vocabularies employed at those service academies.

In defending its design approach, SOM contextualized the Air Force Academy in mythic terms that related to modernism, flight, and its Colorado site. Richard Slotkin, in discussing the role of myths in defining America's West, has written that myths are stories, drawn from history, that acquire a symbolizing function over time. As their structure is increasingly conventionalized and abstracted, they become part of our language, in the form of encoded metaphors that contain various "lessons" or elements of a supposed worldview. The power of myths is their ability to appear transcendent and timeless. Their recounting implies a connection between past and present, but they also carry a heavy ideological charge. By reducing imperatives to a simple set of choices—"either/or" decisions—this process makes decisions appear preordained and relegates the audience to the role of passive participants. As Slotkin has observed, myths always have a concealed historical foundation, and it is only through careful analysis of that history that the agenda of a myth can be ascertained and recognized: "The myths we inherit carry the marks of past reworking, and beneath their smooth surfaces they conceal the scars of the conflicts and ambivalences that attended their making."[5] Slotkin's observation is appropriate when placed within the complex context of the cold war and the Air Force Academy's sleek, modernist design. The complexity of the era was reflected in debates in the public and political realms over the academy design.

In 1954, the United States was in a period of relative tranquility and prosperity, bracketed on the one hand by events of 1953—Stalin's death in March and the armistice ending the Ko-

Figure 3. United States Military Academy, West Point, New York. McKim, Mead, and White, 1897–99; Cram Goodhue and Ferguson, 1903–10+. The cadet chapel overlooks the academy. Courtesy United States Military Academy Archives.

rean War in July—and on the other hand by the October 1957 launch of Sputnik, which catapulted the Russians and the Americans into the space race and intensified the cold war. That brief tranquility, coupled with the fact that the United States had emerged as the world's most powerful nation following World War II, could lead a casual observer to conclude that the academy project resulted during a climate of nearly euphoric optimism. However, the reality was more complicated: the escalation of the cold war, the inconclusive settlement of the Korean War, and the continuing specter of nuclear warfare all were eroding the public's faith in simple political and technological solutions to society's complex problems.

The debates swirling within the architectural community over a suitable design for the academy were no less complex and were also informed by the sociopolitical conditions of the times. That the academy was realized using a modernist vocabulary—one that SOM consciously linked to the International style through presentations of its work at such prestigious institutions as New York's Museum of Modern Art—could also lead to broad conclusions: that the International style had triumphed in the battle of architectural styles in the United States and that the style's legitimacy had been established for public and national monuments. In fact, the International style was a "style" that was often contested even by its advocates, and it was only one of many strains of modernism. While it is true that debates raged in the architectural community between advocates of modernist or regionalist approaches to design, architects and critics by no means agreed about what constituted the distinctions between the two. In fact, in many cases the two areas overlapped. Debates within the military hierarchy, Congress, and the public realm also undermine any notions that SOM's modernist approach, with its technological allusions, was a preordained choice for the academy. As congressional and public critics of the design aligned and identified themselves, it became clear that a consensus on the design would never occur. Central to that discussion was the thorny issue of having the academy serve as a national monument. The association of monuments and monumentality with both Fascism and Communism during World War II and the cold war era had created a crisis of architectural meaning. How could the academy represent the United States and its history in symbolic fashion without resorting to more traditional historic styles? By linking classicizing, historicist styles with the totalitarian regimes of Fascism and Stalinist Communism, modernists had presented their case for an alternative architectural vocabulary. The question remained as to whether the glass walls, steel frames, and functional design that defined SOM's technological mandate could create a monumental presence.

Arriving at a design solution that would metaphorically represent an air academy while addressing its Colorado location created additional concerns. Metaphors of flight could be evoked to create an association between a modernist technological mandate and an air academy, but justifying a modernist design in the American West meant confronting one of America's most potent myths. SOM would need to convincingly integrate ideas of individualism, exploration, and the Western frontier in its presentations if the firm expected congressional and public approval for its design. To address these myriad concerns, SOM would draw on its past experience in mass culture and world's fair design, museum exhibition design, and the rhetoric of earlier modernists.

Curiously, although this highly visible project commanded continual media attention during its construction, little has been written about it since. While several histories, mostly produced by persons affiliated with the academy, have discussed the academy's realization in immediate terms, the project's

Figure 4. United States Naval Academy, Annapolis, Maryland. Ernest Flagg, begun 1898. The domed chapel is behind the Bancroft Hall complex that faces the harbor. Courtesy United States Naval Academy Archives.

larger historical significance has seldom been addressed in either articles or books. The academy project came to be judged
as a typical example of corporate modernism—a product of the
military-industrial complex, predictable in its goals and fail-
ures. Charles Jencks, for example, blamed the academy design
for causing cheating scandals within the institution, explaining
that the modernist quest for a transcendently objective utopia
in fact realized a regimented distopia.[6] The academy's unpopu-
larity as a subject of critical study may also be explained by a
general hostility to the military in the wake of the Vietnam War.
Richard Gid Power's 1974 article "The Cold War in the Rockies:
American Ideology and the Air Force Academy Design," informed by both the cold war and the Vietnam War, examined
the academy as a symbol as well as a result of government bureaucracy and the regulatory nature of military institutions.
Judith Stiehm's 1981 feminist text *Bring Me Men, and Women*
focused less on architectural issues than on the antiquated
and patriarchal institution of the academy itself.

Compounding these issues is the problem of critically addressing SOM's work. As early as 1949, Henry-Russell
Hitchcock defined SOM's work within the parameters of the
"architecture of bureaucracy," explaining that "by bureaucratic
architecture I mean all building that is the product of large-
scale architectural organizations, from which all personal expression is absent."[7] The impetus for such organizational principles had been provided by Frederick Taylor, in his book *The
Principles of Scientific Management.* Writing in 1911, Taylor outlined a method of factory organization that removed the conceptual and decisionmaking power from the average workers
and created a hierarchical management system. Adopted by
Henry Ford, the system soon spread to white-collar industries
and became a model for bureaucratic systems. Large architectural firms quickly adopted a similar organizational style. Working for Ford and other car manufacturers during the first decades of the century, Albert Kahn Associates (one of the
applicants for the academy commission) also equated a hierarchical organization with efficiency.[8] SOM adopted a similar
office structure, to the point that the names of individual designers were often obscured. During the academy construction,
the major partners in the firm (specifically Louis Skidmore,
Nathaniel Owings, and John Merrill) signed all the architectural
drawings, although the designs for the academy buildings were
the product of numerous persons within SOM. Even the contributions of Gordon Bunshaft and Walter Netsch, the SOM partners who attended the major design meetings and were in
charge of the academy project, have gone essentially unrecog-

nized.[9] Netsch, who oversaw the academy design, was simply
identified in SOM's proposal for the project as a "coordinator"
of an efficiently organized team. Although the firm's organizational charts created a hierarchy of authority, at no point in
these job definitions did one sense the importance of any
single individual; all worked together in their collective goal.

The division of labor among the various SOM offices also
contributed to the perception of corporate anonymity. Chicago
was the location of the original firm of Skidmore and Owings,
begun in 1934 by Louis Skidmore and his brother-in-law
Nathaniel Owings (it was not until 1939 that John Merrill, an architect-engineer, joined the firm, resulting in the new firm of
Skidmore, Owings, and Merrill). Skidmore subsequently
opened a New York office in 1937, and in 1946 Owings opened
a San Francisco office. A Portland, Oregon, office was set up in
association with Pietro Belluschi in 1951, after Belluschi accepted the job as dean of the School of Architecture and Urban
Planning at the Massachusetts Institute of Technology and approached the firm of SOM to complete the projects his firm had
begun.[10] All those offices were functioning during the academy
project. Although design directives issued from the Chicago
office, academy personnel were often confused as to what
office and which individuals within the SOM hierarchy were
"running the show."

The first publication to sort through these issues and analyze the importance of, and underlying factors behind, the
academy project was *Modernism at Mid-Century: The Architecture of the United States Air Force Academy,* edited by Robert
Bruegmann and published in 1994. The publication challenged
and questioned the modernist rhetoric that had veiled discussions of the academy, substituting specifics for generalities
and revealing the complexities of the project. However, as a
collection of chapters by various authors, it lacked a cohesive
thesis. To create that narrative required a more comprehensive
examination of archival records and primary sources to document the circumstances surrounding the academy's construction. Fortunately, both SOM and the Air Force Academy Construction Agency kept many of the records of the academy
design and construction process, ranging from isolated memoranda recounting the selection processes for the site and architectural firm, to records that trace the construction process.[11]
Those records have been supplemented by materials contained in the archives of the United States Air Force Academy
Library's Special Collections Branch in Colorado Springs. In addition, minutes of congressional hearings and comments of
both the architectural community and general public, as re-

ported by the mass media, are essential documents. They provide invaluable insights into the political and public processes that informed the academy project.

Chapter 1 of this study investigates the academy's origins. From the start, the academy project was informed by bureaucratic processes, beginning with the efforts to establish the air force as a separate service branch with its own service academy. Bureaucratic processes also lay behind the determination of the academy's location, the selection of an architect-engineer team, and the appointment of a design advisory board by the secretary of the air force to work in conjunction with the selected firm. Concerns over specific architectural approaches to the design, or how the design would relate to any given geographical location, were broached only in the vaguest of terms during this early process.

Chapter 2 deals with SOM's first public exhibition of the academy design, in May 1955. That exhibition, presented at the Colorado Springs Fine Arts Center and mounted at a cost of nearly $100,000, was ostensibly funded by the air force to introduce the academy design to members of Congress, the press, and the general public. It was envisioned as both presentation and propaganda—as a means of encouraging congressional and private funding for the academy's construction, and as a media tool to encourage youth to enlist in the air force. It was used by SOM, however, as an opportunity to increase its own visibility and to promote its modernist agenda. This chapter recounts SOM's experiences in world's fairs and museum exhibitions and the effect they had on its Colorado presentation, as well as the presentation's intersection with myths of modernism, flight, and the American West.

Chapter 3 analyzes the political response to the May 1955 exhibition, specifically as it pertained to funding the entire project. The chapter focuses upon the testimonies given before various congressional appropriations committees by members of the military hierarchy, SOM, and other involved parties. The testimonies reveal the nature of the concerns that arose regarding the academy's ability to function symbolically as a national monument and to relate to its Colorado site. This chapter also explores the manner in which SOM employed a modernist rhetoric in attempting to convince Congress to fund the project and adopt the firm's design. Although the academy project included housing for staff and families, a community center to serve their needs, and an airfield, it was the Cadet Area that became the focus of congressional and public debate. It is that area, therefore, that is the focus of this study.

Chapter 4 deals with the actual construction of the Cadet Area. In it I not only discuss the architecture as it was realized, but also outline the sources and causes of contention that accompanied the project. SOM had to deal with continual congressional debates that jeopardized the project and also found itself in conflict with the Air Force Academy Construction Agency. This chapter also addresses the circumstances that led to the selection of Walter Dorwin Teague Associates as the interior design firm and the addition of Dan Kiley as the landscape consultant.

During the construction phase, attention ultimately focused on the buildings in the Court of Honor, the most public portion of the Cadet Area, where the academy chapel became a focus of controversy. Within the context of the cold war and "godless Communism," the decision to have a chapel as the central element of the academy design was never questioned. The building's design, however, was controversial from the first public exhibition and brought its creator, Walter Netsch, into the spotlight. Chapter 5 addresses the issues surrounding the chapel—which became the most visible and recognized element of the academy design. In addition, the chapter discusses the importance of the photographic image to SOM. Photographs not only reinforced the technological attributes of the architecture, but also served to represent the abstract and formal tenets of the firm's modernist vocabulary.

A short epilogue to the book contains discussion of some of the additions and alterations that have taken place at the academy since the 1963 chapel dedication.

The United States Air Force Academy project was one of the largest of the cold war era, but it merits attention for other reasons. Its evolution provides insights into modernism and the crisis of architectural meaning during the period. Behind the technological metaphors that are often used to fit the project's forms to the academy's program lies its reality, a reality that unfolds within a cultural, social, and political context. Those dynamics were important from the project's inception, as an examination of its early history reveals.

BACKGROUND TO THE ACADEMY
The Bureaucratic Processes

The events that led to the realization of the United States Air Force Academy included sociopolitical arguments for an air academy; a site selection process for an appropriate academy location; early considerations for an academy master plan and an appropriate architectural style; and a search for an architectural firm that could handle so large a project. These processes were often bureaucratic in nature, combining practicality, economics, and political maneuverings and alliances. The people most involved in that bureaucratic process were not representatives of the architectural world but members of the military hierarchy whose decisions were informed and influenced by congressional pressures.

ESTABLISHMENT OF A SEPARATE AIR FORCE BRANCH AND AN AIR ACADEMY

The increased role that aerotechnology would play in national defense had concerned the United States since World War I. After the outbreak of the war in Europe, the Army Signal Corps's Aeronautical Division had been redesignated as the Aviation Section, which was subsequently renamed the Army Air Service.[1] Soon there were suggestions for the establishment of an air academy, whose goal would be the training of an officer elite. Early air academy feasibility studies addressed such concerns as curriculum content (whether flight training should be included, and if emphasis should be placed on technical, scientific, military, or academic studies), cost, and location. As the potential impact of aerotechnology became clearer, several Air Service officers advocated the need not only for an air academy, but for an independent air service branch.

In December 1918, Robert E. Vinson, president of the University of Texas, in conjunction with the Texas legislature, offered to donate a parcel of land near Austin as the site for an air academy. When John Ryan, who had recently resigned as the director of aircraft production for the Manufacturers Aircraft Association, reiterated the proposal a month later, he compared the role of such an air academy to that of the military academies of West Point and Annapolis. In July 1919, Representative Charles Curry of California introduced House of Representatives Bill 7925, calling for the establishment of an air academy.[2] By then, though, the war had ended, and within a year Air Service personnel had been cut from a wartime peak of 185,000 to 17,500.[3] As a result, interest in an air academy waned.

The involvement of the United States in World War II again catapulted discussions of a separate air service branch and air academy to the forefront of the political arena. The aerial attack on Pearl Harbor and awareness of the superiority of both German and English air power underscored President Franklin D. Roosevelt's 1939 charge that United States air forces were "utterly inadequate."[4] Congress responded with a $300 million air corps appropriation. Addressing the changing nature of modern warfare and the need to maintain the United States' world leadership in the field of aerotechnology, President Harry Truman signed the National Security Act, creating a separate air force branch, on July 26, 1947.[5] Within months, on January 1, 1948, the Air Policy Commission's Finletter report (named for its chairman, Thomas Finletter) urged that the air force budget be doubled. Subsequent events, including the 1948 Berlin airlift and Russia's successful detonation of an atomic device in 1949, only intensified the country's resolve to strengthen its newest military branch.[6]

At the same time, arguments for an air academy resurfaced. On August 8, 1948, at the request of Secretary of the Air Force W. Stuart Symington, a conference of fifteen civilians and officers was convened under the direction of General Muir Fairchild, vice chief of staff, to establish guidelines for such an air academy. The guidelines of the Fairchild Board, as it came to be called, were reviewed the same month and acted upon by Major General Robert Harper, commander of the Air University. On August 21, 1948, he proposed, in accordance with the board's recommendations, that the academy be established as an undergraduate institution but that it not include flight training as part of its curriculum. He made the following arguments opposing flight training: efficiency of flight training would suffer due to conflict with academic interests, and attention to academic subjects would suffer due to the nervous strain of flight training; the academic curriculum would have to be reduced drastically to accommodate flight training; scheduling problems would result because some cadets would be taking flight training and some would not, creating an academic dis-

advantage for those taking time out for flight training; and programs providing both flight and academic instruction would be formidable to administer and operate. On August 16, the Air University itself, located at Maxwell Air Force Base, Alabama, was given the overall responsibility for the early academy planning. Shortly thereafter, General Harper created the Air Force Academy Planning Board. It consisted of five task forces that examined all aspects of the academy program.[7]

On March 4, 1949, Secretary of Defense James Forrestal established the Service Academy Board to study the service academy system. The chairman of that board was Robert Stearns, president of the University of Colorado in Boulder; the vice chairman was Dwight Eisenhower, president of Columbia University. The board's recommendation, given in its final report in January 1950, was to establish a separate air academy with a four-year educational program similar to that of West Point or Annapolis.[8] That report emphasized the importance of an educational environment that would instill a sense of honor and duty, and a curriculum that would include practical experience, the development of physical stamina, and offerings in the liberal arts and sciences.

Congressional debate over the academy was heated. At issue was not only its feasibility, but its eventual location and the amount of federal funding that would be allocated to the various service branches. United States involvement in the Korean War interrupted the process, and it was not until March 29, 1954, that the academy bill was passed by Congress. On April 1, 1954, President Dwight D. Eisenhower signed Public Law 325, that provided for the establishment of a United States Air Force Academy.[9] The bill's provisions included the formation of a selection commission to determine a permanent location for the academy, and it authorized the secretary of the air force to arrange for the design and construction of the academy.

SITE SELECTION

The question of the permanent location for an air academy was hotly contested. The issue was political, since Congress members throughout the country sought to have the academy located in their particular state. Congressional debates addressing the issue had begun after World War I but intensified after a separate air force branch was created in 1947. In response, the military, attempting to exert as much control as possible over the process, adopted a bureaucratic model. Committees were formed and choices were made in an atmosphere of relative secrecy that excluded both Congress and the general public.

In November 1949, Secretary of the Air Force Stuart Symington had created a Site Selection Board to choose a suitable location for an air academy.[10] Carl Spaatz, a retired general who had served as the first chief of staff of the newly formed air force, from 1947 until 1949, was selected to chair the board.[11] Lieutenant General Hubert Harmon was also a member of the board.[12] The following month, Harmon was appointed head of the Office of Special Assistant for Air Force Matters, an office responsible for placing pressure on Congress to establish an academy.[13] Three hundred fifty-four potential academy sites were submitted to the selection board for consideration. One of the sites was Randolph Field near San Antonio, Texas, which had been suggested as a possible air academy site in 1945 and again in 1947. Completed in 1930, it had become the Air Corps Training Center and was known as the "West Point of the Air." The Randolph site was problematic, however, because it was only a 2,300-acre installation and could not be expanded by more than 2,000 acres. As early as May 1948, Colonel Leo J. Erler, acting director of installations, had suggested that the Randolph facility would be inadequate because the proposed air academy site would have to equal West Point's 15,000 acres.[14]

With the Chicago architectural firm of Holabird, Root, and Burgee serving in an advisory capacity, the selection board narrowed the list of potential sites to eight. Of those sites, five were in the western United States (including two in Colorado Springs) while the other three were located east of the Mississippi River.[15] In its April 15, 1951, report, the firm included cost estimates for the construction of an academy in each area, assuming an initial cadet population of 2,500. The average cost, including consideration for air-conditioning, was over $182 million. Complicating the site selection process was Symington's announcement in April 1950 that flight training would be included in the academy training, a reversal of the Fairchild Board's recommendation of 1948.[16] Symington's decision also substantially increased the construction budget. In a report dated February 28, 1949, the total cost for constructing an academy had been estimated at $161 million, assuming the proximity of an already existing airfield and that the academy would be built without air-conditioning.[17] Since no legislation had yet been passed providing for the establishment of an academy, none of the recommendations was acted upon.[18]

The 1954 act establishing the Air Force Academy contained a provision for the appointment of a five-member commission to select the academy site. It also stipulated that if the members agreed unanimously on a site, that location would be accepted by the secretary of the air force. If there was not consensus, the commission would select three sites and the secretary would make the final choice.[19] Within a week after the passage of that act, Secretary of the Air Force Harold Talbott appointed the Site Selection Commission. The findings of the earlier Site Selection Board were made available and two of its members, Harmon and Spaatz, were appointed to the new commission. In addition, three new members were named: Dr. Virgil M. Hancher, president of the State University of Iowa; Mr. Merrill C. Meigs, vice president of the Hearst Corporation; and Reserve Brigadier General Charles A. Lindbergh, by then retired but one of America's most renowned aviators.[20] No documents have been recovered that indicate how the membership of that commission was determined. Harmon and Spaatz had been deeply involved with academy issues from the start. One can speculate that Lindbergh was chosen for his prestige with the American public, as well as for his lengthy affiliation with the air force. In testimony before a congressional subcommittee in 1955, Talbott stated that Meigs had been "active in aircraft work for many years."[21] In addition, the Hearst Corporation had long supported the establishment of an Air Force Academy. Meigs's media experience was used to advantage by the air force hierarchy, as he handled the press relations during the site selection process.[22] As for Hancher, it was not unusual to have an advisor from the civilian academic community on these committees. Bruce Hopper of Harvard, for example, had served on the earlier Site Selection Board. In testimony before the Committee on Armed Services in the United States Senate on February 18–19, 1954, Talbott discussed only indirectly why Hancher was chosen. Responding to a question about the members of the site committee, Talbott stated, "What I have tried to do is to select men as members of this committee who come from states or locations who are not interested in the Academy being in their state." However, when asked which states those might be, Talbott singled out only Illinois, New York, and Idaho.[23]

By April 1954, 582 sites had been submitted to the commission for consideration. Commission members reported that they had visited 34 sites in 21 states and had viewed 33 additional sites in 17 states from the air. The ground inspections took place in states across the country, including Hancher's Iowa and, despite Talbott's earlier testimony, Illinois.[24] By June 3, 1954, the commission had narrowed its choices to three possibilities: Lake Geneva, Wisconsin; Alton, Illinois; and Colorado Springs, Colorado.[25] In their report, the commissioners listed the following considerations in evaluating locations: available acreage (at least 15,000 acres); topography (both the site's natural beauty and its suitability to flight instruction); community aspects (including accessibility to educational, religious, recreational, and cultural resources); climate (including providing student pilots experience in all seasons); water supply; utilities; transportation (including proximity to railway, airline, and highway systems); cost; and flight training. The section of the report headed "topography" included the following guidelines: "The Air Academy will become a national monument as are West Point and Annapolis. In selecting the permanent location, consideration will be given to the natural beauty of the site and of the surrounding country."[26] Ultimately, in reviewing the three sites, the commission members admitted they found none "superior in all respects to all others."[27] In their report to Talbott, they recommended he choose one of the three sites "without preference or priority."[28] On June 24, 1954, Talbott announced the selection of Colorado Springs as the home of the future academy. Denver's Lowry Air Force Base would serve as the interim home for the cadets during the construction phase.

The political aspects of the final site selection are unclear, but there is substantial evidence to indicate that both Talbott and Eisenhower had a hand in the Colorado site selection. Within days of the Site Selection Commission's June 3 memo, Governor Dan Thornton of Colorado wired Talbott stating, "I notice through press reports that you are the one to make the decision as to where the Air Force Academy is to be located. If there is anything I can do to be of assistance, I await your call. If you would like to come to Colorado and keep it on the quiet side, Jessie [Thornton's wife] and I will be happy to have you and Peg as our guests."[29] On another occasion, on June 19, a presidential aide recorded in his notes: "After golf . . . President and Talbott got into a lengthy discussion about the Air Force Academy and its site. While the President did not say so, the manner in which he discussed it proved to me at least that the President favored Colorado Springs as the location . . . and two or three times said he did not believe that the Air Force Academy should be located in the Middle West. . . . From Talbott's conversation, the choice has now narrowed down to Colorado Springs or Alton, Illinois. Lake Geneva, Wisconsin is definitely out."[30]

The reason for the elimination of Lake Geneva can be surmised: Eisenhower and Talbott shared a well-documented disdain for Senator Joseph McCarthy of Wisconsin.[31] Placing the prestigious academy—a "plum" facility—in his state was probably not an option either supported. In a letter to Talbott dated July 14, 1954, the outraged members of the Madison Chamber

of Commerce cited commentaries from leading newspapers and magazines noting presidential preference for a Colorado location. As further proof of bias in the selection process, they contended, "We remember your statement that the Lake Geneva Site was so completely satisfactory that you would have announced your selection of it with no further doubt, had you not been placed upon Notice by Mrs. Talbott that she assuredly would File Separation Papers the same day that you Announced Sending Anything to Joe McCarthy's jurisdictional area [capitalization in the original]."[32]

In addition to those factors, Eisenhower's fondness for the state of Colorado has been well documented. His wife's family lived there, and for years he had vacationed in Fraser at the ranch of his friend Aksel Nielsen, a Denver millionaire, where he fished and painted. Colorado Governor Thornton had also enthusiastically supported Eisenhower's nomination for the presidency.[33] During the summer of 1954, Eisenhower spent even more time in the state, moving his office to Lowry and spending a substantial amount of time at Nielsen's ranch or at Cherry Hills Country Club, where he golfed.[34]

Not all citizen groups were enthusiastic about having a military installation and flight training school in their backyards. Before the final site was selected, letters flooded into the offices of Eisenhower and Talbott protesting academy construction in their vicinity and even threatening legal action if it was considered.[35] In contrast, the Chamber of Commerce and citizens of Colorado Springs had actively campaigned to have the academy located in the area. As Lindbergh noted, "there was no other suitable site where little opposition would be encountered."[36]

Although the Colorado Springs site favorably impressed the military members of the commission, the two civilian members were opposed to it. Meigs, in particular, questioned its relative distance from other educational centers and its inaccessibility in general, a factor that seemed to fall short of the "community aspects" requirement.[37] Practical factors, however, favored the Colorado Springs site: the city had agreed to supply three million gallons of water a day to the academy, thus meeting that criterion; the site's topography and climate met the criteria for selection (in fact, the surgeon general of the air force had determined that the Colorado site had the most desirable climate of any of the sites under consideration); and it was reasoned that the academy would be in the vicinity of enough smaller population centers to satisfy the "community" criterion.[38]

The choice of an academy site in the country's western region also seemed expedient given the economic and industrial development of the American West during and following World War II. War industries had created an economic boom in the western United States, particularly on the Pacific Coast. This boom transformed the West from an area with a colonial economy, based upon the exploitation of raw materials by the eastern states, into one with a diversified economy, dependent upon the location and development of industries and government installations in the region.[39] Several writers of the period urged an economic model that would draw upon free enterprise and a mythic frontier heritage, defined by a democratic and progressive spirit. In 1946, for example, Wendell Berge noted that a key aspect in attaining western economic freedom from the East would be the successful reconversion of war plants and the employment of new technologies developed during the war in the manufacturing of new products.[40]

The growth of new technological industries, particularly aerospace and electronics, combined with the growth of aluminum and steel manufacturing needed for building ships and aircraft, put the western United States in the vanguard of postwar economic development.[41] Corporate and government investments subsidized the economic base of the region. Companies such as San Francisco's Bank of America, which had invested heavily in the aircraft industry in the West during the war and was one of the nation's largest financial institutions by the war's conclusion, began international expansion into the Pacific Rim. Bank of America opened new offices in the Philippines, Bangkok, Shanghai, and Tokyo, an expansion that depended on the establishment of American air power as a formidable peacekeeping force in the postwar political arena.[42] The aerospace industry seized the opportunity, urging the 1948 Finletter Commission to double the air force budget. Lucrative government subsidies resulted, and by 1953, with federal assistance, the aeroindustry had become the nation's largest industry, with many of its major production plants located in the western United States.

The West's transformation into a diversified economy was also due in large part to federal decision-making. The federal government had invested over $40 billion in the West during the war and had, in effect, made it a federal province. The open spaces of the region's interior became terrain for scientific experimentation and development, and the area's remoteness made it well suited for numerous military installations and training sites.[43] The West's vast expanse was also used as an argument by advocates proposing the academy be located in that region. In the November 30, 1948, editions of Hearst newspapers, an editorial argued: "It [the Air Force Academy] should be established somewhere in the great and vast Western area of the United States, preferably in California or Texas. . . . There is such a vast expanse of land and sky and sea, of mountains and desert, of climatic range and technical and tactical challenge, that air fighters trained in such an atmosphere would be without peer in the world."[44]

Colorado was similarly affected by these economic and industrial developments. The state had received numerous federal contracts and became the home to a number of military bases during the war, including Fort Carson and Peterson Air Field in Colorado Springs, Buckley Field in Denver, Pueblo Air Base, and La Junta Army Air Field.[45] The Rocky Mountain Arsenal was established in 1942 in the Denver area, and during the 1950s the state attracted many corporations associated with the aerospace industry.[46] At least part of that development was fueled by the possibility of nuclear attack and the subsequent implementation of Truman's decentralization program. The December 11, 1950, issue of Newsweek had commented, "If an atom bomb should wipe out Washington, or any other major city, what then? That grim possibility has sent top government officials on nationwide tours. . . . Recently, the search for safety has centered on one largely undeveloped region—the Denver metropolitan area."[47]

Colorado's economy was dependent not only upon federal contracts, but on eastern-based financial institutions. During the war, many of the state's defense plants, established by the federal government, were operated by out-of-state companies; following the war it was eastern, and particularly New York, capital that was invested in the region. That fact would later prompt Colorado's Governor John Love to comment: "From the beginning of the development of this community, capital came into Denver from the East, and we and the whole West were a province or possession of the money centers."[48] Interestingly, it was in his role as president of the Colorado Springs Chamber of Commerce that Love attempted to redress that situation by campaigning to have the academy located near that city. Since 1940, Colorado Springs had been concerned about a sagging tourist industry, and city supporters envisioned the academy as a boon to the economy both directly, through the cadets, and indirectly, as a tourist site.[49]

The selection of the Colorado Springs site for the academy, however, would prove problematic in ways unforeseen. Even as the site was announced, a selection committee was working on the problem of choosing an architectural firm to design the academy. That firm would eventually have to address the academy's spectacular Colorado location. More important, however, it would have to respond to the pragmatic requirements and economic constraints that had been the subject of both military and congressional attention for several years.

ARCHITECTURAL DESIGN AND MASTER PLANNING

Early discussions of the specific architectural needs of an air academy took place within a bureaucratic context. As with the site selection, the military hierarchy attempted to maintain control over the process by creating committees comprised of its own members to address those issues. The primary concerns were pragmatic—what specific buildings were needed for this new academy and how much they would cost—since those were the factors that would determine cost projections to Congress. Decisions regarding the appropriateness of a specific architectural style or design were subordinated to, and only considered after, more practical issues of master planning—a process that would continue even after an architectural firm was selected. Certainly there was no association between architectural forms and metaphors of flight or technology during this phase.

Several memoranda written years prior to the site selection provide insight into early design considerations. A memorandum dated January 5, 1949, was one of a series of documents that offered opinions without defining precise guidelines. While warning that ornamentation would increase the cost of the architecture, the memo also predicted that if "the extremes in modern architecture be used, it may result in a group of buildings which would become obsolete some 15 or 20 years in the future."[50] Recommendations were framed in terms of functional planning and economic concerns; prior to the passage of the bill creating the academy, efforts were made to convince congressional appropriations committees that their constituents' tax dollars were not being spent irresponsibly on unnecessary ornament, or on artistic expressions that would require costly revision in the near future. Ultimately, the memo recommended that "the exterior architectural appearance of the buildings would be pleasing by virtue of ingenious handling of mass, choice of materials, and the correct proportions and orientation of fenestration," which would allow myriad options for the yet-to-be determined architect. A month later a similar memorandum was sent to General R. E. Nugent, acting assistant deputy chief of staff personnel, from the Air Force Academy Planning Board. That board had been established by General Harper in August 1948 and consisted of five task forces that examined various facets of the academy's feasibility. The memo stated, "Structures were envisioned as substantial and of pleasing architecture, free of unwarranted mars [sic] and costly ornamentation."[51]

There was a broader context for these comments, rooted in federal architectural programs. During World War II, new federal buildings in the nation's capital had been constructed quickly and efficiently, with functional flexibility provided as inexpensively as possible (elements such as movable interior partitions, for example, became commonplace).[52] By 1949, the national architecture program had been transferred from the Federal Works Agency to the newly created General Services Administration, whose function it was to "simplify the procurement, utilization, and disposal of Government property."[53] W. E. Reynolds, the GSA's commissioner of public buildings, stated that "the design of future Federal buildings will be greatly simplified to achieve economy in construction and maintenance costs." Emphasis on efficiency and economy translated to "clean lines."[54] A branch post office that was constructed in Denver in 1952 reflected those concerns. Stark glass and corrugated asbestos cement panels were used on the exterior, while the interior was "a bare box," capable of being "subdivided and arranged as desired."[55]

Design criteria published in architectural magazines reflected similar concerns. An article in the January 1952 *Architectural Record* entitled "Air Force Buildings" began with the following observation: "Architects anxious to turn their talents to buildings for the Air Force will find a well formulated program, complete with planning criteria, awaiting them. . . . Planning aids take the form of 'definitive drawings' for various types of buildings (there are more than two hundred drawings), plus a set of outline specifications." That introduction further noted that these were not working drawings and that they allowed for interpretation by the individual architect, but the statement was qualified: "Architects are called upon to work to rigid dictates of economy, in fact the word 'austerity' is heard frequently in the Pentagon. In spite of the ease with which Washington talks about billions . . . military architects are extremely sensitive to murmurs of extravagance." The next page elaborated: "Of course, should the design urge run to useless embellishments or nostalgic doodads, the Engineering Corps, which makes contracts for the Air Force, will give it a crisp veto." The introduction, however, ended with a comment that encouraged regional adaptations of design within those budgetary constraints. It said of the prospective architect: "In other words, even though he may be called upon to follow floor plans with near exactness, he must determine architectural styling, must adapt plans to local climate, and will find considerable range in fenestration, overhang, materials and colors. He is still expected to be an architect, and to think as such."[56]

By 1953, in preparation for Congress's passage of the bill to establish an air academy, Harold Talbott, then newly appointed as secretary of the air force, asked the New York architect Ellery Husted to submit plans and a model for the academy. Husted had just returned from Paris, where he had been working on air force construction projects. On May 26, 1953, the combined firms of Gugler, Kimball, and Husted, and Harbeson, Hough, Livingston, and Larson of Philadelphia were awarded a contract for the substantial fee of $106,000 to prepare "Architectural and Engineering studies for an Air Academy situated on a hypothetical site."[57] Husted had previous experience with the design. In 1947, Secretary of the Air Force Symington had commissioned him to submit preliminary designs for an air academy, although those sketches have never been located. In 1953, however, air force planners and the associated firms identified the major functional units of the complex, and on February 15, 1954, they submitted two documents: "Cost Data Analysis Sheets and Diagrammatic Drawings for Preliminary Estimate" and "Study of Proposed Air Force Academy, Hypothetical Site."[58] In addition, they made a preliminary model of the academy.[59] The plan reflected the influence of two renowned campus architects—James Gamble Rogers and Paul Cret. Husted had trained in the office of the former, while the firm of Harbeson, Hough, Livingston, and Larson was the successor to Cret's office.[60]

In those early academy designs (figures 5 and 6), a U-shaped, open-ended quadrangle reminiscent of Thomas Jefferson's University of Virginia design replaced the medieval type of enclosed quadrangle of Rogers's Yale design. Like Jefferson's campus, the so-called "Husted plan," or "Husted-Kimball plan," was an axial plan centered on a large domed building at its closed end—in this case, the cadet dining hall. Although many Beaux-Arts campus planners of the time admired Jefferson's University of Virginia plan, most found his pure, single-axis plan insufficient to accommodate the more complex programmatic concerns of twentieth-century educational institutions.[61] Husted's plan, which included the major facilities of the academic area, employed secondary axes and the whole was ringed by outlying buildings, a plan type that had also been used at Randolph Air Force Base (figure 7). Comparisons may also be drawn between the Husted-Kimball plan and Cret's 1908 University of Wisconsin plan (an early example

of campus design that consisted of a major axis and cross-axes, with domed edifices serving as focal points), or Eliel Saarinen's design for Cranbrook Academy at Bloomington Hills, Michigan, constructed in the 1920s and 1930s.[62]

The specific architectural style of buildings in the Husted plan was vague, as were the construction specifications. A memorandum following a November 1953 meeting of Husted, General Harmon, and Colonel Herbert C. Person, chief of the Planning and Programming Division of the Department of the Air Force, stated that "the treatment of details of building were not of great importance as long as the buildings were intelligently planned and contained the information to support a budget figure."[63] Thus, the design for the Roman Catholic chapel was indicated simply by a Latin cross. Many of the building plans revealed a strong preference for symmetry, complementing the Beaux-Arts composition of the whole. The general style, as suggested only on diagrammatic drawings, seems to have been a sort of stripped-down classicism, close to the federal architectural styles that had been favored in the 1930s.[64] Above all, the Husted plan was intended to provide a model for addressing the primary components of the project—its programmatic and functional needs—which were identified as the Cadet Area, housing, and the airfield. In this regard, the designs parallel Rogers's approach. Rogers, trained in the Beaux-Arts, believed that the architectural character or style of specific works should be expressed only after the plan had been efficiently organized according to the client's functional demands and after appropriate materials and the larger context of the work had been examined.[65]

Afraid that their own lack of expertise might lead to "grave and irreparable blunders," air force personnel made visits to other university campuses. In June 1953, for example, key personnel arranged to visit and study the University of Mexico campus, then under construction, with the intent of returning with ideas that might inform their own.[66] Their written request for permission to make the trip to Mexico, however, indicated they still thought of the academy design in the vaguest of terms: "We believe the plans should also take into account the advantage of providing buildings and grounds of beauty which will inspire young men to strive for an Air Force career."[67] The University of Mexico project, initiated in 1950, was smaller than the proposed academy undertaking, encompassing approximately 1,730 acres and having a budget of just over $20 million. But its programmatic concerns were similar to those of the academy: the site would be divided into academic, recreational, and residential sectors, with a separate stadium loca-

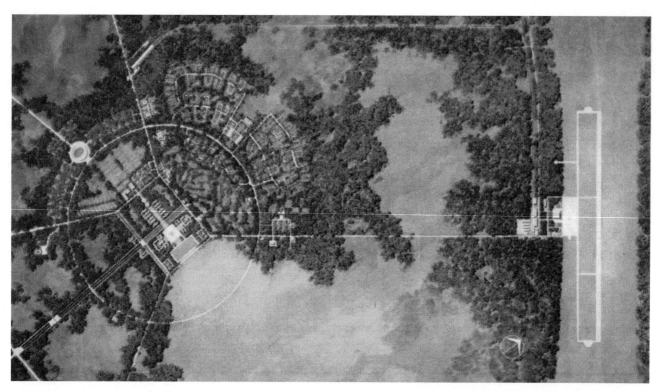

Figure 5. Husted-Kimball plan for Air Force Academy, 1954. Courtesy United States Air Force Academy Special Collections Branch.

Figure 6. Husted-Kimball plan for Air Force Academy, 1954. Courtesy United States Air Force Academy Special Collections Branch.

tion. In addition, it was a coordinated effort of approximately 150 architects, engineers, sculptors, and painters, realized over a three-year period.[68]

In his report written after studying the Mexican campus, Colonel George Dany mentioned that although the project cost only $22 million, it would have cost ten times that amount if constructed in the United States, hinting that perhaps it was too expensive a solution to be employed in the United States. While Dany commented that the architecture blended harmoniously with its locale, he also stated that whether this "massive-column type of architecture can be scaled down to be effectively used in the construction of a smaller facility is problematical."[69] Colonel Dale Smith, on the other hand, reported that the campus was "functional," noting its division into six zones, and that the exterior materials—brick, glass, and concrete—would require little maintenance. In terms of ornamentation, he was struck by the dramatic use of murals in the design.[70] These reports, addressing concerns of function and economic feasibility, indicate not only a critical approach to campus design, but a concern with how the project would be presented to members of Congress for approval.

Talbott's activities during this time indicate similar concerns. On October 19, 1953, Talbott made a trip to Colorado Springs to consult with Lieutenant Colonel Arthur E. Boudreau

about the academy project, because he had received little information regarding it. Boudreau had served as project officer of the Air Force Academy Planning Board from 1948 to 1949. Two days later, he met with Harmon and several other air force personnel to discuss the matter of the academy's projected cost, in preparation for congressional hearings. Advised by Harmon that the cost could be substantially reduced by adopting "a much cheaper type of architecture," Talbott stated he wanted only the best, and costs would be cut only through the elimination of "non-essentials." His list of "non-essentials" did not relate to architectural style. Talbott targeted the flight training program, stating that the initial cost for aircraft alone would be $25 million. He also thought costs could be reduced by funding the construction of facilities such as the library, museum, hospital, and field house through private sources.[71]

At the January 1954 House committee hearings, which focused on the academy bill, Talbott stated, "the Academy design should become a national monument as are West Point and Annapolis. We hope to make of it an institution in which the people of America will have faith and pride. In my opinion, this requires fine engineering[,] design and construction."[72] His discussion focused upon curriculum, site, and budgetary constraints. In his January 13 appearance before Congress, Talbott gave cost estimates for an air academy at just over $125 mil-

Figure 7. Randolph Air Force Base, San Antonio, Texas, 1931. USAF Photograph.

lion. Yet, several weeks later the firms of Gugler, Kimball, and Husted, and Harbeson, Hough, Livingston, and Larson, which Talbott had paid handsomely to do preliminary cost analyses of the proposed academy, projected the cost at over $145 million.[73] Talbott confided to air force personnel that he thought Congress would not approve such a large figure. Nonetheless, the following month Major General Lee B. Washbourne, who was director of installations and probably aware of the Husted figure, testified before Congress that the projected cost of the academy would be $145 million.

Harmon, who recommended to Talbott a "cheaper style of architecture," expressed various opinions regarding possibilities for the academy's architectural style during this time. Early in the process, in 1951, he had cited modern edifices as admirable models for the academy, equating an unornamented modernist style with cost efficiency. He specifically singled out Edward Durrell Stone's recently constructed El Panama Hotel, which he mentioned he had seen in the April 1951 issue of *Architectural Forum,* as an example, stating that "the general style might very well be adapted."[74] But he also continually made references and comparisons to West Point, including its "classic traditions." His use of the word "classic" to refer to the collegiate Gothic forms of West Point can be understood only generically, perhaps reflecting his conservative preferences in planning. In a letter of March 1954 to Lieutenant General Laurence Kuter, he referred to the Christ Church quadrangle at Oxford University and noted, "I, myself, like the idea of enclosed area or areas, i.e., one or two large buildings each in the form of [a] quadrangle with a large open 'patio' in the middle."[75] As late as April 1955, after Skidmore, Owings, and Merrill had already been selected for the project, Harmon submitted his own proposed plans for the academy to the firm, with the major buildings arranged symmetrically along an axis.[76] Gordon Bunshaft later recalled that Harmon recommended a Spanish colonial style of architecture for the academy.[77]

All of these events indicate that the issue of architectural style in these early discussions was, as expected, less important than issues of budget and function. After Eisenhower signed the academy into existence and a search began for an architecture-engineering firm to tackle the project, pragmatic concerns continued to be the focus of discussion. It was important to select a firm that could effectively and efficiently construct the academy within the allotted budget. It is not surprising that the military hierarchy wanted to control that selection, and that the process would be carried out within a bureaucratic context.

ARCHITECT SELECTION PROCESS

The primary concern of members of the air force hierarchy in selecting a firm to design and construct the academy was to choose an entity that would work with them efficiently and co-operatively, in order to meet their goal of opening the academy by June 1957. As a military campus, the academy would have different needs than those of a civilian college, and the choice of a firm that had previous dealings with the military establishment would facilitate meeting the goal. More important, an experienced architectural firm would presumably avoid embarrassing cost overruns that would have to be explained to Congress and would lead to damaging publicity in the public sector.

These concerns were especially important to Secretary of the Air Force Talbott, who was responsible for every aspect of the academy project. He had overseen the site selection, was responsible for any additional land acquisition, and was ultimately responsible for all the contracting that would lead to the construction of the academy. Like many of Eisenhower's cabinet members, Talbott was very shrewd when it came to business matters. Many of Eisenhower's appointments in the Department of Defense came from the corporate sector, which had sometimes led to problems in Senate confirmation hearings due to conflicts of interest. Talbott's selection as secretary of the air force in February 1953 had been a matter of controversy, since he had holdings in the Chrysler Corporation and North American Aviation. Secretary of Defense Charles E. Wilson had been president of General Motors, and Deputy Secretary Roger M. Kyes had been associated with General Motors as a vice-president of procurement and schedules. In defending himself against conflict-of-interest charges before the Senate Committee on Armed Services during the confirmation proceedings, Wilson made his famous statement, "I thought what was good for our country was good for General Motors, and vice versa." Secretary of the Navy Robert Bernerd Anderson had affiliations with Associated Refineries, while Secretary of the Army Robert Ten Broeck Stevens had connections to a textile factory that sold uniforms to the military.[78] These men were comfortable with the corporate world—a world that measured its effectiveness in terms of organizational skills. In 1956, C. Wright Mills termed these men the "power elite." They were men, Mills observed, who were able to move among the hierarchies of the military, political, and industrial worlds because they had the administrative and organizational skills that were valued in each of those sectors, and thus they controlled much of the decisionmaking process in the United States after World War II.[79] As a member of that "power elite," Talbott had hired a management consultant team two months prior to the 1952 presidential elections "to determine which posts it would be necessary for a Republican administration to take over in order to control the government of the United States." Eisenhower received a fourteen-volume report of the findings several days after his election.[80]

Talbott would have had little tolerance for an architectural firm that was more concerned with artistic expression than with the organizational and administrative skills that he himself possessed. Since he ultimately answered to Congress and the public, it is small wonder that Talbott wanted to exert as much control as possible over the architect selection. As Mills wrote, "the formation of the power elite rests upon . . . the increased public secrecy behind which great decisions are made without benefit of public or even Congressional debate."[81] Talbott could ill afford to have that decision made in a fashion that would allow an unknown firm to gain the commission; this was not the project for an inexperienced firm. Nor would he have been adverse to the corporate manner of doing business—through personal contacts and over business lunches. It was in that domain that he felt most comfortable and most able to determine whether he could personally get along with those in the firm of his choice.

Preparation for the selection of an architectural firm to design and construct the academy had begun years prior to Eisenhower's signing Public Law 325. In 1950, General Myer's office had issued a memo stating that a conference had been held with Leopold Arnaud, dean of the architecture school at Columbia University, "with reference to proper procedure for a national competition for the selection of an architect to prepare plans for the construction of the permanent Air Academy."[82] An air force memo dated July 1951 provided two scenarios for the eventual selection of an Air Force Academy "architect-engineer firm." Those procedural guidelines were based on an American Institute of Architects (AIA) brochure entitled *Architectural Competitions,* which had been published the previous month. The first method was the one of which the Myer's memo spoke—one that would require a twelve-to eighteen-month selection period. The second, "desirable from the standpoint of cost and time," was termed "selection by negotiation." Using this procedure, firms were to be evaluated on the basis of "technical qualifications, experience, organization, availability, reputation, and financial responsibility." A planning group would then be established by the air force to work in close contact with the selected architect-engineer; that group "should make recommendations to the commanding general regarding the approval of such matters as style of architecture, layout of the base, and all plans and specification."[83]

There was a substantial difference between those two methods of architect selection. In the first, the architectural firm would determine an appropriate style for the academy—a decision presumably based upon its expertise—and the appropriateness of the style would be judged by "a Professional Advisor and a Jury of at least three prominent members." Using the second model, "the contracting officer together with parties responsible for the project" would meet with the selected firm or firms and negotiate cost figures and oversee the design. It is not clear in the memo which parties within the military hierarchy would be responsible for selecting those firms, but the memo did note that this process "may be subject to charges of favoritism." In any case, it would be a military planning group that would have the task of determining an appropriate style for the academy, with the selected architect(s) realizing those recommendations.

On January 29, 1954, Colonel Person enclosed the 1951 AIA brochure in a memo to Major General Washbourne and recommended the first option. He suggested a national competition similar to those that had been held for other government projects, such as the United States Military Academy, the Smithsonian Institution, the Jefferson National Expansion Memorial in St. Louis, and the Oregon State Capitol. The purpose would be to choose architectural and engineering talents worthy of the commission, as well as to forestall congressional criticism and pressure during the selection process.[84] Washbourne's response to Person's two-page typed memorandum was a cursory handwritten note, advising they wait until the bill approving the academy had passed. Washbourne added, "Would site selection limit your competition?"[85] His question most likely referred to a point raised in the AIA brochure. In the discussion of the "selection by negotiation" process, it was noted that "emphasis is placed on the employment of local firms when practical and feasible." In fact, it would be suggested on several occasions during the selection process that the architectural firm that received the academy contract would have to retain a local firm as part of a joint venture.[86]

The architectural community, of course, had not been oblivious to the impending passage of a bill calling for the establishment of an academy. Well aware of the monetary gain and prestige that would be afforded by the huge commission, firms from around the country had begun to inquire about it in the late 1940s. For example, on March 28, 1949, William Delano of the firm Delano and Whitney had written to his friend Cornelius V. Whitney, assistant secretary of the air, asking about the project.[87] The first record of SOM's interest in the academy project is a memo of December 22, 1953, which John B. Rodgers, a partner in SOM's San Francisco office, wrote to the other partners in the firm. He alerted them that Colonel Simon Lutz, an air force liaison officer in San Francisco, had mentioned that Eisenhower's administration favored the establishment of an Air Force Academy and that SOM would be in a good position to get the commission. Rodgers, who had negotiated SOM's Guam and Ryukus Islands air force contracts in Tokyo with Lutz in 1950, also identified other air force personnel whom SOM might contact, including General Washbourne and Colonel Leo J. Erler.[88] At the time, Erler was deputy director of installations under Washbourne and had been director of installations for SOM's work in the Far East.[89] Rodgers also confided that Lutz felt SOM was in good position for the academy contract due to previous work it had done for the military (he specifically cited the Navy Postgraduate School and the Air Force Institute of Technology at Dayton) and the fact that the firm was not presently involved in working on the Spanish bases.[90] The memo, which reveals SOM's use of a network of acquaintances to get an inside track on the commission, also suggested a list of previous projects that might be used as references, and it put a hypothetical cost on the project (given to Rogers by Lutz at $50 to $75 million).

Within the week Rodgers had consulted with Owings and had again contacted Lutz to ascertain the timing of the academy contract. According to a January 7, 1954, interoffice memo initiated by Rodgers, Owings had told Rodgers of his friendship with James Douglas, under secretary of the air force and a confidant of Talbott.[91] The communiqué also mentioned that Harmon would be heading the site selection process. On February 5, 1954, Rodgers sent another interoffice communication to "All Partners" stating that he had maintained contact with Lutz, who was informing him of the progress of the academy bill. He had also contacted Lieutenant Colonel Charles Busbee, an air force liaison officer for medical buildings, and received information on possible sites, including locations in Texas, California, and Missouri.[92]

On March 9, 1954, Owings submitted a formal request to Talbott asking that SOM be considered as architects-engineers for the United States Air Force Academy. He included a brochure that outlined SOM's office organization and its work experience during the past ten years. Although declining to com-

mit to engineering associates until the academy bill was officially signed and a specific academy site was selected, Owings mentioned his preference for the following firms, with whom SOM had worked on previous government projects: Syska and Hennessy; Moran, Proctor, Mueser, and Rutledge; and Weiskopf and Pickworth.[93]

Two days later, the criteria to be used for the preliminary screening of the architect-engineer for the Air Force Academy were sent through air force channels. Those criteria included: must be a United States firm; must be experienced in handling large-scale projects; must have completed projects for the armed forces; and must have an adequate staff to complete the project.[94] No mention was made that the preliminary process would include the submission of any specific design proposals. That same day, March 11, the Air Force Academy Project Office was established "to commence the planning for the design and construction of the Air Academy."[95]

Within a week, Rodgers lunched with Lutz and then conveyed more information to Owings regarding the project. According to Lutz, the most likely academy site was now Peterson Air Force Base in Colorado Springs, with Camp Beale, California, and an unnamed site in Texas being considered as other possibilities. Lutz had informed Rodgers that Harmon and Spaatz were to be on the Site Selection Commission, and he had added that any firm getting the job would likely have to associate with a local firm from the state where the site was located. Past association and familiarity with air force procedures would be viewed favorably, leading Rodgers to suggest to Owings that SOM stress its work on Andersen Air Force Base in Guam. According to Lutz, Erler and the air force liked the efficient manner in which the firm handled that project. In his memo to Owings, Rodgers noted that SOM's work in Guam was "one of the few, if not the only instance, in which an architect-engineer has worked on the contract directly with the Air Force on a project of this size."[96] Most important, the memo implied, would be a firm's knowledge of, and ability to work with, a government bureaucracy.

Stressing the work the firm had done in Guam, SOM now began to compile a résumé of completed projects and continued to contact people close to the academy project. A memo from William Hartmann, an SOM partner, to Owings on April 2, 1954 (the day after Eisenhower signed the bill establishing the academy) advised him to call James Douglas and arrange for a meeting with Douglas and Talbott the following week.[97] A memo from "Jim" [Douglas] to "Nat" [Owings], dated March 17, had previously confirmed that Douglas would be glad to introduce Owings to Talbott.[98] Jack Hennessy, a partner in the engineering firm of Syska and Hennessy, was also asked to attend the meeting. Syska and Hennessy had worked on numerous projects with SOM and had also established Washington connections with its government work at air bases (including Lowry in Denver) and West Point.

Talbott, meanwhile, wrote a letter to the Air Force Chief of Staff on April 2 recommending that an Architect-Engineer Selection Board made up of three "distinguished and disinterested" civilians select the architect for the commission: "Professor Talbott Hamlin, Professor of Architectural History at Columbia University; Lewis Mumford, architectural critic on the staff of the *New Yorker Magazine*; and Pietro Belluschi, Dean of the School of Architecture at MIT, a practicing architect until his selection as Dean."[99] The entire process for choosing the architect-engineer, he wrote, was expected to be completed within two weeks of approving the selection board. How Talbott or his advisors arrived at the list of civilian advisors is unknown. Eisenhower had served as president of Columbia University, and perhaps he recommended Hamlin. Mumford would have qualified as a distinguished committee member as well. In addition to his work at the *New Yorker,* he had written numerous publications by this time that addressed issues of urban planning. Belluschi not only had the highly visible position of dean at the Massachusetts Institute of Technology (MIT) but also was a member of the Commission of Fine Arts, which had jurisdiction over public works in Washington, D.C. His career as an architect was connected with SOM. Belluschi's firm in Portland had been acquired by SOM in 1951, and (until 1956) that part of the firm operated as Belluschi/Skidmore, Owings, and Merrill.[100] In January 1954, he had been invited to serve on the four-member Architectural Advisory Committee to recommend appropriate architectural styles for prospective United States building projects overseas.[101] That Talbott's committee had a decidedly East Coast bias was to be expected in a committee chosen by Pentagon-based officials.

Within days, memoranda indicated that the composition of the selection board had been rethought, reflecting the increased role the air force hierarchy sought in determining the architect. Colonel E. V. N. Schuyler, chief of the Engineering Division and Directorate of Construction of the Air Force, responded to a memo from Lieutenant Colonel C. A. Eckert, officer in charge of the newly established Project Office of the academy, which required that the selection board be comprised of both civilian and military members. Eckert asked the engineering division to nominate at least six civilians who

might serve on the board. Schuyler nominated eight, including Belluschi and Walter Gropius, the latter identified as "Former head, School of Architecture, Harvard University."[102] Eckert narrowed the list to four: Belluschi; Clair Ditchey, president of the AIA; Allen Thorn, supervising architect of the Public Building Service in Washington, D.C.; and Ernest Langford, dean of the Department of Architecture at Texas A & M.[103] The basis for those choices is a matter of conjecture. While Belluschi and Thorn were highly visible in the capital's decisionmaking bureaucracy, and Ditchey occupied a prominent and prestigious position in the architectural world, the reason for the choice of Langford is unclear. Eckert also tentatively named three military members for the board—General Harmon, General Washbourne, and Chief of Staff A. W. Milton—and forwarded the list to Talbott.[104]

On April 8, James Douglas convened a meeting in his office, which was attended by Washbourne and members of the general's staff. At that meeting, it was suggested that a selection board of seven military members evaluate the architect-engineer applicants and submit nominations of the three foremost firms to the secretary of the air force by May 15. The proposed selection board was comprised of Generals Harmon, Washbourne, and Milton, Colonel Schuyler, and Mr. Carl Sanford, Mr. Richard Rio, and Mr. John Ferry.[105] While some of the proposed members had experience with architecture, planning, or engineering, others were simply administrators or upper-echelon officers in the military establishment. In addition, a design advisory board composed of three members of the architectural community—Ditchey, Belluschi, and Skidmore—was suggested "to ascertain the style or the prospective styles of architecture most appropriate to the locale of the Academy." How Skidmore came to be included on this list is unknown. It could have been because of his architectural background, his firm's work for the military, personal connections, or a combination of all of those factors. But one thing was peculiar: two of the appointees were technically members of the same firm, since Belluschi was still legally a partner with SOM. Whether the group at the meeting realized the implication of its decision is unknown. Douglas certainly knew that SOM had asked to be considered for the commission—on April 9 Owings wrote him, thanking Douglas for setting up a meeting between SOM representatives and Talbott.[106] Ultimately, Talbott decided he would rather wait to appoint the design advisory board until after the working architect had been designated.[107]

Events of the following few weeks reveal that architects at SOM continued to work on personal contacts and acquaintances to gain the inside track to their appointment as official academy architects. Their method of doing business certainly would not have seemed inappropriate or unusual in the corporate world of the Eisenhower era. On April 9, Owings sent a memo to Jack Hennessy, of Syska and Hennessy, stating, "I hope you'll go to work on Ferry."[108] Hennessy answered Owings within the week, stating he would indeed go to Washington and see Ferry, and that his son knew people in the installations section of the Pentagon whom he would contact.[109] On April 13, Owings "dropped in" on Colonel Erler. He also notified Erler in a memo that the SOM team that would be involved in the academy project would include John Merrill, a partner in the firm, and "associate partners Tallie Maule, Walter Netsch, John Weese and Carl Russell," all of whom had worked in Okinawa with Erler.[110] Erler replied six days later, assuring Owings that "I shall be most happy to indorse [sic] the capabilities of your organization for this job should the opportunity permit."[111] Upon receiving Erler's letter, Owings responded, saying that he would be "taking the liberty" of sending Netsch to show Erler the material SOM would be presenting for its application.[112] A letter to Owings from Hennessy dated April 26 stated he had contacted Ferry and Rio, who told him that a selection board had not yet officially been chosen, but that after it was established its membership would be kept confidential.[113]

In the meantime, on April 6, a form letter had been mailed by the Department of the Air Force to all the architectural firms that had expressed an interest in the academy project. Attached to it was a questionnaire, to be completed and returned by May 1—a deadline that was later extended pending the determination of the site. The letter stated: "The selection of an architect-engineer will be made by the Secretary of the Air Force, assisted by a qualified Selection Board, using as a basis the information contained in brochures [submitted by the firms] and the attached questionnaire." Information in the packet stated that Congress and the president had approved a bill authorizing the appropriation of $125 million for the construction of the academy on a site to be determined. The project, to design an academy to educate and train future air force officers, would include: administration, academic, laboratory, training, and office buildings; cadet and airmen barracks and mess halls; library, museum, hospital, and chapels; housing; gymnasium, field house, swimming pool, and other athletic and recreational facilities; shops, warehouses, power and heating plants, utilities, roads, airfield pavements, and other operational support facilities. The letter further stated that the air force would provide descriptive outlines of materi-

als and methods of construction and schematic plans of typical and special buildings. All working drawings for facilities were to be approved by the air force. The completed questionnaire, to be mailed to General Washbourne, would contain a description of the organization of the responding architect-engineer firm, including the responsibilities of each member of the joint venture, and a listing of the firm's principals along with their experience in design and construction work with the armed services; the firm's experience, including a listing of commissions during the past five years and a description of how such commissions were handled; the capability and staff of the firm, including the size of the organization, who in the organization would assume responsibility for the project, and who would perform tasks such as materials tests and drafting work; projected time of completion, including when the work could be started; and work supervision at the job site, identifying who would represent the firm at the job site and who would be the liaison between the firm and the air force.[114]

Later in April, John Ferry wrote a letter to the secretary of the AIA informing him of the selection process for the architects of the academy. His letter included the following provision: "No formal design competition is planned as it is our view that the past record of achievements is the major factor in the determination of the selected firm."[115]

On May 25, 1954, SOM submitted its completed questionnaire and a company brochure to Erler, Eckert, and Lieutenant Colonel J. R. White for a preliminary review. Eckert, as previously mentioned, was in charge of the newly formed Project Office for the Air Force Academy, while White served under him in the same office. On May 27, the completed proposal was officially presented to the air force by Robert Cutler, a partner in SOM's New York office; John Weese, an associate partner in the Chicago office; and John Hennessy.[116] The proposal identified the firms of Moran, Proctor, Mueser, and Rutledge, consulting engineers, and Syska and Hennessy, incorporated engineers, as SOM's joint venture partners. Still looking for opportunities to make a last-minute favorable impression, Weese wrote Cutler on the same day, May 27, advising him that Owings thought he should hand-deliver to Washington some missing information on the Connecticut General Life Insurance Building in Bloomfield, Connecticut, an SOM project then being built: "He [Owings] thought we should get the sheets that are missing from the second brochure for Connecticut General and have somebody take them to Washington, using that as an excuse for making another contact with the people in the Air Force Academy Project Office."[117]

On June 1, the Air Force Academy Project Office was super-seded by the newly created Air Force Academy Construction Agency (AFACA). Its mission, like that of the Project Office, was "to direct the planning, designing, and construction of an Air Force Academy."[118] Erler, who had replaced Schuyler on the architect selection board days earlier, was appointed its director, and on June 25 (the same day Talbott announced the academy site) he mailed a formal invitation to SOM representatives to appear before the board. That interview, to be scheduled between July 7 and 9, was to include a "general discussion regarding your proposed architectural and structural concepts for the Air Academy."[119] On June 29, Weese called Erler to confirm the time and the specifics of that meeting. The presentation would be one hour long, with an additional half hour reserved for discussion or questions.[120]

On June 30, SOM was again contacted by Lutz, who mentioned he had been transferred from San Francisco to Erler's office in Washington. Lutz advised the firm that, for political reasons, Erler had mentioned the firm might want to associate with a local (Colorado) architect.[121] James Hammond, an SOM associate partner, suggested the firms of Temple Buell, Burnham Hoyt, or Fisher and Fisher.[122] The following day Skidmore advised Owings that a former classmate had worked for Hoyt, and he also mentioned Fisher and Fisher and Gordon Jamieson.[123] There is no indication that any of these suggestions were pursued.

FINAL INTERVIEWS AND THE ACADEMY ARCHITECT SELECTION

Over three hundred firms applied for the academy commission. They included some of the most prestigious architectural offices in the country: Mies van der Rohe; Philip Johnson and Pace Associates; Holabird, Root, and Burgee; Albert Kahn; William Lescaze; Neutra and Alexander; Perry, Shaw, and Hepburn; Reinhard, Hofmeister, and Walquist; and Shepley, Bullfinch, Richardson, and Abbott (for a partial listing of the applicants, see appendix 1).[124] By late June, the roster of applicants had been reduced to a short list of eight finalists. Exactly what procedures were used to arrive at the short list is unknown, although presumably emphasis was placed upon previous government work. In an SOM interdepartmental memo dated July 1, Hammond wrote that Rodgers had told him that Lutz (via Erler) had stated that preference would be given to firms with broad experience in designing academic institutions, including master planning.[125] In the letter officially informing the finalists of the day and time of their interviews, Erler stated that the issue of the fee for the commission would not be discussed at the interview, and that the final decision on the architect-engineer would not be made before July 26, since Talbott would be in Europe at the time of the interviews.[126]

The following eight firms were interviewed by the selection board at the Pentagon Building in Washington, D.C., on July 8 and 9, 1954: Pereira and Luckman; Harrison and Abramovitz; York and Sawyer, Kiff, Colean, Voss, and Souder; Eero Saarinen and Associates; Kittyhawk Associates; T. H. Buell and Company; Voorhees, Walker, Foley, and Smith; and Skidmore, Owings, and Merrill (for more information regarding the finalists, see appendix 2). The list of finalists favored firms with government or corporate connections. This underscores the probability that these firms pursued the same bureaucratic channels as SOM in attempting to land the prestigious academy commission.

Pereira and Luckman had worked on government commissions as recently as 1952, when they designed facilities at Camp Pendleton in California. Having been warned in mid-May by Colonel Eckert that preference would be given to joint venture applicants, they associated with the Detroit firm of Giffels and Vallet, Inc., L. Rossetti, a firm that had also worked on government commissions.[127] During World War II, Giffels and Vallet had done work for the Atomic Energy Commission and the National Aeronautic Advisory Commission. In its August 1955 issue, *Architectural Forum* reported that Pereira and Luckman were eliminated from the academy's finalist list because they were designing the Spanish air bases, although the magazine's sources of information are questionable since the same sentence stated that Eero Saarinen had not been selected as one of the finalists for the academy commission.[128] More likely, Pereira lacked the political contacts and experience with government commissions that SOM had amassed.

Wallace K. Harrison and Max Abramovitz had served as directors of planning for the United Nations Permanent Headquarters (appointing Louis Skidmore as one of their consultants). By the time of the academy competition, the firm had worked on myriad corporate and government projects, including commissions for the United States Navy and several United States embassies. Included in its joint venture were the following firms: Gugler, Kimball, and Husted; Harbeson, Hough, Livingston, and Larson; Praeger and Cavanagh; and Ammann and Whitney. Gugler, Kimball, and Husted, in association with Harbeson, Hough, Livingston, and Larson, had prepared both the earliest plans for the proposed air academy, in 1947–48, and preliminary sketches and a scale-model of the academy, in 1953–54. Their absorption into a larger joint venture was probably undertaken for practical reasons. At the time of their 1953–54 work, Talbott had confided "he did not think the present architect, Mr. Hustead [*sic*], was large enough to handle the architectural designs."[129] Husted also did consulting work for various government agencies, such as the Federal Civil Defense Administration, while the firm of Harbeson, Hough, Livingston, and Larson served as consultants to the American Monuments Commission and designed hospitals for the United States Navy. Ammann and Whitney had worked with Gugler, Kimball, and Husted in preparing cost estimates for the proposed academy in 1954.

Kiff, Colean, Voss, and Souder, the successor firm of York and Sawyer, had designed United States naval facilities in 1950 and 1952. The other firms in their joint venture included Anderson and Beckwith; Masten and Hurd; Huber and Knapik; Adache and Case; and Fay, Spofford, and Thorndike. The architectural firm of Anderson and Beckwith was headed by Lawrence Anderson and Herbert Beckwith, both of whom taught at MIT and had designed laboratory facilities there.

Eero Saarinen had worked during the war for the Office of Strategic Services in Washington, D.C. The largest postwar project of Saarinen, Saarinen, and Associates was the General Motors Technical Center, done in association with Smith, Hinchman, and Grylls, Inc., Architects and Engineers, the same firm with whom it associated for the academy project. The $160 million project was one of the two largest projects of the 1950s; the other was the Air Force Academy. At the time of the academy project, Eero Saarinen was completing the United States Embassy in Oslo, Norway. The engineering firm of Knappen, Tippetts, Abbett, and McCarthy completed the joint venture team.

Kittyhawk Associates consisted of members from various firms around the country.[130] The group was supervised by M. G. Probst, president of Graham, Anderson, Probst, and White of Chicago. The conglomerate firm seems to have had few government contacts at the time of the academy competition. Its joint venture team included the following firms: Mitchell and Ritchey; E. J. Kump of Kump and Falk, Architects-Engineers; Richard Hawley Cutting and Associates; Harold Bush-Brown of Bush-Brown, Gailey, and Heffernan, Architects; Robert and Company Associates, Architects and Engineers; Burns and Roe, Inc.; George B. Cunningham; and R. J. Tipton. Mitchell and Ritchey had earlier collaborated with Harrison and Abramovitz;

Ernest Kump, of Kump Associates, Architects, in San Francisco, was best known for his school designs; and Richard Hawley Cutting and Associates of Cleveland had designed a number of housing projects and had served as consultants to the air force for air fields in England and France. Harold Bush-Brown, of Bush-Brown, Gailey, and Heffernan, Architects, was director of the Department of Architecture at the Georgia Institute of Technology, where the firm had designed an engineering building and a library. Early in the selection process for the academy, he had been recommended as a civilian consultant. The Atlanta firm of Robert and Company had designed a variety of civilian projects, including hospitals, offices, and museums; Burns and Roe, Inc., of New York was an engineering firm that had designed jet-testing facilities and other aerodynamic installations in the United States; George B. Cunningham had liaison experience with air force construction and had been involved with air base, school, and hospital designs; and R. J. Tipton of Denver was a water authority.

Controversy surrounded the Kittyhawk group. The August 1955 issue of *Architectural Forum* reported that Frank Lloyd Wright was approached by Richard Hawley Cutting of Cutting and Associates of Cleveland to head a joint venture group that had named itself Kittyhawk Associates. In July 1954 Wright had reportedly withdrawn from the competition because the National Americanism Commission of the American Legion threatened to reveal his past antimilitaristic activities and associations with Russia.[131] In a telegraph to Cutting, he complained, "I assume that an architect . . . shouldn't be asked to plead his own case or tell who he is. The world knows what I can do in architecture. If officials of the air force have missed this, I can do no more than feel sorry for what both have lost."[132] Several years later, responding to an inquiry by Congressman Glenn Davis on this issue, Lieutenant Colonel Noonan, liaison officer of the AFACA, wrote, "There is no information available in the Liaison Office, Air Force Academy Construction Agency, that would indicate that Mr. Frank Lloyd Wright was not awarded the design contract for the Academy on account of un-American activities."[133] In any case, the notice sent by Erler to Kittyhawk Associates on June 30 informing its representatives of the time of their presentation did not include Wright's name in the heading, and a two-page document submitted to the air force by Kittyhawk Associates as part of its questionnaire did not include Wright's name in the heading or in the list of firms comprising the joint venture. The opening paragraph of that introductory document simply stated, "They [Kittyhawk Associates] will be supervised by Mr. M. G. Probst, President of Graham,

Anderson, Probst and White of Chicago, who, with his assistants, will be directly responsible to the principals and the Air Force."[134] It is unclear whether Wright was simply to serve as a senior outside consultant whose association with Kittyhawk was to be informal, or if he was insulted that he had not been approached directly by the air force. In any case, by the final interview date, Kittyhawk Associates was a joint venture that did not include Wright.

Temple Buell stands out as the most unlikely finalist for the academy commission. He did not enter into a joint venture, and his résumé of projects, when compared to those of the other finalists, was brief. As a Denver architect and land investor, he had designed several theaters, schools, shopping centers, and hospitals. A short article that appeared in the November 18, 1966, issue of *Time* magazine, written upon the occasion of his $25 million donation to Colorado Woman's College, may provide insight into the reasons for his inclusion as a finalist. The article identified Buell not only as an architect and real estate investor, but as "a frequent golf partner of Dwight Eisenhower."[135] One can only speculate that Buell's inclusion was either a political move to include an architect from the state of Colorado, a political move to appease a prominent and wealthy citizen of the state, or both. As mentioned, SOM had earlier considered associating with Buell.

Voorhees, Walker, Foley, and Smith was a prominent New York firm, primarily recognized for its laboratory and research center designs, producing dozens of such facilities after the war for corporations such as Bell Telephone, IBM, GE, Ford, DuPont, and Westinghouse. The firm had also worked on army bases and airfields and for the Atomic Energy Commission. It formed a joint venture in association with Gibbs and Hill, Inc.

The specific content of the presentations of these firms seems not to have been preserved. The first four firms listed presented their ideas on July 8; the last four firms presented on July 9, with SOM presenting last. The selection board kept little material from the interviews, and no record of the procedures of the selection process has been located. The statement of purpose submitted by Kittyhawk Associates has survived and provides insight into the sort of comments that group made regarding the proposed academy design—vague and generic remarks, capable of allowing for any range of design possibilities:

> It is felt that the magnificent site affords opportunities for combining natural beauty with modern design. It is not desirable to preconceive a design for an important project

such as this until all of the contributing elements have been thoroughly examined, together with the requirements of the Air Force. However, preliminary studies have been made of the limitations of West Point and Annapolis and several members of the organization have visited the site. It can be said that there are certain basic considerations which are sound, namely, that the theme should be modern but not so extreme that it will ever become dated; it must be completely compatible with the beauty of the site; it must symbolize the purpose for which it is designed; and it must be worthy of the pride which the people of America will hold for the Academy which is to train our Air Force of the future.[136]

As for SOM, Owings later wrote in his autobiography, "Our SOM presentation was a national effort. The result was a hard-backed brochure exactly two inches larger in each direction than any known file drawer or wastebasket in existence. Our brochure would be kept on top of the desk—not in or under it."[137] The brochure outlined the extensive experience amassed by the firms of that joint venture.

Listed under SOM's "particular specialty" was the following: "Creative design and administration of large scale projects involving master planning, site development, and technical building groups constitute the major part of our practice. Our recent and current projects include work of this nature for the Armed Forces, government agencies, such as the Atomic Energy Commission, hospitals, industrial corporations, and academic institutions."[138] SOM had a long history of government-related projects. During the years 1936–41, SOM had experimented with prefabricated, low-cost housing, culminating in such projects as the community of over six hundred homes that it built for Martin Company, a corporation that produced bombers during World War II, in Middle River, Maryland.[139] During the war, the firm was also commissioned to design the Manhattan Project town of Oak Ridge, Tennessee—a city of thirty thousand inhabitants—as well as other governmental projects, such as the Great Lakes Naval Training Station in Illinois (figure 8).[140] After the war, SOM was awarded numerous additional government projects, including theaters, barracks, libraries, recreation centers, and chapels at air bases in Guam, Okinawa, and French Morocco. In listing its experience when applying for the academy contract, the firm emphasized its military and academic projects, such as Oak Ridge, Los Alamos, the air bases in French Morocco and Okinawa, the Ohio State University Medical Center, and the United States Naval Postgraduate School. SOM's references included Colonels Erler, Person, and Lutz (Lutz had provided the firm with the latest navy photographs of the buildings it had constructed

Figure 8. Great Lakes Naval Training Station Reception Building, Illinois. Skidmore, Owings, and Merrill (Gordon Bunshaft, designer). Photograph by Hedrich-Blessing, 1942. Courtesy Chicago Historic Society; Hedrich-Blessing #HB-07226-E.

in Guam).[141] The listing of the firm's major projects over the previous five years occupied over thirty pages and totaled more than seventy projects.

Moran, Proctor, Mueser, and Rutledge had worked on a number of projects with SOM during the five years prior to the academy competition. Those projects included the Bellevue Medical Center in New York, the Heinz Plant in Pittsburgh, the Ford Administration Building in Dearborn, the New York Life Insurance Company Building in Chicago, the Hoffmann Beverage Company Plant on Long Island, the United Air Lines Hangar in San Francisco, and various projects in Okinawa. The firm had also worked on the United Nations Buildings in New York, as had the firm of Syska and Hennessy.[142] A list of the group's achievements added another six pages and nineteen projects to SOM's academy brochure.

Syska and Hennessy had also worked with SOM on several projects since 1949, including the Bellevue Medical Center in New York, the Lake Meadows Apartment project in Chicago, a naval hospital (no location given), several elementary schools (no locations given), Manufacturer's Trust Company in New

York, the Connecticut General Insurance Company in Bloomfield, the MIT Laboratory, and work in Bogota, Columbia. Another five pages and fourteen projects were added to the SOM brochure listing its work.[143] In total, the members of the joint venture had amassed an impressive forty-page dossier listing more than one hundred projects accomplished between 1949 and 1954. The military and education projects they listed, as well as the fact that the firms had worked together on numerous projects, would have impressed the selection board. SOM's organizational hierarchy was important as well and was outlined in the brochure.

During the postwar period, SOM structured itself in terms of specific duties and responsibilities, functioning as a collective of partners, associate partners, and participating partners. In its application for the academy project it differentiated the functions as follows: ten partners "assume responsibility of the general partnership in regard to client relationships, business management, and execution of architect-engineering services"; thirteen associate partners "share in varying degree the financial responsibility of the firm, develop contract documents, supervise engineering and construction cost control, and assume management of particular projects"; twenty-one participating associates "act as project managers and department heads, supervising design, working drawings, specifications, cost estimates, and construction of building projects."[144] SOM's application specifically identified the associate partners and participating associates who had experience that related to the Air Force Academy project and who might be assigned to that project.

SOM's office structure was one that could be immediately conveyed by charts and diagrams, which were included in the application. The firm practiced the type of management by committee that would have appealed to Talbott, as both a businessman and a representative of the military bureaucracy. While organization and project efficiency are not necessarily synonymous, this type of organization would certainly have been perceived as being effective, efficient, and necessary to coordinate the more than nine hundred architects, engineers, designers, and landscape specialists required at the height of the academy project.[145] SOM's organizational approach to architecture had been—and would be throughout the academy project—recognized by the architectural community as exemplary.[146]

In SOM's academy proposal, a board of directors, consisting of Skidmore, Owings, Merrill, Mueser, and Hennessy, headed the firm's organizational chart. Answering to that board was John Merrill, identified as "Executive Director," and a group labeled the "Air Force Academic and Technical Consultants." The general manager under Merrill was Robert M. Wagner, an associate partner of the firm from the New York office. The air force liaison was Albert Lockett, a participating associate of SOM. Wagner had been one of the principals in the work for the Lever House project. Under his scrutiny were six separate categories: administration was the task of the SOM business manager, Thomas Flavin; master planning was headed by Fred Craft, an SOM associate partner who was a member of the Chicago office and one of the principles responsible for developing the Oak Ridge master plan; construction supervision was overseen by an SOM associate partner, Edward Merrill (John Merrill's brother), who had been in charge of field operations at Los Alamos; site engineering was the responsibility of the firm of Moran, Proctor, Mueser, and Rutledge, while utility engineering was the responsibility of the firm of Syska and Hennessy, Inc. Finally, building design and engineering was headed by Gordon Bunshaft.

SOM's future had been most clearly charted by Bunshaft,

who introduced a specifically European modernist approach to the firm's work. Bunshaft had joined the firm of Skidmore and Owings in 1937, and his approach to design made an immediate impact on the firm. As Owings noted in his autobiography, "of the original nucleus [of SOM], he [Bunshaft] was the acknowledged designer."[147] Regarding a 1939 hospital design in Petosky, Michigan, Owings wrote, "the central portion of this northern Michigan phenomenon, which might be described as American brewery style, is almost pure Owings; and anyone familiar with the contemporary architecture of the Bauhaus and the international style would know that the sloping wing was almost pure Bunshaft."[148] Although Owings generalized in associating Bunshaft's modernism with the Bauhaus, his recognition of a European influence was correct.

Bunshaft, like Skidmore and Merrill, had studied at MIT.[149] Although modern architecture and theory were not part of the MIT curriculum while Bunshaft was a student, he recalled being heavily influenced by the writings of Le Corbusier. Bunshaft later stated that although he was influenced by Le Corbusier's work, Le Corbusier had a more purely aesthetic approach to architecture, whereas he had a more practical approach in order to better suit the client's programmatic needs.[150] Bunshaft's work for the 1939 New York World's Fair included the Venezuelan Pavilion—a project he regarded as "semi-good" (figure 9). Its design, a glass box with walls supported by steel columns, gave a preview of Bunshaft's later work with the firm.[151] Bunshaft insisted on living in New York rather than Chicago and became SOM's chief designer of the New York office and a full partner in the firm in 1949. He came to regard Eero Saarinen, Wallace Harrison, Philip Johnson, and I. M. Pei as "fellow students of European modernism," and it was the milieu of New York, not Chicago, that inspired his most famous SOM designs of the early 1950s.[152] Those works included the iconic Lever House of 1951–52 (figure 10), the Manufacturers' Hanover Trust Company building of 1953–54 (figure 11), and the Connecticut General Life Insurance building of 1954–57 (figure 12).[153]

Although Bunshaft played an active role during meetings in which the Air Force Academy design was discussed, Walter Netsch was listed in the questionnaire as resident architect of the project, responsible for architectural coordination.[154] Netsch had also been a student at MIT. By the time he graduated in 1943, the school had adopted a Bauhaus approach to design. Many of the faculty had taught at the Bauhaus or at Chicago's Institute of Design under the auspices of László Moholy-Nagy, a former Bauhaus teacher.[155] Netsch was also

Figure 9. Venezuelan Pavilion, 1939 World's Fair, New York. Skidmore and Owings (Gordon Bunshaft, designer).

influenced by the historian and modernist advocate Sigfried Giedion, who in 1938 had delivered his Charles Eliot Norton lectures at Harvard (later to be published as the modernist text *Space, Time, and Architecture*), and by Walter Gropius, who had been teaching at Harvard since 1938. In addition, Netsch studied with the Finnish architect Alvar Aalto, who was teaching at MIT at the time. Netsch joined the firm of SOM in 1947, at the age of twenty-seven. He worked at Oak Ridge designing garden apartments and in 1950 was placed in charge of SOM's Okinawa project, responsible for the designs of warehouses, town centers, chapels, schools, and other buildings.[156] He was chief of design in SOM's San Francisco office from 1949 to 1954 and oversaw the design for the United States Navy Postgraduate School in Monterey, California, employing a modernist vocabulary for a complex that included classrooms, laboratories, an auditorium, and a library (figure 13).[157] Fortuitously, the month prior to SOM's academy interview Netsch had published an article entitled "Programming the U.S. Naval Postgraduate

School of Engineering" in *Architectural Record,* providing an analysis of the factors that determined that school's design.[158] Just before the academy competition, Netsch was transferred to the Chicago office to begin work on the Inland Steel Building.[159]

SOM's presentation to the selection board can be only partially reconstructed. The firm of Henning and Cheadle was hired to coordinate SOM's presentation, which was augmented by color and black-and-white photographs by acclaimed architectural photographers such as Morley Baer.[160] In his autobiography, Owings stated that their presentation "consisted of a fifteen-foot-long, six-foot-high folding screen divided into three-foot panels, each devoted to one aspect of the total problem: research, programming, scheduling and design of the academy. A different partner explained each section of the screen."[161] Although not present at the interview, Netsch later claimed that the idea for the screen came from armed forces work he had done in Japan and at the United States Post-

Figure 10. Lever House, New York. Skidmore, Owings, and Merrill (Gordon Bunshaft, designer), 1951–52. Photograph by Ezra Stoller, © ESTO.

Figure 11. Manufacturers' Trust Company, New York. Skidmore, Owings, and Merrill (Gordon Bunshaft, designer), 1953–54. Photograph by Ezra Stoller, © ESTO.

graduate School.[162] Reminiscing about the process, Owings stated that several factors were key in SOM's appointment. One was his association with James Douglas. Owings recalled that the presentation took place in front of "a ten-member board of heavily starred generals, chaired by Jim Douglas."[163] As noted earlier, the membership of the selection board was not comprised solely of generals, nor did it include Douglas, although perhaps he sat in on the presentation. Bunshaft, in later recollections, presented a different version, based on secondhand information given to him by Skidmore. That account had the presentations all taking place in one day, with Talbott informing Skidmore at the day's end, on a ride back to New York in his private plane, that SOM had received the commission. According to Bunshaft's account, Talbott gave Skidmore two reasons for the firm's selection. First was the influence of Mrs. Talbott. SOM had designed the New York Infirmary, and

she chaired the board. The second was the recommendation of Frazer Wilde. He was head of Connecticut General and a friend of Talbott, and, as noted earlier, SOM had designed the Connecticut General Life Insurance Company headquarters in Bloomfield.[164] Bunshaft's narrative contradicts earlier memos stating that Talbott would be in Europe at the time of the selection process and would not make the final selection until his return.[165]

SOM was officially awarded the academy project on July 23, 1954.[166] A preliminary contract, signed on August 4, allocated $23,527.50 for services to be rendered by the firm, with a clause providing for a more definitive contract to follow. Minutes from a meeting on August 2–3, 1954, between representatives of SOM and the air force record that the air force was reluctant to negotiate a contract with a joint venture operation; instead it drew up a contract exclusively with SOM, which then

Figure 12. Connecticut General Life Insurance Company Headquarters, Bloomfield, Connecticut. Skidmore, Owings, and Merrill (Gordon Bunshaft, designer), 1954–57. Photograph by Ezra Stoller, © ESTO.

employed Syska and Hennessy; Moran, Proctor, Mueser, and Rutledge; and Robert and Company as associates for specific phases of the project.[167] Robert and Company, whose specialty was dealing with water issues, had initially been part of the Kittyhawk group during the academy competition. On August 12, the fee was increased to $29,774.00, with work to commence within forty-eight hours after receipt of notice to proceed. The contract stipulated the following work be initiated: analysis and development of the academic, architectural, and engineering requirements; preparation of an academy master plan; development of sketch designs and preliminary drawings with design analysis and material lists; preparation of scale models as requested; preparation of cost estimates; and site investigation, including topographic and engineering surveys.[168]

Figure 13. Naval Postgraduate Technical School, Monterey, California. Skidmore, Owings, and Merrill (Walter Netsch, designer), 1952. Photograph by Morley Baer.

CONSULTANT SELECTION

Talbott had decided to wait until the academy architect had been chosen to designate a design advisory board to work with the firm. On July 26, 1954, John Ferry wrote letters to Eero Saarinen, Wallace Harrison, and Welton Becket asking them to serve as consultants to the secretary of the air force, "in the review of the major program, planning and design phases of the project."[169] Whether SOM had any input on these appointments is doubtful—no documents indicate so. Reimbursement for the architects' services would consist of travel costs, per diem expense costs, and a per diem stipend of fifty dollars.[170] All three agreed to serve as consultants. Since all the other aspects of the academy, from site selection to architect selection, were enmeshed in political maneuverings, it would not be surprising if the selection of the consultants also had political underpinnings. Saarinen's work for General Motors (figure 14) had been completed under the auspices of its president,

Charles Wilson, Eisenhower's new secretary of defense. Wallace Harrison's association with the Rockefellers has been well documented. In 1926 he had married Ellen Milton, whose brother was married to John D. Rockefeller's daughter. In the 1930s, Harrison and Nelson Rockefeller had been trustees at the Museum of Modern Art and their association continued through the United Nations project.[171] By the time of Harrison's appointment to the academy project, Nelson Rockefeller was Eisenhower's undersecretary of health, education, and welfare. That is not to say political associations were the only reasons for the firms' appointments. Both were highly qualified and had been among the finalists for the academy project. There was little doubt that both could work with SOM; Harrison already had done so in the United Nations project.

Although Welton Becket's firm had applied for the academy commission, it was not a finalist. A summary of the firm's work is not nearly as impressive as that of Saarinen or Harrison. Becket had studied for a year at the Ecole des Beaux-Arts be-

Figure 14. General Motors Technical Center, Warren, Michigan. Saarinen and Associates, 1948–56. Photograph by Balthazar Korab.

fore joining with Walter Wurdeman and Charles Plummer to form a partnership in Los Angeles. Following Plummer's death in 1939, Wurdeman and Becket constructed fourteen thousand low-cost housing units, primarily in California, and emerged after the war as a large firm with eighty employees. In 1949, the firm designed two of its most publicized buildings, the General Petroleum Building and the Prudential Insurance Building, both in Los Angeles. Those designs were praised in the pages of *Architectural Forum* as being "dramatically designed, cannily constructed, and full of new techniques."[172] Welton Becket and Associates, as the firm was renamed after Wurdeman's death in 1949, became best known for its residential, department store, and shopping center designs.[173] During the early 1950s, the firm's commissions were focused in California and included a Hilton Hotel in Beverly Hills (figure 15), a shopping center in San Francisco, a small laboratory in Los Angeles for General Petroleum, a small manufacturing plant in Los Angeles for Lever Brothers, and a small bank in Los Angeles. At the time of the academy competition, the firm was also working on a new recreation center at the California Air National Guard Base at Van Nuys. The members of the firm were also apparently hoping that the work they had done on the UCLA campus, supervising forty projects as master planners, would qualify them for the academy project.[174]

Becket's appointment, however, was probably not based solely on his performance as an architect. In his recollections, Bunshaft wrote, "I think Becket was a political appointment."[175] Documents confirm Bunshaft's supposition. On March 29, 1954, Jack Beardwood, one of the attorneys for Welton Becket and Associates, wrote to Charles Willis at the White House, stating that "anything you can do to call our organization to the Secretary's [Talbott's] attention would be appreciated."[176] Willis was the ultimate bureaucrat in a bureaucratic administration. One of the original "Citizens for Eisenhower," his job was to oversee citizen recruitment for the administration. In 1954, he had initiated a plan called "Operation People's Mandate." Under that system, information was passed on to department heads, identifying persons of merit to whom key positions and appointments should be given. Willis dutifully forwarded excerpts of Beardwood's letter, which stated the accomplishments of the firm, to Talbott with the following note: "For your information, Jack was a volunteer during the campaign at Citizens for Eisenhower and was head of the press section there. He did a wonderful job. He is very well known and liked by the President and served on his staff in Europe for some time."[177] Several days later Talbott responded to Beardwood, acknowl-

edging the impressiveness of Welton Becket's work and noting that the firm would receive consideration during the academy selection process.[178]

By the end of June, Maxwell Rabb, Eisenhower's cabinet secretary, had intervened in the firm's behalf. He wrote to Colonel Draper of the air force: "Of course, I cannot personally intervene in a matter of this type, but I would appreciate it if you could call the availability of Mr. Beardwood's firm to the attention of those concerned with the construction of the Academy. Mr. Beardwood, you may recall, was the Executive Assistant, for quite a time, to Secretary Hobby."[179] Oveta Culp Hobby, first secretary of the Department of Healthy, Education, and Welfare, was the wife of the publisher of the *Houston Post*. She had used the newspaper to rally support for Eisenhower during the 1952 election and was subsequently rewarded with the position of federal security administrator in the Eisenhower administration. When Becket's firm was not included in the short list of prospective candidates for the academy commission, Beardwood wrote a gracious note to Sherman Adams, assistant to the president, expressing gratitude for the consideration that had been given to the firm.[180] But a letter he sent at the same time to Willis revealed a less gracious frame of mind: "That we were not called for an interview puzzles us somewhat since another Los Angeles firm [Pereira and Luckman], with less experience, was called back as part of a two-firm combination. The Los Angeles firm, incidentally, includes Charlie Luckman who served the previous administration, and who is a close friend of Harry Truman."[181] The letter prompted Willis to add a handwritten note to Adams's letter, stating, "This [the selection process] doesn't appear to have been very objectively handled. Would you want this looked into?" Later, in a letter written to Willis shortly after the announcement of the selection of SOM as the academy architects, Beardwood acknowledged the firm's selection as consultants to the project, noting:

> My concern about the particular political angle I mentioned to you in my letter about the Air Force Academy is no longer great since the architectural and engineering commission for the Academy was awarded last Friday to Skidmore, Owings and Merrill, a fine firm with an excellent record and background. The Democrat-headed firm [Pereira and Luckman] was interviewed but fortunately was not chosen. . . . Friday afternoon John Ferry, Secretary Talbott's assistant on installations, telephoned me to report that the Secretary wanted to appoint Welton Becket as one of three consulting architects to the Secretary on the Academy project. The job of these three consultants, all top American architects, would be to review the Skidmore, Owings and

Figure 15. Beverly Hilton Hotel, Beverly Hills, California. Welton Becket and Associates, 1952. Photograph by Julius Shulman.

Merrill plans to make professionally certain that the design and layout of the Academy are outstanding in taste and function. . . . This means that although we get none of the meat and potatoes we at least get a sprig of the prestige parsley.[182]

THE SELECTION PROCESS AS A BUREAUCRATIC PROCESS

The reconstruction of the selection process for the academy project indicates that it was bureaucratic from its inception. Focused on issues of practicality, economics, and politics, that process was overseen by committees formed primarily of military personnel. The committees were appointed according to criteria known only to themselves, and selections were determined by behind-the-scenes alliances—a process consistent with the appointment of federal positions during that period. As a government-sponsored project, that comes as no surprise. Both Skidmore and Owings unabashedly confirmed that personal contacts and martini lunches were an important part of the architectural world in garnering commissions not only from the government, but from the corporate world. The firm's interoffice memos reveal that SOM employed all its offices' resources, throughout the country, to win this highly prestigious commission. Within a political context in which corporate figures landed many of the country's most prestigious appointments and cabinet positions, SOM favorably positioned itself by emphasizing its corporate organizational methods and approach.

As the project progressed, the bureaucratic process continued. Committees were formed to advise, oversee, and administer, but none assumed the responsibility for articulating in definitive terms the academy design. Instead, one committee answered to another, as the process for funding the academy project tiptoed its way through Congress. While SOM often lamented this lack of accountability, it was just such a bureaucratic labyrinth that the firm had so adeptly negotiated during the selection process. And it was that system that characterized and defined the academy project: not a technological or teleological determinism based on the preference for a specific architectural style, but a bureaucratic decisionmaking process that occurred behind closed doors. It was a system in which decisions were justified and legitimized through campaigns of rhetoric and publicity.

ON THE WINGS OF MODERNISM
The Exhibition of May 13–15, 1955

The rhetoric of architectural modernism, though seldom expressed during the selection process for the architects of the United States Air Force Academy, was quickly adopted by the firm of Skidmore, Owings, and Merrill once the firm began the project. Nowhere was this more clearly demonstrated than in the first public exhibition of the academy design on May 13–15, 1955. In presenting the project, SOM reinforced the myths of modernism, emphasizing the notion that the academy design was an expression of technological achievements that reflected the spirit of the age. In so doing, the architects would draw upon their experience with the world's fairs of the 1930s in presenting their "perfect city."[1] Other myths were woven into SOM's presentation and discussion of the academy project, including those of flight and the American West. In this, SOM's academy presentation was influenced by the 1933 and 1939 world's fairs in Chicago and New York and a series of exhibitions mounted by the Museum of Modern Art in New York.

ARCHITECTURE AND ARTIFICE: SOM AND THE MARKETING OF MODERNISM

Louis Skidmore and Nathaniel Owings had long been aware of the intricacies and persuasive value of exhibition design. Skidmore had convinced the architects Raymond Hood and Paul Cret, members of the architectural commission for the 1933 Chicago World's Fair, to appoint him the fair's assistant general manager in charge of design and construction.[2] His position as "Chief of Exhibition Design," as it was defined in the press, and his subsequent appointment of his brother-in-law, Nathaniel Owings, to oversee its entertainment and concession aspects, had involved them both in marketing campaigns aimed at a consumer-oriented mass culture.[3]

The purpose of the 1933 fair—the so-called Century of Progress—was to emphasize the active role of industry and science in creating the new world order. The fair's *Official Guide* made that clear from the outset, boldly stating that the "Theme of Fair is Science," with a clarifying subheading: "Science Finds—Industry Applies—Man Conforms." In this hierarchy, according to the guidebook, "Science discovers, genius invents, industry applies, and man adapts himself to, or is molded by, new things."[4] Man was defined as a passive participant in history, while science and industry were restructured as separate forces that created their own history. Skidmore himself reiterated that premise: "The Century of Progress is based on an *idea*—that of science as the determining factor in the progress of the past hundred years."[5]

That new world order was referred to both in terms of technological innovations and in approaches to planning. In an article published in the July 1933 issue of *Architectural Forum*, Skidmore praised the members of the fair's architectural commission: "They decided on an asymmetrical plan. They were cutting adrift from the past, breaking away from traditions of balance and symmetry and classical design."[6] The agenda of the commissioners was made clear to visitors in the guidebook. Explaining the buildings' collective character as a visible manifestation of societal changes (brought about by science and industry) that had occurred since the 1893 World's Columbian Exposition in Chicago, the commissioners were quoted in the guidebook: "'It would be incongruous, to house exhibits showing man's progress in the past century in a Greek temple of the age of Pericles, or a Roman villa of the time of Hadrian,' said members of the architectural commission of the Exposition, all of whom are graduates of the Ecole de Beaux Arts [*sic*], home of the classical school. 'We are trying to show the world not what has happened in the past, because that has already been effectively done, but what is being done in the present, and what may happen in the future.'"[7] The implication was that the planners had progressed beyond historicist nineteenth-century architectural solutions and the teachings of the Ecole des Beaux-Arts and were structuring an approach reflecting the modern condition of twentieth-century America.

The fair indeed reflected American society, but not necessarily in the fashion explained by its planners. While its organizers underscored themes of educating the public, they were targeting the public as consumers, as the fair was conceived from the beginning as a commercial enterprise. Skidmore, describing the design of the fair in the May 1933 issue of *Architectural Record*, stated as much: "The Exposition's exhibit of the Basic Sciences in the Hall of Science established a nucleus around which the commercial exhibitors could build their dis-

plays."[8] That the issues of consumerism and commercialism extended to the architects themselves was made clear several pages later by Owings. In discussing the exposition's amusement features, he noted, "Existing economic conditions assisted in producing these features. Architects and engineers rendered professional services for a chance to get a twenty per cent bonus plus their usual fee out of gate receipts."[9] Both Skidmore and Owings addressed those issues succinctly, moving on in their respective articles to discuss the innovative approaches to structure or planning taken in the fair. Owings, for example, discussed the Skyride and observation towers at the fair in terms of architectural design and structural components, drawing comparisons to the Eiffel Tower, built for the 1889 Paris Exposition, and the Ferris wheel at the Columbian Exposition. But Owings later acknowledged that in actuality the 1933 fair represented American consumerism. In his autobiography, he reflected on the monumental presence of the Skyride: "Although the ride was as aesthetically out of keeping for us as the Eiffel Tower must have been for Paris, its size and volume marked a presence for the fair, producing a kind of giant bracketing—ugly, big, and popular."[10]

Issues of economy, practicality, and efficiency were of primary concern to a country in the depths of the Great Depression, and they were also themes at the fair. In an article written in May 1932 and published in October of that year, for example, Skidmore had previewed Cret's Hall of Science Building to be built at the fair, with its engineering and structural innovations, in terms of its economic feasibility—the building would stand only for five months, so "economy was a vital consideration."[11] Throughout, the fair's guidebook emphasized that prefabricated and mass-produced materials were used as a matter of practicality and economics. The one-page discussion of the administration building, for example, read like a construction manual: the trustees' room was "famous for its modern simplicity"; the walls were flexwood veneers, made possible by industrial technology; the table was "utilitarian"; the building utilized the most efficient heating and ventilation systems; the roof insulation employed new technologies (processed cornstalks); and the wall insulation—a two-and-three-quarter-inch space between an outer asbestos cement board and inner plaster board filled with asphalt and wood—provided better insulation than a brick wall thirteen inches thick. Most important, it was noted that the cost per cubic foot for construction was less than half of usual building costs.[12] The guidebook explained that the fair was to stand for only 150 days and could easily be dismantled using new industrial methods. Furthermore, the fair had been realized without cost to the taxpayer, with industry itself "presenting the drama."[13] The technological future was revealed through a series of showrooms behind a veneer of prefabricated walls—a futurist dream conveyed through lights and rhetoric.

Indeed, if there was a single aspect that defined the 1933 fair, it was the spectacle of lighting. The 1893 Chicago fair, which had used more electrical lighting than any city in the country, served as its inspiration. The lighting there was not intended to illuminate the architecture for visitors so much as to set buildings off against shadows, creating aesthetic objects best presented through photographs and postcards. David Nye has summarized the effect of the electric lighting: "Whereas Burke had imagined light as a minor element of architectural design, as a contrast to darkness, the electrical sublime was a manufactured experience that reduced the night to a background. Whereas Kant had expected the individual to draw the correct transcendental conclusion from a sublime encounter with nature, the electrical sublime produced awe on demand and insured it would be understood within the interpretive framework of the impresario."[14] Owings himself mentioned how the lighting elements in the amusement features contributed to the 1933 fair's overall effect. It was, as the guidebook noted, from the observation platforms atop the towering Skyride that one could best appreciate the overall design of the fair. But it was an abstracted view. At night you gazed "upon a magic city that seems to float in a vast pool of light," while during the day the pattern was like "a gigantic, gay rug, or a vast garden of colorful flowers."[15] Visitors in the Skyride, hovering above the fair, its perimeter blurring into that of the surrounding city, could extend the fair's utopian promises into the world at large.[16]

Not only did the lighting contribute to the spectacle of the 1933 Chicago fair, but it enhanced the scenographic aspect of the exhibition buildings. That Joseph Urban, an architect with stage design experience, had been called upon to coordinate this architectural ensemble is not surprising. The fair's guidebook explained his intent: "Joseph Urban, famous architect and stage designer, sought to achieve a harmony of color on the building exteriors that might express the Exposition's deeper, more lasting implications and purposes."[17] The definition of architecture as a series of carefully disposed tableaux may also be applied to a discussion of other world's fair designs, including the 1893 Columbian Exposition in Chicago—a constant reference point for the 1933 fair. But organizers of the 1933 fair were anxious to distinguish between the

Beaux-Arts classicism of the earlier fair and the scientifically rational theme of their own. The theme was not a recollection of the past, but a projection into the future. Ultimately, the scenographic effects and the spectacle of lighting hid the economic exigencies of the 1933 exposition. Although Owings decried his experience at the fair as qualifying him for nothing more than "an itinerant hawker of snake-bite-cure medicine" and defined the uses of color, motion, and light at the fair as "primitive devices," the lessons he learned there were to be refined and reemployed throughout his career.[18]

Six years later, Skidmore and Owings were again involved with a world's fair, where their role was that of architectural and exhibition designers for specific participants. The firm's clients at the 1939 New York World's Fair included the Radio Corporation of America (RCA), Westinghouse, Swift and Company (figure 16), Continental Baking Company (producers of Wonder Bread) (figures 17 and 18), Agfa Ansco Corporation (figure 19), and Gas Exhibits, Inc. (which included United States and Canadian gas utility and appliance manufacturers).[19] The New York fair's theme—"Building the World of Tomorrow with the Tools of Today"—was reinforced by its architectural program and its overall emphasis on technological solutions to the world's problems.[20]

In the August 1940 issue of *Architectural Forum,* the critic Douglas Haskell prophetically commented that the overall planning design of the 1939 fair, specifically its division into functional zones, was of interest "because there are parallel problems in the laying out of new towns that will be needed for our defense and other industry. A town, too, has its characteristic functional zones."[21] Haskell entitled this section of his article "Nuclear Zoning." Ironically, within two years, SOM (by that time Skidmore and Owings had entered into a limited partnership with John Ogden Merrill) would be asked to apply those lessons in designing the town of Oak Ridge for workers involved in developing the atomic bomb. As Joseph Corn has noted, the fair's utopian plan had precedent. Its radiating design was based on historical models of utopian cities of the seventeenth and eighteenth centuries, such as those of Tommaso Campanella (City of the Sun, 1623) and Claude-Nicolas Ledoux (Chaux, 1773–79). Also, Emil Kaufmann's recently published text *Von Ledoux bis Le Corbusier,* comparing the work of Le Corbusier to Ledoux, may have influenced the planning of the 1939 fair.[22]

The utopian architectural program of the 1939 fair was used to underscore the role of commerce and consumerism in determining the future. Walter Dorwin Teague was a member of the

Figure 16. Swift and Company Building, 1939 World's Fair, New York. Skidmore and Owings.

board of design for the New York World's Fair. He noted that the function of the fair was to serve "as a place where merchants come to display their wares to possible purchasers," but he still idealistically thought it could also be "aesthetically beautiful—a vast, magnificent work of art."[23] The architecture itself often served as large billboards, either directly or through allusion. The exterior of Skidmore and Owings's design for Continental Baking Company's Wonder Bakery, for example, was decorated with balloon shapes in primary colors like those on Wonder Bread's wrapper, while the sandwich bar on the interior incorporated actual balloons as a design motif (figures 17 and 18).

The role of architecture in creating a product image was, of course, not unique to this fair, but the role of the observer within this spectacle of consumerism was redefined.[24] That role was a passive one, to a much greater extent than in previous fairs. Haskell noted that "the architects of this Fair went further than architects had ever gone before in taking care of the visitor's every requirement, not to mention his guidance."[25] Teague compared the exhibition designs to a craftily planned maze, saying that "people must flow in an exhibit"—the exhibits had to be designed "in such a way that the spectator's interest is stimulated and his responses are involuntary."[26]

Figure 18. Continental Baking Company Building, 1939 World's Fair, New York. Skidmore and Owings.

Figure 17. Continental Baking Company Building, 1939 World's Fair, New York. Skidmore and Owings.

Figure 19. Agfa Ansco Corporation Communications Building exhibit, 1939 World's Fair, New York. Skidmore and Owings.

The architecture itself was lit, not by floodlights, but by exterior lighting incorporated more subtly into the architectural designs themselves. The result was architecture that appeared quite different at night—not merely illuminated, but transformed.[27] Light was also a factor in interior design. Haskell especially noted the manner in which the Westinghouse exhibit, designed by Skidmore and Owings, "carries the visitor through a subtle progression of light and dark, so modulated to a purpose that only a professional observer is aware of the subtleties."[28]

Missing at this fair were the typical representations of the "exotic other"—the colonized third world countries that had been such prominent fixtures at past fairs. Whereas the 1933 Chicago exposition had extended its boundaries into the sur-

rounding city fabric through the spectacle of lighting, the New York fair extended itself metaphorically. The viewing public was itself presumed to be the "other," and the city beyond the fair's perimeter was to be the next area of colonization, fulfilling the promises of the exhibitions. Those promises were presented and represented in the form of scale models and dioramas of a world that supposedly could be realized within the immediate future. The viewers, however, were given an elevated perspective that literally distanced them from the specifics of economics or function. In the General Motors Futurama exhibit (figure 20), for example, the designer Norman Bel Geddes orchestrated a sequence of spaces through which the viewer was carried on a conveyer belt of chairs. Small

Figure 20. Norman Bel Geddes's General Motors Futurama exhibit, 1939 World's Fair, New York. Courtesy General Motors Media Archives; used with permission of General Motors Corp.

speakers were attached to the chairs, which hovered above the dioramas, and a narrator explained to the audience what they were seeing. The publicity for that exhibition stated that observers would "enjoy a thrilling scenic ride into the future, a tour through what seems to be many miles of landscape. Past them streams a realistic miniature countryside, with cities and towns, rivers and lakes, valleys and mountains, forests and fertile fields executed in perfect detail. Through this landscape run super-highways of the future."[29] These were idealized pastoral landscapes, depicted without urban blight, mediating between the fair's technological theme and the romantic evocations of a Jeffersonian rural America.

If SOM's experience in designing world's fairs represented one thread of events that was to influence the firm's 1955 academy exhibition, museum exhibition designs, particularly those mounted by New York's Museum of Modern Art (MoMA), represented another.[30] Similar structures of thought informed both: the realities of the present were displaced by the rhetoric of a technologically manifested future. Skidmore and Owings would have been keenly aware of the architectural exhibitions at MoMA and their enormous impact upon the course of modernism. They would also have known how those exhibitions had evolved during the 1930s and 1940s to appeal to a larger public—a change that drew world's fairs and museum exhibitions into the common arena of marketing to a mass public. Addressing the relationship between modernism and mass culture,

Beatriz Colomina has proposed that it was through the techniques of mechanical reproduction in the mass media that modern architecture increasingly came to represent itself. Analyzing Le Corbusier's engagement with mass media, she located an American equivalent, or translation, in the 1932 MoMA exhibition *Modern Architecture*.[31]

Organized by three Harvard graduates, Alfred Barr, Henry-Russell Hitchcock, and Philip Johnson, the 1932 exhibition grew out of a rewriting of Hitchcock's 1929 publication *Modern Architecture: Romanticism and Reintegration*.[32] Architectural modernism was presented at this exhibition as an aestheticized image, separated from its social, political, or cultural contexts. The exhibition codified the formal criteria of a modernist architectural vocabulary as represented in photographs, models, and drawings.[33] Alfred Barr, director of the museum, established the link between expositions and exhibitions in the first sentence of his introduction to the exhibition's catalogue, where he wrote, "Expositions and exhibitions have perhaps changed the character of American architecture of the last forty years more than any other factor."[34]

In his "Memorandum on the Architectural Exhibition," dated September 24, 1931, Johnson listed the proposed itinerary of the exhibition, including stops at museums in Philadelphia, Seattle, San Francisco, Los Angeles, Buffalo, Cleveland, Toledo, Cincinnati, Milwaukee, Cambridge, Pittsburgh, St. Paul, Rochester, Worcester, Omaha, and Houston.[35] Earlier that spring, Johnson had noted, "Judging from the keen interest abroad in new ideas in Architecture emanating from America, the unique character and selectivity of the Show will necessitate a European and Japanese itinerary."[36] (Johnson used the terms "Exhibition" and "Show" interchangeably throughout his memoranda.) Johnson and Hitchcock also planned a series of proselytizing lectures on modernist design, not only at museums, but at department stores.[37]

In the exhibition itself, models of architectural projects were presented along with photographs, plans, and text. Although MoMA does not publish its budget figures for exhibitions, the proposed budget "was enormous."[38] The models were meant to represent works in progress or projected works, augmented with photographs of actual buildings. In the tradition of connoisseurship, the exhibition and catalogue were presented as artistic images—as equivalent to paintings. Johnson, appointed exhibition director in January 1931, made that clear in his February 10 proposal, writing that the photographs "which are mounted on plywood, will be hung in the same way as paintings."[39] The enlarged photographs, typically three feet high and hung at eye level, were the focal point of the exhibition—so much so that later historians have stated the exhibition could have been more accurately described as a photographic exhibition.[40] The images were carefully cropped and were, for the most part, devoid of human presence. In other words, the photographs abstracted the architecture and separated it from any specific cultural, social, or geographical context. There was an element of restraint in the exhibition design—the future was displayed in the sanctity of the museum as "high art." Although the critical response to the exhibition at the time was cool, more than thirty-three thousand people viewed it.[41]

While the 1932 exhibition was understated in its dependence on spectacle as a method of attracting the public, future exhibitions incorporated that aspect to greater and greater degrees. By 1940, Beaumont Newhall had been named as MoMA's curator of photography. If photography was an implicit aspect of exhibition design prior to that time, it now became explicit. For the department's first exhibitions, David McAlpin, a wealthy stockbroker and chairman of the museum's Committee on Photography, arranged for Ansel Adams to join Newhall as vice chairman of the department with the goal of making photography an object of aesthetic attention. But it was only when photographic exhibitions at the museum overlapped with the worlds of fashion and advertising that the mass public was successfully enticed. That transition occurred under the auspices of Edward Steichen, with the assistance of Herbert Bayer. By the time Newhall was replaced by Steichen as curator of the photography department of MoMA in 1947, Newhall's aesthetic program for photography had been replaced by one that, in employing the psychology of advertising, appealed to mass culture.[42]

In 1942, Steichen had presented his *Road to Victory* exhibition at the museum, employing an installation design by Bayer. In designing the exhibition, Bayer used photography as a form of sublime spectacle to manipulate the audience. At the entrance to the gallery space, a gigantic photomural of a western landscape set the tone for the exhibition. The show's intent was not to engage the viewer in critically or aesthetically defining photography as fine art, but to make the viewer a passive recipient of a propagandistic message. As Christopher Phillips noted in his discussion of MoMA's use of the photographic image, the image was used both for its dramatic impact and to create a narrative with a predetermined thesis. A winding "road" led through enormous documentary photomurals, recalling the photojournalistic techniques of *Life* magazine. Like the dioramas at the 1939 World's Fair in New York, the exhibition culminated in simple positive resolutions to complex problems. As Bayer had stated several years earlier, an exhibition "should not retain its distance from the spectator, it should be brought close to him, penetrate and leave an impression on him, should explain, demonstrate, and even persuade and lead him to a planned and direct reaction. Therefore we may say that exhibition design runs parallel with the psychology of advertising."[43] Jeffrey Meikle has commented that the heirs of the social control developed at the 1939 fair were shopping malls and amusement parks. Overlooked in his statement is the fact that one of the fair's designers was Herbert Bayer, and that his museum exhibition designs during the ensuing years continued that experience.[44]

Bayer's familiarity with the psychology of advertising was firsthand. Prior to moving to the United States in 1938, he had taught at the Bauhaus as a master in design. After leaving the Bauhaus in 1928, he launched a career in graphic design, working as art director for *Vogue* in Berlin. In 1938 Bayer immigrated to the United States and immediately began working with Walter and Ise Gropius on an exhibit for MoMA entitled *Bauhaus 1919–1928.* The following year he was responsible for the exhibition design in the Pennsylvania State Building at the New York World's Fair—a building designed by his Bauhaus compatriots Walter Gropius and Marcel Breuer. Bayer's exhibition space for the 1942 MoMA exhibition was spatially innovative, integrating photography and text and using ramps, photo panels placed at angles above and below the viewer, and dramatic juxtapositions and vistas to lead the viewer through a carefully choreographed sequence of spaces. Still more innovative was the walk-in globe he designed for the 1943 *Airways to Peace* exhibition. These exhibitions drew huge crowds from a previously untapped general public, as did the 1945 *Power in the Pacific* exhibition. The shows could also be used as "editions"—infinitely reproduced to circulate throughout the United States or the world. The *Road to Victory,* for example, traveled across the country and was adapted for other exhibition spaces. It also traveled to London, opening in March 1943 as *America Marches.*[45]

Corporate advertising, so important in the world's fairs of the 1930s, also entered the sanctity of the American museum. Bayer, for example, had close ties to Walter Paepke, president of the American Container Corporation, and in 1945 he designed a promotional exhibition for the company entitled *Modern Art in Advertising,* which opened at the Art Institute of Chicago.[46] In 1949, MoMA launched its "Good Design" program, meant to influence the marketplace and encourage the consumption of products it deemed "tasteful."[47] The first exhibition was designed by Charles and Ray Eames and opened in November 1950. Charles Eames was trained as an architect, as were the designers of the subsequent annual exhibitions: Finn Juhl (1951), Paul Rudolph (1952), Alexander Girard (1953 and 1954), and Daniel Brennan and A. James Speyer (1955).[48] The exhibitions were promoted through the print media and television. Promotions ran for several weeks in early 1954, for example, on Margaret Arlen's *Morning Show* and on the *Camel Caravan* program.[49]

In 1950, the firm of SOM was itself the subject of a MoMA exhibition, the museum's first exhibition of work by an architectural corporation. Using architectural models by Theodore Conrad and photographic images by Torkel Korling, Louis Checkman, and Ezra Stoller, the exhibition was mounted under the auspices of Philip Johnson, director of the Department of Architecture and Design. The catalogue stated: "The single designers who function within this organization have no fear of a loss of individuality. They are able to work within their corporate framework because they understand and employ the vocabulary and grammar which developed from the esthetic conceptions of the twenties."[50] The references to "the esthetic conceptions of the twenties" connected SOM with the early proponents of the architectural modernism, especially Walter Gropius and the Bauhaus.

More specifically, the firm's achievements were directly linked to the 1932 MoMA exhibition, as the first page of the catalogue noted: "We are now rounding out the revolutionary cycle begun by the chief pioneers of the International Style. . . . Their pioneering work is over but the concepts and principles they introduced are today being employed by them [the designers of SOM] as well as by architects throughout the world."[51] On the following page, the concepts and principles of the International style, as codified by Hitchcock and Johnson at the 1932 MoMA exhibition, were reiterated. Like the 1932 exhibition, photographs of in-progress projects (such as Lever House) were displayed along with those of completed works and, like that exhibition, it was the photographic image, carefully cropped and often devoid of humans, that was the focus of the exhibition. The images reinforced the simplicity of the architecture's geometric design, in the process abstracting it into a series of grids. Unlike the 1932 exhibition, however, it was the corporate identity of the firm, not the identity of individual architects, that was underscored. As the catalogue stated, "the firm bears its name like a trademark. It is like a brand name identifying its work which is persistently characterized by the idiom of the firm rather than that of any individual within the firm."[52] The photographic images in the exhibition reinforced that notion of a "trademark," establishing a coherent image of identity—an infinitely reproducible object able to market itself over time and space to an anonymous audience eager to embrace the modern, as defined and codified by a premier cultural institution.[53]

The means were sparse in this exhibition and marked a return to the style of the 1932 exhibition, underscoring the association between the two shows. Both presented architecture as an entity disassociated from social, cultural, or geographic specificities; formal attributes were emphasized through the use of models or photographs. A technologically determinant reading linked both exhibitions, reinforcing the myths and lineage of a specific type of architectural modernism, the International style. Equally important for SOM was that within this "high art" museum setting, status was automatically conferred upon its designs—as sanctioned works of art, they were above reproach or criticism.

The 1950 MoMA exhibition was a high-water mark for SOM, firmly establishing the firm in the vanguard of architectural modernism. Lost in that exhibition, however, were not only the details of modernism's complex and diverse history, but the details of SOM's history. The firm's experiences at the world's fairs during the 1930s and its roots in expositions that specifically appealed to a mass culture were negated by the exhibition's modernist agenda. Those experiences, however, are essential in explaining the first public display of the Air Force Academy design in May 1955—an exhibition that drew upon the utopian dreams of the world's fairs and the expertise of museum exhibition designers. Not only did SOM architects employ the rhetoric of modernism in explaining and presenting their design—a vocabulary to which they had contributed during the 1930s fairs—but they also drew upon their knowledge of the power of spectacle and photography as a persuasive tool in exhibition formats. Finally, they knew the importance of presenting their design within the sanctity of a museum, an institution that they assumed would confer a status of success upon their design prior to its construction, guaranteeing its realization. In short, they knew how to market and persuade; these were key factors in their 1955 academy exhibition.

PROPOSALS AND PRESENTATION: BACKGROUND TO THE 1955 EXHIBITION

Although meetings between SOM and air force representatives began in August 1954, the first meeting that was relevant to the 1955 exhibition design took place at the Pentagon on December 15, 1954. Representatives for SOM at that meeting included Skidmore, Owings, John Merrill, and the designers Bunshaft and Netsch. Representatives of the air force included Talbott, Douglas, Harmon (who by that time was both special assistant for Air Force Academy matters and superintendent of the academy), Washbourne, Erler, and Ferry. Also present was L. W. Robert of Robert and Company Associates, part of SOM's joint venture team.[54] SOM representatives began the meeting by presenting the basic program of the academy as a whole; they next interpreted that program using a flow chart outlining functions of the academy; and they concluded by presenting a master plan, which located the various elements of the program on the site.[55] Owings introduced the format, adding that Netsch would discuss the flow chart, Merrill the physical aspects of the site, and Bunshaft the master plan. The site model that Bunshaft used as a visual aid simply indicated locations of the major elements of the project, primarily so that work could begin on the first phase of the academy project, the construction of the road system within the academy property. It was in the afternoon session that the issue of an exhibition was first broached.

That session began with a discussion of budget issues. Owings stated that, because Congress had not yet allocated building funds for the construction of the academy, the "real buildings" would not be designed and unveiled until late April or May of the following spring.[56] Talbott followed by expressing a concern that was to haunt the academy throughout its construction, that of raising money and funding the project. His suggestions for cutting costs ranged from the practical to the theatrical. Considering Eisenhower's fondness for golf and the administration's proclivity for using the golf course as a meeting ground for bureaucratic decisionmaking, his initial comments were not surprising: "I'm just thinking aloud. . . . The Colorado people want to do something for us. I have been foundering in my mind trying to say what they ought to give to us; what we would like to have. And I have pretty near come to the conclusion that if they say: 'We'll build this golf course—put in this clubhouse,' why that would be the nicest thing we could get."[57] That Talbott also envisioned the course as a marketing tool was revealed by his later remarks: "But I think that a spectacular golf course is going to bring in there a great many of our officers who then will become more enthused about it; and I think it's one of the things that will draw people more than anything else."[58] During Talbott's "thinking aloud" comments, Owings often encouraged him, while subtly promoting SOM's agenda. After a comment by Owings that the golf course could help with landscaping, the conversation continued:

Talbott: Yes; then there's another thing that may sound foolish, but I thought in connection with this nursery and so forth that if we had the right kind of promoter in here we can get a lot of trees donated—with a plaque—

Owings: (interposing) From all over the United States.

Talbott: (continuing)—from all over the United States—get beautiful trees that would be fifty or a hundred feet long—put them on two flat cars, you know. People will say, "Well, I'll give a tree—$500, or whatever you—" If we can put trees out there it will make that place.

Robert: That's not a bad idea; that's a good idea. However, it would be interesting to know what trees would survive.[59]

The remarks here are revealing because they provide insight into Talbott's awareness of the importance of publicity in promoting the academy project. Owings's ideas for publicity, however, did not include cross-country tree hauling. The type of spectacle he envisioned had been made clear in his previous comments: "In general, Mr. Secretary, our plan, subject to this discussion here, was to put on this next show, which will be quite something—and one that the layman could understand—out in Colorado Springs—we hoped at the Fine Arts Center—have the meeting there—and then just blast it out."[60] Owings proposed they wait until May 1 for this "show." Talbott was initially reluctant to wait that long, feeling he might lose support of potential Denver donors. He also questioned the wisdom of having the exhibition in Colorado Springs, instead of in Denver with its larger population. But Harmon also liked the idea of having the exhibition in Colorado Springs, since that would facilitate visiting the actual site.

Following this discussion, Merrill initiated an analysis of the site itself, but the issue of private funding kept recurring. Moments later, Talbott asked about the athletic building, and Owings discussed it in terms of its moneymaking potential as a club. The subject of athletics as a means of funding kept the issue of publicity at the forefront of the discussion. Owings's detailed explanation of the initial exhibition some minutes later, however, revealed that he, in contrast to Talbott, was not "thinking aloud," and that this had been a well-thought-out and coordinated part of SOM's effort: "Our hope was that we would have the kickoff at the Fine Arts Center in Colorado Springs and have the governor and all those people; and then work out a chain across the country in the major museums where this could be shown, as something of aesthetic value, and not just a commercial venture. . . . Because you have all of those people all over the country—some of them with us now . . . thousands of architects you might get into the act"[61] Skidmore and Robert reinforced the remarks of Owings, after

which Owings and Robert neatly tied the proposal to the marketing aspect:

Robert: Mr. Secretary, I was going to make the suggestion that you are going to be drawing students from every state in the Union; and you're not having such success in getting men— you're recruiting everything. If this thing would be flown and shown in every possible center all over the United States by just taking it, like this model here—

Owings: (interposing) We would like to keep it on a high-level basis of the aesthetic and artistic, so that they can't start shooting at it.[62]

Douglas and Owings noted that an additional benefit was that these local exhibitions would draw the attention of the national press.

Bunshaft reinforced the idea that the exhibition present itself on a cultural, and not an advertising, level—although the distinction between the two had by this time become completely blurred. Owings underscored that point: "I had in mind, now, this fine arts center as the basis for the cultural approach; and then lead it from that to the fine museums of the country, like Chicago, and San Francisco, and Boston, and so on around; that would give us everything, I think, we would need in the way of public approach. It's an intellectual thing."[63] More precisely, what Bunshaft and Owings had in mind was the type of architectural exhibitions that MoMA had mounted in 1932 and 1950. Their emphasis was on a traveling museum exhibition that would serve as a marketing tool for the firm of SOM. Within that format the academy design, already qualified as "art" by definition, would be shielded from criticism. Coupled with SOM's 1950 MoMA exhibition, it would solidify the firm's status at the forefront of architectural modernism.

As if on cue, Talbott followed Owings's remarks by expressing concerns about academy enrollments to Harmon, allowing Robert again to tie the exhibition to their concerns: "I meant primarily the recruiting in all services. The interest that this would stir in the Air Force—not necessarily in the Academy, but in the Air Force itself. It would be like showing everyone because the newspapers in every local community will pick it up."[64]

The following month, on January 5, another meeting was held in Washington, D.C., primarily to deal with the boundaries of the academy site. Among those representing the air force were Talbott, Harmon, and Erler, while Owings, John Merrill, Bunshaft, and Netsch represented SOM.[65] Although the focus of this meeting was to determine the amount of land available for the academy, Owings again brought up the issue of the exhibition. Talbott still wanted to solicit private funding by revealing some of the architectural developments to the people at the United States Air Force Academy Foundation later in the month. Harmon also wanted to present the ideas to a symposium of the Air Defense Command, which would include representatives from the aircraft industry.[66] After patiently listening to their arguments, Owings countered: "Mr. Secretary, I would like to suggest this possibility: that you make no presentation until we have something to really show them. Now, you can understand these things and your staff can, but this is highly technical, and to the layman, all they can see is a bunch of trees and hills. . . . Let's just have it a small group of people, confidential, because if we break this, some people are going to get the wrong impression. We ought to plan this presentation very carefully. . . . If we get off base a little bit, it is going to cause a lot of trouble. Everybody is dying to know what this stuff looks like, and we won't be able to show them until late May."[67]

Owings, of course, knew that a broader context existed for SOM's academy design. He realized that, while many of the major architectural magazines in this country supported architectural modernism, a strong, well-publicized presentation would help elicit a favorable response from the press and encourage a favorable reception by the general public, functioning as an invaluable marketing tool for the firm. He was also aware that the major architectural magazines in the country were already interested in the academy project. On July 26, 1954, just three days after SOM was awarded the contract, Owings had received a telegraph from Thomas Creighton, editor of the prestigious magazine *Progressive Architecture,* asking for first publication privileges in presenting the academy design.[68] Owings's remarks to Talbott reflect that awareness: "The only other thing we would like to be sure of is this publicity. The last time I had lunch with you, you suggested we might get a public relations group, and we ought to be planning right now. We should be telling the big magazines that we are going to have this ready for the May or June issues. . . . This thing should sweep the country at the top level, so that people will accept it as a fine thing."[69]

SOM envisioned controlling the publicity surrounding the academy construction. An SOM interdepartmental memo written the same day as the January 5, 1955, meeting noted, "My view is that we might as well have Ivy Lee [a public relations consultant] under sub-contract to us for publicity rather than have him under contract directly with the [Air Force Academy] Construction Agency. In this way we will be able to coordinate and control what is done."[70] SOM's intent was to place the academy design itself at the center of its publicity, but instead

it was air force officials that took control of publicity. They established a public information office as part of the Air Force Academy Construction Agency to handle news releases concerning the academy and assigned Colonel Max Boyd to oversee it.[71]

In a January 24 letter to Harmon, Boyd suggested a date in May for the unveiling of the academy design. It would take place in Colorado Springs and would be timed so that information could be reported in the Sunday newspapers. Besides the members of the press, civic leaders from Colorado would be invited, and briefings would be provided by both air force personnel and the architects. Boyd's letter cited the exhibition as only one of several publicity events that would call attention to the academy. Other events would include the first public showing of the uniforms ("worn by a sharp-looking young man"), the historic entrance of the first class into the academy (an event to take place on July 11 of the same year at the temporary Lowry facility), and the academy's first football game. These events all had the potential to be the subjects of short features that would be shown at movie theaters and on television and that would attract enlistees to the academy. Boyd also supported the idea of a traveling exhibition of the academy models to other cities, complete with pamphlets and photographs available to the public.[72] Boyd's letter reveals a publicity campaign focused more broadly on recruitment, rather than simply on the academy's architectural design. Within that context, the exhibition was only part of the overall plan. Proof of that is the manner in which the new cadet uniform design was unveiled to the public. In February 1955, Talbott announced that the Hollywood producer and director Cecil B. DeMille would design the uniforms—a decision that was reported to the public the following month in *Time* magazine.[73]

SOM's notion of a publicity campaign, however, continued to focus upon the firm, as reflected in an exchange of letters during March. On March 14 James Byrnes, director of the Colorado Springs Fine Arts Center, wrote Owings: "As you will recall, during your last visit here we discussed the possibility of an overall exhibition of the work of your firm. At that time, I expressed the hope that the Air Academy plans and models could be the focal point. Since that time the project has progressed to the point where I feel that it could provide the major theme." Byrnes envisioned a gala opening event, complete with comprehensive catalogues, and planned to have the exhibition tour other cities.[74] Three days later, Owings sent a letter to Talbott proposing an early May date for the opening of the exhibition. He also reiterated that the event should be held in

Colorado Springs rather than Washington, D.C., so that the actual academy site could be visited. Owings explained that, following the presentation to members of Congress and the press in Colorado Springs, the exhibit could be displayed in major art museums around the country—a tour that would span the construction phase of the academy.[75] On March 25, Talbott wrote Byrnes, reserving the weekend of May 13–15, 1955, at the Colorado Springs Fine Arts Center for the initial public showing of the Air Force Academy plans and models.[76] The exhibition was to focus on two main themes: the cadet's curriculum and the development of the site, from regional studies to master plan.[77]

Owings had, in the meantime, requested an extravagant $100,000 budget for the exhibition, an amount agreed upon by Talbott.[78] Several days later, Ferry wrote a memorandum on behalf of Talbott informing General Washbourne that $100,000 would be made available to SOM for the exhibition. Not wanting to cut into the construction budget that had been allocated by Congress for the academy, Ferry requested they search for the money from other sources.[79] Realizing that taxpayers might object to an expensive exhibition, Ferry advised Owings to design "for clarity and simplicity, keeping in mind always that criticism of the waste of taxpayers' funds for the presentation could easily stem from an elaborate and expensively executed affair. For example, a simple stenofaxed fact sheet could serve the same purposes as an expensively printed brochure."[80]

In fact, SOM and the air force spared no expense on the exhibition. A day after Ferry's letter was written, Carroll L. Tyler, general manager of the air force academy project for SOM, informed Herbert Bayer, who had agreed to design the exhibition, that his fee would be $1,800.[81] Based on his experiences at the 1939 World's Fair and the MoMA, Bayer was now recognized as one of the foremost exhibition designers in the country. On April 4, Netsch wrote Tyler that Theodore Conrad's fee for building two models of the proposed design would be over $24,000 and that George Cooper Rudolph would be preparing a series of renderings for $750 each (eventually his fee totaled $7991.94).[82] Both worked out of New York and had been employed extensively by SOM (Conrad had constructed the models for its 1950 MoMA exhibition). Within the week Rush Studios, a model-building firm in Chicago, gave bids of $13,120 and $8,830 for constructing two other models.[83] Eventually, the cost of models for the exhibition amounted to more than half of the nearly $100,000 total cost.[84] At approximately the same time, the photographers Ezra Stoller, Ansel Adams, and William Garnett were hired at fees of $4,547.42, $1,005.62, and $1,171.95 (plus expenses), respectively. The air force had its

own photographers, and certainly an exhibition that would simply display proposed models of the academy did not require the services of a design and photographic team of this caliber. But by this time, SOM and the air force shared the agenda of mounting a high-quality exhibition that newspapers would report on their front pages. Clearly, SOM intended this to be a full-fledged museum exhibition, designed and realized by top professionals in their fields.

However, Colonel Albert E. Stoltz, the new director of the Air Force Academy Construction Agency, was leery about the costly nature of this exhibition. Stoltz had replaced Erler as director of the AFACA on January 31, 1955, and was more critical of the firm than his predecessor had been. On April 13, he wrote John Merrill, stating, "Some concern has been expressed that this presentation may well verge upon 'gold-plating.'" Stoltz informed SOM that he had charged Colonel Fred Drittler of the agency with the specific task of overseeing the exhibition, and he arranged for Drittler to visit SOM's Chicago office "to assure himself of the fact that presentation materials be as austere as is necessary, and yet to further assure himself that completeness of coverage is not diminished."[85] Stoltz's concerns overlapped with the air force's perception of a successful publicity campaign. Associations with football games and designer uniforms or the glamour of high-speed flight were viewed as positive ways to increase enlistment; a scandal over the cost of this exhibition was not.

The same day, Owings drafted a letter and sent copies to Bayer, Bunshaft, and Netsch. Responding to the air force's request for simplicity, he informed them, "I would summarize the theme it suggests to me as monastic quality of rigid and sterile simplicity. . . . It suggests cold, clear austere backgrounds of muslin or monk's cloth with exhibits standing out starkly and simply under effective lighting."[86] The challenge for Bayer, then, was to create a dramatic effect within this "austere" context. He touched on that issue several days later in a letter to Bunshaft (written, as was his custom, in lowercase letters): "i do hope, and this is difficult to foresee, that the many lights which we need in this room to make all perspectives and plans, besides the model, visible, will not brighten up the room so that the dramatic effect will be lost."[87] The dramatic effect that Bayer sought was to be experienced firsthand by the exhibition's visitors, but it was also an effect that SOM wanted to convey through the media.

SOM was not only aware of the potentials of exhibition design, it also recognized the power of the photographic image in the press. Ezra Stoller had taken striking night photographs of

SOM's Lever Brothers Office Building and the Manufacturers Trust Company Bank Building, which had appeared in *Architectural Forum* and *Architectural Record,* respectively.[88] The firm had also employed Stoller to photograph the Conrad models that appeared in the 1950 MoMA exhibit of its work, and the photos appeared in the fall 1950 MoMA bulletin. The effectiveness of Stoller's photographic representations of modernism had not escaped the notice of discerning critics. Commenting on a 1953 MoMA exhibition of postwar architecture, Sibyl Moholy-Nagy wrote, "The triumph of Modern Architecture is the triumph of Ezra Stoller and his colleagues. Architectural photography—from brilliant blow-ups to stereo-optic color shots in special viewers—served as a convincing expression of what the Museum leadership has snobbishly called 'the discovery and proclamation of excellence.'"[89] Stoller's photographs did not merely illuminate architecture but transformed it, much as the dramatic lighting techniques had done with the 1939 World's Fair architecture. The architecture was aestheticized as a transcendent, two-dimensional photographic image. SOM and the air force trusted that Stoller's images of the academy models could be used in marketing "the image" of the academy design in a packet that would be handed out to the press at the exhibition opening. In drawing on elements of the photographic sublime, Stoller's images complemented the heroic photographs of Ansel Adams and William Garnett that would appear in the exhibition.

Adams was a friend of Owings.[90] At the time of the exhibition, Adams was recognized by his peers as the dean of landscape photography. Alfred Steiglitz had mounted an exhibition of his work at the American Place in 1936, the first exhibition Stieglitz had devoted solely to photography since his 1917 exhibition of Paul Strand's work.[91] In 1940, Adams's images were included in the first exhibition of the newly formed Photographic Department at MoMA, which he and Beaumont Newhall curated.[92] His landscape photographs of the 1940s further established his reputation, as magazines such as *Fortune* and *Life* sought his work, and in 1948 his enormous coloramas, commissioned by the Eastman Kodak Company, were installed in New York's Grand Central Station.[93] In these images, Adams drew upon the mythic power of the landscape to create heroic scenes of natural splendor. As John Szarkowski noted, Adams "believed in . . . the deeply romantic idea that the great vistas and microscopic details of the wilderness could be seen as metaphor for freedom and heroic aspiration. Adams's photographs seem to demonstrate that the world is what we wish it was—a place with room in it for fresh beginnings."[94] Adams's

images, though, were as much about the technology of photography as the subject matter itself. In 1954 alone, he wrote three technical books on photography.[95] While his subject was nature, it was formally ordered and arranged by a disciplined sense of structure.[96]

Adams's involvement with environmental issues was perceived as inseparable from the subject matter of his photographs. Serving on the board of directors of the Sierra Club since 1934, he had written extensively on environmental issues and argued his concerns before Congress.[97] Indicative of this union of environmental concerns and photography was the exhibition at the San Francisco Academy of Sciences that opened in May 1955, just one week prior to the Air Force Academy exhibition. Entitled *This Is the American Earth,* the exhibition included a text by Nancy Newhall, encouraging guardianship of natural resources, and contrasted Adams's heroic photographs of unspoiled nature with the chaotic urban sprawl of Los Angeles depicted in Garnett's aerial photographs.[98]

Adams's approach to environmental issues was, however, complex. Like SOM, he had received numerous corporate commissions. Firms such as Kennecott Copper, Pacific Gas and Electric, and Standard Oil used his images as backdrops in their advertising to enhance their corporate image and tie it to associations with the West. He also believed that teamwork between corporate America and the government was necessary to support the national economy and United States military supremacy. In 1951, for example, his photograph of Kennecott Copper Corporation's Bingham mine in Utah appeared in *Fortune* magazine. The image was of the company's huge open-pit mining operation and was accompanied by the text, "They're Rolling Up the Score in the 'Copper Bowl.'" Likening the scarred landscape to a "stadium for giants," Kennecott proudly announced in the ad that its team was pulling together to extract copper for industry and defense. Adams also advocated the use of nuclear-generated energy, which he believed would solve issues of pollution caused by the burning of fossil fuels. In that endeavor he supported the efforts of the Pacific Gas and Electric Company, the same corporation John Muir had fought over the damming of the Hetch Hetchy earlier in the century, to build the now infamous Diablo Canyon power plant.[99] The corporate giant Standard Oil, which Truman accused of collaborating with a German company during World War II to raise rubber costs, used Adams's images to establish links to American postwar patriotism in its "See Your West" advertising series. The landscape photographs associated the corporation with guardianship of the nation's resources.

Figure 21. United States Air Force Academy site, Colorado Springs, Colorado. Photograph by Ansel Adams. Used with permission of the Trustees of the Ansel Adams Publishing Rights Trust. All rights reserved.

Asked to photograph the academy site by Owings less than a month prior to the exhibition, Adams agreed only reluctantly, fearing there was not enough time to do an adequate job for the project. He recommended that William Garnett take aerial photographs to complement his work on the ground.[100] Garnett, while not as well known as a photographer as Adams, was one of the country's first aerial photographers. His photographs, although sometimes described as having "a kind of god's-eye awareness," often reveal patterns of design imposed by man or, if imposed by nature, framed and structured by man.[101] Garnett was also an architectural photographer, but it

was his aerial images that were published by magazines such as *Fortune*. Steichen had included some of his photographs in the *Family of Man* exhibition that opened at MoMA in January 1955, and Newhall featured his photographs in a one-man exhibition later that year at the George Eastman House in Rochester, New York.[102]

Adams and Garnett photographed the academy site under difficult conditions (figure 21). Adams related, "In truth the conditions were awful for good photography! The worst time of the year—and wind, haze and drab trees."[103] Garnett fared as poorly: "I had serious difficulties with air turbulence—which makes low altitude photography uncertain in terms of image definition (especially important when the negatives are to be enlarged to mural proportions)."[104] Bayer received the photographs by the end of April and enlarged them to mural size. He later wrote Adams that the quality of some was so inferior he had to touch them up, optimistically noting that Owings had stated that new and better enlargements could be made when the exhibition was shown in other locations, such as MoMA.[105]

The invitation list for the exhibition opening was compiled by Talbott, and it was extensive and impressive. It included the members of the House Armed Services Committee (40 people), the four representatives and two senators from Colorado, the members of the Department of Defense Subcommittee of the House Committee on Appropriations (15), the members of the Senate Appropriations Committee (19), the Senate Armed Services Committee (14), Congressional Committee staff members (23), air force and Air Force Academy representatives (18), the four members of the Site Selection Committee, the consultants to the architects (along with Becket and Saarinen, he invited Pietro Belluschi, who had been appointed as a consultant after Harrison's resignation on March 3, 1955), as well as the architect Ellery Husted, and members of SOM and the associated

engineers on the project (11 people, including Skidmore, Owings, Merrill, Bunshaft, and Netsch). In addition, various Colorado state, city, and county officials and civic leaders were invited (10), as were members of the advisory committee of the Air Force Academy Foundation and their administrative staff (28). Press invitations were extended to another 70 persons.[106]

The models and photomurals were delivered by van to the Colorado Springs Fine Arts Center on Friday, May 6, at 7:00 A.M., and installed during the following week.[107] It was intended that the members of Congress and their special guests would arrive on Friday afternoon, May 13, and enjoy a reception and dinner at the Broadmoor Hotel in Colorado Springs. The following day they were to be shuttled to the Fine Arts Center, where they would be briefed on the design by the architects prior to touring the exhibition. Tours by van and bus of the academy site would then be conducted. At the same time, members of the press would be given a separate presentation of the exhibition. Their press packets would include a 28-page fact sheet dealing with site and planning data, a 13-page fact sheet on the Air Force Academy, an 11-page fact sheet on the architecture, a 4-page press release that included a Stoller photograph of the Cadet Area model (figure 22), a Rudolph ren-

Figure 22. Architectural model at May 13–15, 1955, exhibition, Colorado Springs Fine Arts Center. The academy chapel appears at the left, the administration building at center, and the cadet social center to the right. Photograph by Ezra Stoller, © ESTO.

Figure 23. George Cooper Rudolph rendering, "The Academy," May 13–15, 1955, exhibition, Colorado Springs Fine Arts Center.

dering of the Cadet Area (figure 23), and a 2-page fact sheet on the Colorado Springs Fine Arts Center.[108] The stage was now set for the unveiling of the Academy design.

THE EXHIBITION

The site of the exhibition, the Colorado Springs Fine Arts Museum, was a noted architectural work by John Gaw Meem, an architect from New Mexico, and had been constructed between 1934 and 1936. The design earned Meem a silver medal at the Fifth Pan American Congress of Architecture in 1940. Meem's regionalist style often merged elements of Pueblo and Spanish colonial styles with a modern stripped classicism. For the Colorado Springs museum, Meem elected to refer to regional architecture in an abstract fashion, while employing a more modern design (figure 24). As he later explained, a Spanish-Pueblo style of architecture seemed out of place "in a modern town

like Colorado Springs. It was decided, therefore, the building must be modern in its design but its masses and simplicity should suggest the regional architecture. The result we felt should be a truly American type of building."[109] Although Meem considered the museum design modern, his design solution in addressing the Colorado locality contrasted radically with SOM's approach.

The academy exhibition took place in the Southwest Museum and Indian Museum Rooms, the walls of which were covered with fabric, negating Meem's interior surfaces. The East Gallery was used as the reception area where groups were briefed prior to their viewing the exhibition. A special exhibition entitled *Man's Aspiration towards Flight,* consisting of fifty prints dating from 1450 to the mid-nineteenth century, had been mounted there.[110] In the absence of any color photographs of the exhibition, we can learn of the colors used in the exhibition by reading letters to SOM firm members in which

Figure 24. Colorado Springs Fine Arts Center, south facade, Colorado Springs, Colorado. John Gaw Meem, 1934–36. Photograph by the author.

Bayer described his design intent. Bayer wrote of using an off-white fabric lining on the walls, accentuated by yellow fabric in the lobby, yellow title panels, blue painted panels at the end of the corridor, and red arches.[111] The use of primary colors was a hallmark of Bayer's design, dating back to his Bauhaus training and the De Stijl influence on that institution. Whether it was feared that the color red had associations with communism in the cold war era, or SOM wanted a more subtle color scheme, the firm objected to the use of red, and Bayer painted the arches white.[112]

Exhibition visitors were to proceed from the reception room (outside the top left corner of the plan in figure 25), cross a corridor, and move in a counterclockwise manner through a series of carefully choreographed spaces presented in scenographic fashion.[113] As the visitors crossed the corridor, they passed an alcove to their right that contained a platform holding a model of the entire academy design. It was mounted at approximately waist height, against the backdrop of a solid blue wall flanked

by curtains. On the wall "THE MASTER PLAN" was written in six-inch uppercase letters (figure 26). This was the only model in the exhibition not backed by a photomural, as the celestial background and authoritative lettering set the mood for the grand plan that was about to be revealed.

The first room past the corridor was devoted to the airfield and academic community areas (figures 27 and 28). Two models, again mounted at waist height, were on opposite sides of the room. The airfield model, to the visitor's right, was backed by an enormous 13'-by-32' Garnett aerial panoramic view of the area, while the model of the community center on the opposite wall was backed by another photomural, this one measuring 13' by 20'. The vistas in both black-and-white murals were photographed facing west, against the spectacular backdrop of the Rampart Range. Brief explanatory texts augmented the models.

Visitors then ascended several steps into the next room, where they faced a Rudolph illustration (figure 29). Rendered with an opaque water-based paint, this 40"-by-60" illustration

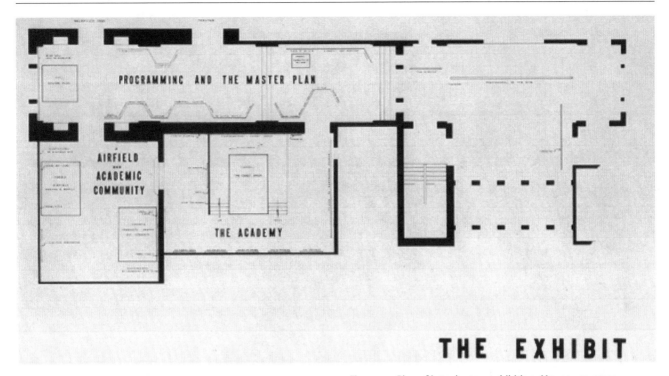

THE EXHIBIT

Figure 25. Plan of introductory exhibition, May 13–15, 1955. Author's drawing.

was one of eight (all the same size) produced for the exhibition, providing colorful contrast to the black-and-white photomurals.[114] This illustration featured cadets in parade formation, marching against a backdrop of the academic building and retaining-wall ramps, with the mountain range again in the background. To the left of this rendering, mounted on an adjacent wall, was another photomural, an 11'-by-12' Adams photograph of Cathedral Rock, one of the outstanding landscape features on the site. Forced by that dead-end wall to continue in a counter-clockwise manner, the visitors proceeded around the corner to reach the exhibition centerpiece, the large model of the central Cadet Area mounted on a low platform (figures 30 and 31). After climbing four steps, visitors circled the model. A 9'-by-24' Adams mural of the area site, again from a vantage point looking west, covered the back wall, completing the sensation of an airborne trip around the site. Upon descending from the platform via another set of four steps, visitors could view five more Rudolph architectural renderings on the opposite wall: "Library Court" (figure 32), "Dining Hall" (figure 33), "Court of Honor" (figure 34), "Gymnasium" (figure 35), and "The Academy" (see figure 23).

Leaving the room, visitors entered the opposite end of the corridor they had originally crossed (labeled "Programming and the Master Plan" in figure 25). Along the corridor's perimeter, panels projected obliquely from the walls. Bearing text,

Figure 26. Model of master plan and its setting in the exhibition, May 13–15, 1955. Courtesy Skidmore, Owings, and Merrill LLP.

graphics, and photomontage, they elucidated the various aspects of the academy's plan and the cadets' curriculum (figures 36–38). On the corridor's right wall, three panels outlined the cadets' educational experience. Just past those was another model of the topography of the site, again mounted at waist height and backed by a photomural—this one a 4'6"-by-

Figure 27. Model and photograph of airfield area, May 13–15, 1955, exhibition. Courtesy Skidmore, Owings, and Merrill LLP.

Figure 28. Model and photograph of community center area, May 13–15, 1955, exhibition. Courtesy Skidmore, Owings, and Merrill LLP.

Figure 29. George Cooper Rudolph rendering, "The Parade," May 13–15, 1955, exhibition. The academic building appears to the left. Courtesy Skidmore, Owings, and Merrill LLP.

Figure 30. Model of the Cadet Area, May 13–15, 1955, exhibition. Courtesy Skidmore, Owings, and Merrill LLP.

Figure 31. Model of the Cadet Area, May 13–15, 1955, exhibition. Courtesy Skidmore, Owings, and Merrill LLP.

Figure 32. George Cooper Rudolph rendering, "Library Court," May 13–15, 1955, exhibition. The academic building's library is to the left and the cadet quarters to the right. Courtesy Skidmore, Owings, and Merrill LLP.

Figure 33. George Cooper Rudolph rendering, "Dining Hall," May 13–15, 1955, exhibition. Courtesy Skidmore, Owings, and Merrill LLP.

Figure 34. George Cooper Rudolph rendering, "Court of Honor," May 13–15, 1955, exhibition. Right to left: the Social Center, the chapel, and a fragment of the administration building. Courtesy Skidmore, Owings, and Merrill LLP.

Figure 35. George Cooper Rudolph rendering, "Gymnasium," May 13–15, 1955, exhibition. The cadet quarters are in the background, to the right. Courtesy Skidmore, Owings, and Merrill LLP.

Figure 36. Exhibition view, May 13–15, 1955. Courtesy Skidmore, Owings, and Merrill LLP.

Figure 37. Exhibition view, "Regional Aspects," May 13–15, 1955. Courtesy Skidmore, Owings, and Merrill LLP.

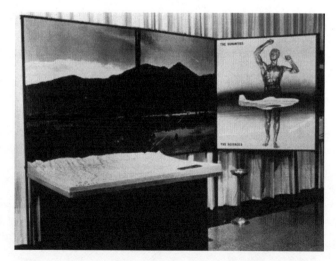

Figure 38. Exhibition view, "The Humanities, The Sciences," May 13–15, 1955. Courtesy Skidmore, Owings, and Merrill LLP

12' view of the site, again photographed facing west. Continuing down the corridor's right wall, elements of the master plan were again outlined. On the left side of the corridor, a series of panels snaked along the wall. The panels described regional issues of zoning, population, transportation, water supply, and climate. The perspective converged at the opposite end of the corridor, where the circuitous journey had begun, at the alcove with its text—"THE MASTER PLAN."

Owings referred to the exhibition in his autobiography as "great theater."[115] Certainly he realized how much the exhibition depended on scenographic spectacle in marketing the academy design. Since the intended audience was comprised of members of Congress (with the expectation that they would fund the project) and the general public (with the intent of drawing attention to the firm's achievements via the national media), the exhibition positioned itself cautiously between the ostentatious spectacles of world's fairs and Steichen's MoMA exhibitions and the sparse, minimalist vocabulary of SOM's own 1950 MoMA exhibition. Bayer's exhibition design combined aspects of both, giving the illusion of economic restraint while drawing on the power of the photographic image. He seamlessly united graphics, the photographic images of Adams and Garnett, and the renderings of Rudolph to reinforce the formalist aesthetics of the architecture.

As visitors left the first room of the exhibition, for example, they encountered Rudolph's rendering "The Parade" (see figure 29). It was an illustration looking west to a mountainous backdrop. In the middle ground, the glass facade of the academic building created a geometric grid, while in the foreground, ordered ranks of cadets marched from the parade ground—silhouetted against the huge ramps that were originally intended to link it to the campus.[116] The exhibition visitors then proceeded to the next room and, after ascending to and descending from the model of the Cadet Area, faced five more of Rudolph's renderings. The first, "Library Court," represented rows of cadets in formation (see figure 32). The men march from the distant right background, seeming to emerge from the mountainous backdrop, to the left foreground, past the chapel and library. The image at once united the natural world, the manmade temple of God, and the temple of technological learning. It also united the present with the classical past, as phalanxes of warriors marched against a backdrop of colonnaded architecture. The four renderings next to that depicted the cadet's life at the academy, conveying a sense of concern for his physical, social, and religious well-being. The last was an aerial rendering, reiterating rational man's role in creating

order out of chaos. Natural forms were minimized, while architectural forms framed the views. As surrounding nature entered the site, it was thinned and regularized to conform to the architectural grid.

A copy of that aerial rendering of the Cadet Area was one of two images included in the press packet for the exhibition (see figure 23). The view was toward the northwest, with the Rampart Range in the background. Basically a reinterpretation of the ensemble of the model and Adams's photomural at the exhibition, it was reinforced by the other image in the packet—a Stoller photograph of the model taken prior to the exhibition (see figure 22). Stoller's image simulated another aerial view of the complex, again looking west. But whereas Rudolph's rendering depicted the academy in a clear, even light, Stoller's photograph showed the mountains as silhouettes in the background against a darkening sky. This was due in part to the fact that the Stoller photo of the model was taken in Chicago, with cardboard cutouts serving as the mountainous terrain, and yet the image reinforced the sublime nature of the western site.[117] Coincidentally, the shadows also served to soften the stark appearance of the modernist design (in the process, perhaps, softening public resistance to the design). Both the Rudolph and Stoller images appeared in numerous publications following the exhibition, including *Architectural Forum, Architectural Record, Progressive Architecture, Art News, Newsweek, Time, U.S. News,* and newspapers across the country.

Bayer's sequence of graphics in the corridor further reinforced the notion of technology in the service of humankind. Like the rationalist grid of the academy, they underscored the role of reason in organizing and ordering the natural site. Facing the small site model on the right side of the corridor, for example, was a panel that displayed a large figure of a man—a classical nude—with a jet plane superimposed across his midsection (see figure 38). To the upper left of the image were the words "The Humanities," while at the bottom left, the same bold uppercase type read "The Sciences." Technology was, quite literally, inscribed across the geography of human existence and contrasted to the image and model of the undeveloped site—"humane science" would order the master plan and ensure world peace and prosperity.

THE EXHIBITION: RHETORIC AND MYTHIC ANALOGIES

This vision of an Air Force Academy, based on the notion of an heroic western past progressing toward a utopian and technologically determined future, was supported by a mythic context that overlapped with the rhetoric of architectural modernism, flight, and the American West. In his short introductory speech that prefaced the exhibition viewing, Owings set those myths in motion. He began his speech by stating SOM's design approach: "The challenge—our challenge—is to produce for generations to come—not just for today or for fifty years hence—an efficient, flexible, and simple solution to the design of your Academy; and yet—and above all—beautiful, lastingly beautiful. In other words, our challenge is to produce a timeless beautiful thing that works." Owings then credited the involvement of others in the design, first citing Talbott and the consultants, in the process presenting the consultants as representative of the nation at large: "Eero Saarinen from the Middle West, Welton Becket from the West Coast, MIT's Pietro Belluschi, who recently took the place of Wally Harrison of New York"). He continued, naming the engineering firms, Harmon, and the academy staff. "There has been," Owings noted, "teamwork from the beginning and still is." This was followed with comments emphasizing how thorough the firm's site and regional analyses had been, addressing such issues as climate, terrain, soil conditions, and water supply (aspects addressed in the exhibition by Bayer's graphics).[118]

Owings then turned his attention to the site itself: "And now about the site. What a site! Magnificent!" Owings presented it in contrast to an age "of enforced decentralization, of congested cities, snarled traffic, creeping slums . . . 17,500 acres of untouched nature . . . a virtual island of unspoiled country. . . . With Academy boundaries strategically located so as to make intrusion into this area an actual impossibility in perpetuity. . . . A natural solution seems to have come out of all this. On our wonderful site we found a natural mesa or finger of land resting high up against the mountains—a veritable Acropolis, a perfect series of plains on which to rest the Academy proper." Careful to prepare his audience for SOM's architectural response, Owings stressed the fact that the defining issues for the academy superseded regional concerns: "The site is a magnificent section of Colorado, of the Rocky Mountains. It establishes on the magnificent scale of a 7,000-foot high to mile wide backdrop the local environment and character of the Academy. On the other hand, as we see it, the cultural and educational aspects of the United States Air Force Academy are in no way local—they are national, or in our minds, really global in scope." He then tied those comments more specifically to SOM's design approach:

We believe that the architectural concepts of the Academy buildings should represent this national character of the Academy, that they should represent in steel and glass, marble and stone the simple, direct, modern way of life—that they should be as modern, as timeless, and as style-less in their architectural concept, as efficient and as flexible in their basic layout as the most modern projected aircraft. . . . We believe that this Academy, tucked in among the mountains, proudly standing on our modern Acropolis, will create a vibrant cultural and spiritual sense of forward-looking accomplishment in these young people.

The exhibition content and design reinforced Owings's remarks, giving the impression that SOM's design solution was not just a viable one for the program of an air academy and its Colorado location, but was in fact the only appropriate solution. SOM's experience with expositions and museum exhibitions, and its familiarity with modernist rhetoric, is paramount to this discussion, creating the context for the vital myths that were incorporated into SOM's design presentation.

The overlap of modern approaches to architecture and flight had many precedents. Allusions to flight and aircraft had been used in collaboration with visions of technological utopias and as an apologia for modern design since the early twentieth century. One of the best known such texts was Le Corbusier's *Vers une architecture* of 1923. Of particular relevance to the later academy discussions were the analogies he made between flight and architecture, reducing both to technological imperatives.[119] He also juxtaposed text and image in reinforcing those analogies—a technique that the firm of SOM employed in its academy presentation.

In the United States, flight represented an envisioned future that included easier lifestyles and more leisure time, the result of a flourishing capitalistic system and mass production of consumer goods.[120] The American mania for flight was given impetus by Charles Lindbergh's historic crossing of the Atlantic on May 20, 1927.[121] A year later, Amelia Earhart became the first woman to fly across the Atlantic (although two men actually flew the craft), and in 1932 became the first woman to fly across it solo. The enthusiasm for flight grew during the 1930s, as exemplified by the world's fairs of that decade and reflected in various publications that repositioned Le Corbusier's writings within an American context. Two such publications were Norman Bel Geddes's *Horizons* of 1932 and Walter Dorwin Teague's 1940 text, *Design This Day*. Geddes's book included a section on airplane design. Like Le Corbusier, he emphasized standardization, mathematical proportions, and unadorned geometric forms, while his insistence upon efficiency and economy had special relevance for Americans in the throes of the Great Depression.[122] Teague's text compared the formal properties of industrial aircraft design to classical and Gothic structures, again underscoring associations between architectural and technological forms.[123]

The world's fairs of 1933 and 1939 also celebrated flight. At the 1933 Chicago exposition, for example, George Keck's "Home of Tomorrow" incorporated a planeport into its design. The futurist theme of the 1939 New York World's Fair was predicated on the belief that a new dynamic and technological society would be realized by 1960. That fair's descriptions of the future were in large part inspired by writers of the late nineteenth and early twentieth centuries.[124] Those authors included H. G. Wells, who wrote the article "World of Tomorrow" for the March 5, 1939, issue of the *New York Times*. His article was accompanied by a rendering of a bird's-eye view of a futuristic city, emphasizing the fact that the vision of the future would, quite literally, be from the vantage point of an airplane. The most popular dioramas of the fair itself included elevated vantage points. They included Democracity, a city of the year 2039 designed by Henry Dreyfuss in Harrison and Fouilhoux's Perisphere, Geddes's Futurama in the General Motors "Highways and Horizons" exhibit (mentioned earlier), and Walter Dorwin Teague's futuristic diorama for United States Steel.[125]

Certainly the placement of the architectural models at the initial academy exhibition, with the huge photomural backgrounds by Garnett and Adams, simulated aerial vantage points—an effect emphasized in the centerpiece model of the Cadet Area, which was exhibited at a much lower height than the other models. Circling that model, the viewer assumed the position of a pilot, tacitly taking responsibility for a new world order in which technology would be at the service of humankind.[126] One can imagine a voice in the background intoning, "Now we approach a modern university center. Here, in buildings of simple but functional architecture, the youth of 1960 study for their future in a world of still greater progress and achievement." That, in fact, had been the accompanying soundtrack at Geddes's 1939 World's Fair Futurama exhibit as the visitors observed the future from their aerial vantage point.[127] The difference between the two events was that the 1939 World's Fair and Futurama were subsidized by industry, which, as noted at the beginning of this chapter, positioned itself at the forefront of technology while man conformed or adapted to those changes. The academy exhibition, while em-

phasizing the new technologies employed by the air force, more specifically emphasized the role of man (the trained cadet) in applying and managing those technologies.

Predictions for the future included aircraft ownership by the average citizen. In the 1943 MoMA *Airways for Peace* exhibition, a film presented a vision of the American future in which businessmen commuted to work in private helicopters.[128] These images persisted into the 1950s. The February 1951 cover of *Popular Mechanics*, for example, portrayed a businessman pushing a small private helicopter into his garage. The notion of individuals traveling in privately owned helicopters was an idea reiterated by Frank Lloyd Wright. In his book *The Living City*, first published in 1958, he noted that the decentralization of cities was more feasible than ever, since man now had the means to travel "in his motorcar, copter, or plane." In that text, an illustration of Broadacre City depicted flying saucer–like helicopters hovering over the Broadacre countryside.[129]

World War II created a more complicated context for the myth of flight than for technological utopias. The Civilian Pilot Training Program was initiated in 1939 in response to the German invasion of Poland. The program established preflight ground school training at many American universities, and by 1943, preflight aeronautic courses were being taught at over half of the nation's high schools. Postwar education emphasized international flight. "Air Globes," showing only dots for cities and lacking features such as national boundaries, were used as teaching aids. Students were taught key phrases in various languages, as a world of enduring peace was envisioned—a world shrunk by the phenomenon of air travel.[130] By the 1950s, however, the American public's fascination with flight had been tainted by the events of the war and the realization that a private plane in every garage was impractical, from the standpoint of both economics and safety. From a year of peak sales in 1946, when thirty-three thousand private planes were sold, 1947 sales were half that figure, and 1948 saw another 50 percent drop.

As sales in private airplanes slumped, however, the aerospace industry found a larger market for its services. Spurred by concerns over national defense and by global investment possibilities, aerospace corporations flourished, and by 1953 the aerospace industry was again the country's largest commercial enterprise. The enhanced role of the air force in protecting and watching over the world during the cold war was couched in both political and economic terms—the world was made safe for both democracy and capitalistic investments. This renewed emphasis upon the air force's international significance reverberated in Owings's introductory speech, in which he reminded listeners that the cultural and educational concerns of the academy were truly "global in scope."

In planning the May exhibition, Walter Netsch had originally intended to present the significance of the air force in different terms, overlapping a summary of the evolution of the armed services with overt references to a technologically determinant reading of modernism. In a memo written during the exhibition planning stages, Netsch noted: "West Point was designed for the defense of 13 states and for slow and tedious land war, emphasizing traditional tactics and uncomplicated equipment; Annapolis focused on war at sea, employing more extensive operations and recognizing a new way of life; the Air Force was realized as a force to attack and defend throughout the world, using complicated equipment and new tactics—new something all the time."[131] Although it was decided to avoid comparisons to the other service academies because it might "easily elicit public debate and stir up a service controversy," the analogy was always implicit. Commenting on the exhibition, for example, the May 16 issue of the *New York Herald Tribune* stated, "Just as West Point, with its medieval fortress-like appearance, symbolizes the traditions of land warfare, so does the sharplined and soaring Air Force Academy represent the newest and swiftest military science."[132]

Owings's concluding remarks again established an analogous relationship between the air force and modernism. He stated that the academy buildings should be "as modern, as timeless and as style-less . . . as efficient and as flexible in their basic layout as the most modern projected aircraft." Owings emphasized an architecture that would be "timeless" in part to avert criticism of the design by members of the air force. As early as 1949, an air force memo had expressed concern that too modern an architectural treatment for the academy would soon look dated.[133] The desire for a design solution that would be "style-less" was a continuation of the modernist invective against revival and historicist styles. Owings's analogy to modern aircraft reinforced a technologically deterministic view of history. His remark alluded to methods of mass production and the employment of new building techniques, although methods of mass production (as applied, for example, to the auto industry) were never feasible for the aircraft industry, due to the complexities of the designs and constant technological changes.[134] His remarks were reminiscent of the modernist rhetoric that he and Skidmore had used in discuss-

ing the architecture of the 1933 World's Fair. In a July 1933 *Architectural Forum* article, Skidmore wrote, "Certainly this architecture is free from the shackles of the past. . . . The economy of construction, the use of new materials or the new uses of traditional materials . . . in ways hardly imagined before may forecast a new era in building . . . a building era that forgets the limitations of the past and designs buildings which are basically honest, which express the task they are performing, and which actually perform the task."[135]

Owings's remarks on the role of teamwork in the design process were also rooted in modernist rhetoric. Walter Gropius had promoted the notion of teamwork in architecture since his association with the Bauhaus. He envisioned that institution as a revival of the medieval tradition of guilds, with the notion of cooperative teamwork replacing the competitive system advocated by the Ecole des Beaux-Arts. In his 1943 publication *Scope of Total Architecture,* Gropius thrust the issue of teamwork back into the forefront of architectural discussions: "The architect of the future—if he wants to rise to the top again—will be forced by the trend of events to draw closer once more to the building production. If he will build up a closely co-operating team together with the engineer, the scientist and the builder, then design, construction and economy may again become an entity—a fusion of art, science and business. . . . Synchronizing all individual efforts the team can raise its integrated work to higher potentials than is represented by the sum of the work of just so many individuals."[136] Gropius reiterated those concerns in a series of articles he wrote for *Architectural Forum* in the early 1950s.[137]

Having related the academy design to a technological present, Owings also established a context by which the design could connect to a sense of tradition. He twice related the academy to the "Acropolis"—an apparent reference to the Athenian Acropolis—in his speech. Situated against the backdrop of the mountains at an elevation of approximately 7,175 feet, the Cadet Area served as the most public expression of the academy. It was sited to be highly visible from the east and to provide a panoramic view out to the plains. While the architects often talked about the manner in which the housing areas were nestled in the valleys on the site, the prominent location of the Cadet Area justified the Acropolis analogy. The decision to build the Cadet Area on the mesa seems to have been made by the architects and consultants at least as early as December 1954. Owings mentioned it at the December 15 meeting at the Pentagon, at which time Talbott expressed surprise that they would not build in the flatter areas of the site. In response,

Owings made it seem that the decision was preordained: "The thing that was amazing to us was that we took the ideal plan without reference to the site—which takes a certain amount of discipline to keep from thinking about the site—and when we applied it to the site we found we didn't have to make compromises, which is damned unusual."[138] Judging by Owings's remarks at the May exhibition, it seems more likely that, from the outset, SOM had envisioned that the Cadet Area be prominently located. Owings's reference to the Acropolis-like setting of the Cadet Area was also reinforced by the manner in which the primary model of the area was displayed at the exhibition. Elements of dramatic approach, disclosure and enclosure, ascent and descent, all presented against a natural backdrop, made the analogy to the Acropolis all the more forceful. The evocation of Athena, Greek goddess of wisdom and defense, was particularly appropriate for a military and educational institution. The associations between classical architecture and democracy, a tradition that extended back to this country's earliest public architecture, were also relevant. The mythic references allowed SOM to connect its building program to a classical tradition without having to resort to a revivalist style, such as academic classicism.

Finally, SOM integrated one of the most potent American myths into its discussion and presentation—that of the American West. Although SOM had applied for the academy commission prior to the final site selection, the firm's initial public presentation of the academy design incorporated myths of the American West into an architectural approach that itself rejected stylistic regional associations. Owings's intent was to squelch arguments that the modernist design was incongruous with its site. Those concerns were first voiced when preliminary design sketches for the academy were presented at meetings in March 1955 between members of the air force and SOM. After seeing the sketches, Colonel Stoltz wrote to John Merrill: "Personally, I am impressed with what appears to me to be the development of functional layouts to conform to a preconceived architectural style. This style, as evidenced by the model study in your Chicago office, seems to me to be equally indicative of Lake Geneva, Wisconsin; Alton, Illinois; or even New York City or Washington, D.C. I see nothing, except the terrain features, which are characteristic of the Pike's Peak Area or Southwestern United States."[139]

Ever since its earliest meetings with air force representatives, SOM had been concerned with establishing the academy boundaries to preclude "intrusion" into the area, creating in the process "a virtual island of unspoiled country." At a meet-

ing on October 4, 1954, Owings presented the case to Talbott. The architect was concerned that at some future date the city of Colorado Springs might expand, and that the only way to protect the parameters of the academy site from developing "into something highly objectionable to us" would be to pick a natural division—an escarpment—to create a visual separation. Talbott, explaining that the extra property Owings sought was privately owned, steered the conversation to other matters.[140] Not to be dissuaded, Owings addressed the issue in passing when they met on December 15 and in earnest at the beginning of the meeting on January 4, 1955. Talbott again objected to the proposal of attaining the additional land, citing the possibility of complaints from the current landowners and resultant ill will toward the air force. Owings persisted and, with the backing of Erler, convinced Talbott to increase the total acreage of the academy to 17,500 acres from 15,000, giving the architects the entire valley as their drawing board. At the end of that meeting, Talbott stated that until they cleared the decision with Daniel Thornton, then governor of Colorado, it might be a good idea to keep their decision confidential. To his surprise, Talbott was informed by Owings and Erler that the information had been published by newspapers after the October 4 meeting. Owings placated him by stating, "My point is that I think the more publicity you get, in a way the softer the opposition gets."[141]

It was after having attained this vast tract of land that SOM incorporated it in mythic fashion into its May 1955 exhibition, hiring Ansel Adams and William Garnett to provide the evocative images the architects sought. Despite programmatic requirements that provided for an academy located near a cultural center, accessible by highway, with available utilities and a water supply, the photomurals of Adams and Garnett purposefully eliminated traces of human presence.[142] They depicted a pristine environment of mountains, foothills, mesas, valleys, and plain, recalling the vast "uninhabited" tracts of the frontier West. The murals, in conjunction with the models and renderings in the exhibition, engaged various themes associated with the West: notions of wilderness and the frontier; the role of technology and industrialization in defining the West; and the myths associated with the inhabitants of the region.

In his discussion of the American wilderness, Roderick Nash noted the "complex and often contradictory" nature of its definition.[143] On the one hand, wilderness was associated with darkness and danger—a dwelling place of wild men and beasts, a barrier to progress. On the other hand, it was associated with the concept of Exodus—as a testing ground for men and women and their faith. The attachment of aesthetic, spiritual, and patriotic meanings to the American wilderness developed during the nineteenth century, reinforced in the literature of the Transcendentalists and the painters of the Hudson River School and the American West.[144] By the late nineteenth and early twentieth centuries, the romantic concept of wilderness as virtuous had been extended to incorporate notions of virility, as reflected in the works of hosts of artists, poets, and writers, the attitudes of Theodore Roosevelt, and the success of the Boy Scout movement. The relationship between ideas of wilderness and a utopian and democratic society was also given impetus by Theodore Roosevelt, who viewed the wilderness experience as a means to recapture that which made us uniquely American. Paralleling those developments was an increased concern for wilderness preservation—concerns which led to the creation of a National Parks system.[145] By the time of the academy presentation in 1955, the subject of wilderness preservation was again a topic of heated debate in Congress.[146]

If the concept of wilderness defined one set of attitudes in contributing to Western mythology, the concept of the American frontier represented the other. Frederick Jackson Turner's essay "The Significance of the Frontier in American History," which had been read before the American Historical Association at the 1893 World's Columbian Exposition, articulated the issue. Defined as the line of settlement that had moved from east to west—"the meeting point between savagery and civilization"—the frontier, according to Turner, no longer existed.[147] Turner noted the role that the frontier had played in defining this country's citizens, fostering traits such as individualism and self-reliance, and that the development of the frontier had been the major determinant in establishing our democratic political system, in the process turning Europeans into Americans. Turner perceived the frontier as a beneficent influence upon civilization—a "fair, blank page on which to write a new chapter in the story of man's struggle for a higher type of society."[148] During the twentieth century, notions of the frontier were expanded. As the nineteenth-century concept of Manifest Destiny was applied to issues of world leadership and foreign investment abroad, the frontier association took on international implications. Adlai Stevenson framed it within that context in a speech delivered during his 1952 campaign: "This era may well fix the pattern of civilization for many generations to come. God has set for us an awesome mission: nothing less than the leadership of the free world."[149]

Recognizing the agrarian emphasis that formed the base of Turner's thesis, other historians have defined American attitudes as they related to industrialization, emphasizing the role of transportation and communication systems in settling the country. Leo Marx, for example, identified the pastoral ideal, or "middle landscape," as a symbol of agrarian America, and the incorporation and intrusion of machine imagery as a symbol of American progress within that sphere. Recurring images of the contradictory alliance between the nostalgic evocation of a mythic rural past and the reality of a technological present framed his discussion. His "middle landscape" may be contrasted with the "frontier community" conceived by Richard Slotkin, a site that exists at the boundary between education, order, and civilization and its untamed, uncivilized counterpart.[150] On the one hand, the photomurals at the 1955 exhibition allowed the academy to function metaphorically as a "middle landscape," in the same fashion as did the utopian pastoral landscapes in the Futurama exhibition at the 1939 New York World's Fair, mediating between technology and a romantic evocation of rural America. On the other hand, the academy could be framed within the context of a frontier community, situated at the edge of the wilderness.

Characterizations of the inhabitants of the West were also part of its mythology.[151] Henry Nash Smith has recounted the attitudes in American thought that led to and supported the Turner thesis—that is, that Americans had developed a perception of themselves and of the West as unique. By the end of the nineteenth century, the image of the cowboy as Western hero had been formalized in paintings by artists such as Frederic Remington and Charles Russell, as well as in the ubiquitous "dime novels" of the time.[152] During the twentieth century the fascination with the image and myth of the cowboy grew, and by the 1950s millions of Americans were reading westerns, listening to them on the radio, seeing them at the movies, and, with the advent of television, seeing them in their homes. In 1951, Marshall Fishwick commented: "The American cowboy has come to symbolize freedom, individualism, and a closeness to nature which for most of us has become a mere mirage."[153] The image of the cowboy was also employed in the corporate sector. In January 1955, for example, the first Marlboro Man advertisement appeared on television, using the cowboy as symbol for freedom and individuality. The cowboy came to symbolize individualism and freedom in an age when many Americans feared a loss of those qualities to the norms of suburbia, and a closeness to nature at a time when American wilderness areas were dwindling.[154] Inhabitants of the West were likened to cowboys—rugged individualists within a natural domain. A typical example was the 1942 publication entitled *Fair Is Our Land,* which extolled the beauty of the American countryside. The introduction to the chapter entitled "The Great West" noted the following: "The Westerner has a right to self-confidence. He has spanned the wilderness with rail and highway, tunneled the mountain barriers. . . . Daily he meets the challenge of hostile nature, and daily he gets the best of her."[155] Furthermore, associations of the West as a geographical location within this country to "the West" as a geopolitical label analogous to "the Free World," evoked, in both cases, images of freedom and individualism. Taking the analogy a step further, the image of heroic cowboys fighting the savage red men could easily be extended to heroic pilots protecting a democratic nation against the "Red Menace." In his acceptance speech for a civil rights award in 1953, Eisenhower himself had evoked that myth. Mentioning that his birthplace was Abilene, home of Wild Bill Hickok, he urged Americans to face their cold-war foes as would that Western hero.[156]

Within the context of architectural modernism, references to the frontier and its heroic pioneers could function at yet other levels. Like the pioneers of previous centuries, the academy designers perceived the Western landscape as ideally vacant and uninhabited. Extant architecture in the area was of no consequence. In a 1958 interview, Walter Netsch stated as much. Replying to an interviewer's question, he said:

> Don't you remember the night you ridiculed the idea that there was a Colorado architecture? You asked whether it was Mesa Verde? The dismal shacks of the silver towns? The Victorian opera houses . . . ? The fire station in Georgetown, Colorado? The quaint wooden houses in Leadville . . . ? You asked whether it was the imported Swiss chalets of the motels of Aspen, or the imported modern architecture of Herbert Bayer in the same town, or the brick of Klauder's university at Golden, or Meem's museum at Colorado Springs, or the Broadmoor Hotel, or Ieoh Ming Pei's Mile High Center in Denver? I agree with you when you insist that there is no such thing as Colorado architecture in the sense that there is New England architecture, or even Prairie architecture, à la Frank Lloyd Wright. No, in the narrow sense, there is no Colorado material, no Colorado architecture. The mountains are the architecture of Colorado . . . What is Coloradan is the land and the sky and the flora.[157]

Owings's comments on the site's beauty and unspoiled nature placed the academy design within that context. The terrain was an arena of conquest available for development by a new group of architectural pioneers determined to bring order to

random nature. Owings's reference to the mesa as a "veritable Acropolis" indicated a desire to place the academy design within the context of an abstract interpretation of classical inheritance—that of European modernism. The architectural grid of the Cadet Area was a reinterpretation of the "regulating lines" of which Le Corbusier had written in *Vers une architecture:* "he has taken measures, he has adopted a unit of measurement, *he has regulated his work,* he has brought in order. For, all around him, the forest is in disorder with its creepers, its briars and the tree-trunks which impede him and paralyze his efforts. He has imposed order by means of measurement [italics his]."[158] The models of the academy, framed against the mountains in the photomurals, ultimately presented a variation of the utopian cities envisioned several decades earlier at the 1939 New York World's Fair—also located somewhere in an ideally vacant West. As visitors descended over the mountains in the Futurama exhibit at that fair, they saw a city of the future as they heard it described in the following terms: "The city of 1960, with its abundant sunshine, fresh air, fine green parkways—all the result of thoughtful planning and design."[159]

THE EXHIBITION: REACTIONS AS A PRELUDE TO DEBATE

By interweaving various myths into their presentation, SOM's architects sought to gain support for their design by appealing to universal themes. Myths of architectural modernism, supported by analogies to flight, were interwoven with myths associated with the West in such a convincing manner that writers and critics still discuss the design as if every aspect had inexorably developed in predestined fashion. Through the careful orchestration of the May 1955 exhibition environment, Bayer and the architects of SOM created a vision of the United States Air Force Academy that mirrored the country's hopes for a future of opportunity and tranquillity. The exhibit simultaneously recalled the country's history while underscoring the appropriateness of the modernist architectural vocabulary. Notions of a Western heritage were evoked through the landscape photographs of Adams and Garnett, while the political agenda of the United States in the mid-twentieth century—one of overseeing a peaceful and harmonious world order through a position of technological superiority—was maintained and reinforced. The real situation, of course, was not so simple. The country had emerged victorious from World War II only to get involved in the Korean War and the indeterminate cold war. By drawing attention to the Western landscape, however, an abstracted narrative could be read that was as simple and uncluttered as the architectural designs themselves. Such a reading appealed to a nostalgic public yearning for simplicity and security in a world that was becoming increasingly complex and threatening.

In its incorporation of aspects of the sublime (both natural and technological), its reliance upon spectacle, and its merging of the idealistic rhetoric of "high art" with the language of marketing and advertising, the academy exhibition represented a logical continuation of the exposition and exhibition experience of Bayer and SOM. But while Bayer's exhibition design expressed the Bauhaus belief that the artist could lead mass culture to a higher plane of understanding, if not existence, SOM architects during their meetings with air force personnel seemed to be wary of the masses and the media. From the latter point of view, the exhibition seems to have been mounted for two reasons: to reinforce SOM's stature within the architectural community and to deflect possible public criticism by means of a museum exhibition. In that regard, the firm fell short.

As expected, architectural magazines glowingly described the project. In its June 1955 issue, *Progressive Architecture,* referring primarily to Stoller's photographs, called the design "one of the most remarkable and natural accommodations of an architectural complex to terrain that has ever been achieved in any major complex."[160] Employing a two-page Stoller photograph of the model as introduction, the June 1955 issue of *Architectural Record* referred to the design as a "Little Acropolis," while noting its sensitivity to its site.[161] The June issue of *Architectural Forum* began with a two-page Adams photograph of the site. Using primarily Stoller's images, the article commented, "SOM's models indicated their Air Force architecture will be traceable directly to the dynamic tradition of the great airplane hangars and the airplanes themselves."[162] Both *Architectural Record* and *Architectural Forum* connected the academy design to the western landscape and ended their articles with Adams's photograph of Cathedral Rock, the most prominent landscape feature on the site.

The response to the exhibition from members of Congress, as reported in newspapers and magazines, however, was more critical than expected, with the chapel design attracting the most negative response. The legislators and the general public viewing the Colorado Springs exhibition were not, for the most part, the same viewing public as the New York elite who enthusiastically visited SOM's 1950 exhibition at MoMA. In general,

those at the Colorado exhibit were less informed about contemporary art and more conservative. And, unlike the New York exhibits, this exhibition displayed edifices that could be modified with a critical voice, as the disappearance of the original chapel design would soon confirm.

Although other elements of the academy design, such as the airfield, housing areas, and community center, were presented at the exhibition and discussed in architectural magazines, it was the Cadet Area itself that became the focus of congressional and public debate. Senator Herman Welker of Idaho commented that the buildings should include "more Western architecture—more good red Colorado stone." Representative Porter Hardy of Virginia reported that he had heard someone say "the academy looks like a cigarette factory."[163] Representative F. Edward Hebert of Louisiana tied his criticism of the design to the site, declaring, "I've hardly recovered from the shock of these futuristic and modernistic designs in these beautiful mountains." Criticism was specifically leveled at the chapel. Hebert said of the chapel design, "when you think of the rustle of angels' wings, it is incongruous," while Representative Dewey Short of Missouri thought it "should be higher, a spire of national aspiration."[164] Governor Edwin Johnson of Colorado castigated its design, calling it an "ugly duckling" and "monstrosity." He added: "The paganistic distortion conceived by them as a place of religion is an insult to religion and Colorado."[165]

Letters to Talbott from congressional representatives during the ensuing month reiterated those views. Representative William Hill of Colorado, for example, noted that opposition to the design was based on both choice of materials and the "moderistic [sic] buildings." Representative Charles Bennett of Florida attacked the chapel design, as did Welker (who also repeated his plea for the incorporation of native stone). Senator John Stennis of Mississippi expressed disappointment "in the modernistic and futurist type of architecture," saying it looked "like New York City architecture" rather than western architecture, and that the chapel gave "a cruel twist to the whole subject of religion." Senator Sam Ervin of North Carolina called the proposed buildings "monstrous abominations."[166]

SOM had previously arranged for New York's Museum of Modern Art to display the exhibition from October 18 through November 27 of the same year. A catalogue, explaining the project with photographs, plans, and text, was to accompany the exhibit. A formal opening and garden party had even been planned. The cost of the exhibition, not including the production costs of the models or drawings, the catalogue, or the garden party, was to be a mere $2,500.[167] On June 9, 1955, Talbott gave his approval to go ahead with the exhibition. But congressional pressure and public criticism caused Ferry to cancel the exhibition on August 12. In a letter to SOM, he explained his decision:

> The whole question of the design of the Air Force Academy became controversial with both the Congress and the general public following the public exhibit we had at Colorado Springs Museum of Fine Arts. I see no value to the Air Force in giving an opportunity for critics to reopen the controversy over the design. It is my belief that an exhibit at the Museum of Modern Art would produce another wave of protest and debate that will divert attention from the fundamental objective, which is to get ahead with the design and construction of our Air Force Academy in time to receive students in the fall of 1957.[168]

It would not be until February 1957 that the academy design would be included in an exhibition at MoMA.

The exhibition in Colorado Springs was originally scheduled to remain open to the public until June 12, but SOM asked James Byrnes to extend the exhibition at the Fine Arts Center until June 19. The primary purpose of the extension was to allow SOM architects and the consulting architects an opportunity to have a private conference and discuss the design on June 20 and 21.[169] Stoltz, in his capacity as the director of the AFACA, received a copy of SOM's request for an extension, and on June 6 he responded, stating the exhibition would have to be closed on June 16 and moved to Lowry Air Force Base in Denver, where the architects could have their conference on June 20 and 21.[170] Disregarding Stoltz's reply, Carroll Tyler of SOM wrote to the Fine Arts Center the following day, stating that the AFACA had granted permission to leave the exhibition up at the center until June 19, and that SOM would be removing the exhibit on June 21, after the conference.[171] Even as the exhibition was closing, the debate over the academy design had entered the more politically charged and potentially volatile arena of congressional hearings and public discussion.

THE DESIGN DEBATE
The Congressional Process

The construction of the United States Air Force Academy was scheduled to begin on July 1, 1955. Although $126 million had been authorized by Congress to fund the construction, only $15 million of the amount had actually been appropriated by that date.[1] That amount was intended to cover preliminary construction of roads and utilities, and some of the airfield work. The remainder of the allocation was, from the outset, intertwined with and hampered by funding concerns addressed in Congress. Those concerns were fueled by adverse criticism of the overall design. Prior to the May 1955 exhibition of Skidmore, Owings, and Merrill's academy design, that criticism had been limited to a few remarks within the air force hierarchy, but after the exhibition, criticism mounted.

The complaints fell primarily into three categories, and may be defined alliteratively as issues of meaning, materials, and the monument. First, there were critics who spoke of the design in terms of cultural meaning—how the academy should draw on a tradition of American architectural history, respond to its Western site, represent or symbolize a military institution, or reflect the technological concerns it promised to address. Another group of critics argued over the choice of materials. Although their arguments were phrased similarly to those of the first group of critics, their criticism also targeted special-interest groups, such as the masonry and bricklayers unions. The third group was reacting to the problem of the monument and monumentality, an issue related to the cold war context of the academy project.

The remarks by Representative John Fogarty, a member of the Appropriations Committee, were typical of many congressional comments. Testifying before the House of Representatives on June 20, 1955, Fogarty stated, "The design is not American in conception and is unworthy of the tradition of this Nation." Comparing the design to "shrines" such as West Point and Annapolis, Fogarty complained that "it is difficult to find any trace of American heritage in the cold, impersonal, and mechanical appearance of these buildings." Basing his authority on "several leading architects who studied the drawings and photographs of the models," he asserted, "the design is not American. It is based on a hodgepodge of European and Near Eastern influences." Turning to the use of materials, he added "the taxpayers should not be saddled with an initial cost of 126 million dollars for construction . . . and heaven knows how much more for maintenance over the years, to build a monument to experimental materials. . . . Glass and metal, of course, are alien to American monumental design—even to European."[2] He noted the incompatibility of the materials to the Colorado climate, the inadequacy of the materials for fire protection, and the relatively high cost of maintaining glass, as compared to brick, stone, or masonry.[3] While Fogarty expressed concerns over meaning and materials, those issues were subsumed by a larger issue: the problem of the monument and monumentality—the notion that the academy should function as a national monument and project an appropriate image of the United States during the cold war.

THE MONUMENT, MONUMENTALITY, AND MODERNISM

In the United States, symbolic associations between architectural forms and political and ideological dogma had been expressed since the country's independence, with classical forms of antiquity creating associations between a mythic, glorious past and the aspirations of a fledgling country. For example, Benjamin Henry Latrobe, one of the architects of the nation's Capitol, believed that since no public fine-arts tradition had existed in the colonies, an appropriate symbolic form would be one that looked back to antiquity. In an address to the Society of Artists of the United States in 1811 he stated, "The Apollo of Phidias, the Venus of Praxiteles, the group of the Laocoön, are in fact monumental not more for the arts, than of the freedom of Greece; monuments which are not more perfect as examples to architects, than as lessons to statesmen, and as warnings to every republican to guard well the liberty that alone can produce such virtues."[4] Latrobe's declaration expressed a Jeffersonian preference for the incorporation and adaptation of neoclassical elements into an architectural vocabulary as symbols of democracy.

At the beginning of the twentieth century, due in large part to the impact of the 1893 exposition in Chicago, architectural classicism as a bearer of democratic meaning enjoyed a resurgence. The 1902 planning proposals for Washington, D.C., submitted by a group chaired by Daniel Burnham, employed a ver-

sion of Beaux-Arts classicism. Lois Craig writes of its impact, "In its most conspicuous national institutional image, at least, the Beaux-Arts style adorned the architecture of a prideful and confident nation, returning federal architecture to the classical traditions that had been briefly interrupted by the eclectic forays of the Victorian era. For the next half century some form of classicism would dominate official architecture."[5] Architectural classicism in the United States was eclectic, incorporating classical sources as they had developed in European countries as well as neocolonial and Georgian revival styles. Antoinette Lee, in her study of federal architecture, defined this early twentieth-century style as "Academic classicism."[6]

During the 1930s, a vocabulary of restrained classicism came to be favored in governmental building projects, in part reflecting the influence of the architect Louis A. Simon. Simon was placed in charge of the Supervising Architect's Office, which oversaw federal building projects, in 1934. In his AIA fellowship proposal, it was noted that Simon's work was "characterized by an effort toward simplicity and restraint . . . rather than by excess of elaboration or non-functional expression."[7] Reflecting the influence of modernist tendencies in its stripped-down, undecorated surfaces, that general architectural style was applied to large federal buildings that served the nation's growing bureaucracy. As described in the pages of such publications as the *Federal Architect,* the designs were defined in terms of efficiency and conservatism, of vestigial classicism and the "moderne."[8] Monumental classicism, as it was deployed in the seventy-four-acre Triangle Project in Washington, D.C., was said to have created "an environment thoroughly suited to express the dignity and sovereign power of the United States government as it comes into contact with its workers and citizens, and with those representatives of foreign governments located in Washington."[9]

That notion would be questioned, however, as Adolf Hitler rose to power. The agenda of Hitler and the Third Reich was to instill a sense of pride and community in the German people, visually represented in architectural form. German medieval and Gothic styles were used to evoke nationalistic associations with Germany's medieval past; vernacular forms were associated with an agrarian past, and hence "German soil." A classical vocabulary, with its associations to imperial Rome and its military might, was adopted on an enormous scale to create highly visible symbols of state power. The classical vocabulary was used for public projects that incorporated a sense of theater, ceremony, and spectacle. It would be that classical vocabulary, employed in monumental fashion, that Hitler's favorite architects would adopt. Examples were the House of

German Art in Munich, begun by Paul Ludwig Troost in 1933; the Zeppelinfeld in Nürnberg, designed by Albert Speer after Troost's death in 1934; and the Reichchancellery in Berlin, designed by Speer in 1938.[10]

Complicating the political readings of architectural monumentality was the Soviet Union's adoption of a classical vocabulary as its official state style. Joseph Stalin denigrated modernist architecture, which he perceived to be elitist. After Stalin's rise to power in 1925, the Soviet Union adopted historicist forms—"pillars for the people"—as writers such as Anatole Lunacharsky embraced Stalin's Socialist Realist project.[11] While Germany's defeat in World War II marked an end to that country's aggrandized architectural projects, the Soviets continued to use a vocabulary of monumental classicism as a symbol of state political power after the war. In the ensuing cold war era, it was this Soviet association, as much as associations to the defeated Third Reich, which informed the reactions against classicism and monumentality.

By the end of World War II, it had become apparent to architecture critics, particularly in Great Britain and the United States, that the issue of architectural monumentality had to be addressed. The problem was to identify what constituted monumentality in the postwar era, and to question whether monumental architectural forms could still be employed by democratic societies. If so, what general architectural elements could replace the discredited forms of classicism? Elizabeth Mock addressed this problem in her discussion of monumentality in the 1944 MoMA publication *Built in U.S.A.: 1932–1944:*

> One source of confusion seems to be the shifty word "monumentality," which cannot possibly mean the same thing in every country. A totalitarian nation demands buildings which will express the omnipotence of the State and the complete subordination of the individual. When modern architecture tries to express these things, it ceases to be modern, for modern architecture has its roots in the concept of democracy. . . . [A] democracy needs monuments, even though its requirements are not those of a dictatorship. There must be occasional buildings which raise the everyday casualness of living to a higher and more ceremonial plane. . . . Can modern architecture answer the need for buildings which will symbolize our social needs and aspirations? . . . The need is apparent, but the answer is still nebulous. The question for suitable scale is a delicate one, and the old arguments about ornamentation in modern architecture again become relevant. Can the desired effect be achieved solely through the drama of bold and innovative structure and the richness of revealed material?[12]

Mock's claims for the democratic roots of architectural modernism were supported by a selective editing of history. While noting the use of "the most pompous version of neoclassicism" in Russia's 1931 competition for a Palace of the Soviets and citing Hitler's rejection of modernist architecture, Mock disregarded the adoption of a modernist vocabulary by leftist groups such as the early Bauhaus, or in Fascist projects such as Giuseppe Terragni's Casa del Fascio (1932–36).[13] Having made her argument, however, she was still unsure as to how monumentality, in conjunction with modern architecture, could be achieved as a means to define public space and community.

In the same year as Mock's publication, Sigfried Giedion, in collaboration with Fernand Léger and José Luis Sert, published an essay entitled "The Need for a New Monumentality." Giedion traced the rebirth of a new monumentality to modern painting, with its emphasis on simplification and a powerful "primitive" force. Like painting, modern architecture "had to begin anew," looking to industrial or engineering forms for inspiration. But beyond simply addressing technical concerns, contemporary architecture had to create a sense of community and relate to the general public. Giedion advocated festivals and "spectacles" within civic centers, in combination with contemporary architecture, as a means of attaining a new monumentality. His focus was similar to Mock's, in that they both envisioned civic centers or plazas as the sites for ceremonial activities that would incorporate monumentality. But whereas Mock sought forms that would celebrate and represent democracy, Giedion's was a search for public spectacles that would create community within the context of mass culture.[14] He used the example of the aerial displays of water, light, sound, and fireworks at the 1939 New York World's Fair, where the use of color and light combined with smoke ("which gives it volume and scale") to create a sublime spectacle of monumentality. But now, he wrote, it must be civic centers that provide those spectacles: "Those who govern must know that spectacles, which will lead people back to a neglected community life, must be re-incorporated into civic centers."[15] A year earlier, in his 1943 essay "Nine Points on Monumentality," Giedion had outlined other possibilities: "During night hours, color and forms can be projected on vast surfaces. Such displays could be projected upon buildings for purposes of publicity or propaganda. These buildings would have large plane surfaces planned for this purpose."[16]

Given the publication dates of his articles, and their emphasis upon community festivals and the roles of propaganda and spectacle within the context of mass culture, Giedion may seem uncomfortably close to expressing the tenets of fascism. It is difficult not to associate his comments, for example, with images of Albert Speer's Zeppelinfeld in Nürnberg, built to accommodate over one hundred thousand people. The sublime image of its stagelike stand, lit at night by 150 searchlights, had been immortalized by the director Leni Riefenstahl in her 1935 film *Triumph of the Will*.[17] But Giedion's intent was to position modernist architecture as an alternative to the monumental classicism of fascism and its political associations. In his 1944 essay he referred to the use of large-scale classical forms as "pseudomonumentality," stating that historically they were employed by groups seeking to imitate ruling-class tastes. Giedion associated true monumentality, on the other hand, with "the taste and emotions of the public." Pseudomonumentality was often achieved, according to Giedion, by simply placing a curtain of columns before a structure. Like Mock, he developed his argument by selectively editing history, looking back to "nineteenth-century Napoleonic society" (J. N. L. Durand's plan for an ideal museum, 1801–5) and then jumping forward and citing works such as Troost's 1933 Hall of German Art in Munich and the 1937 Mellon Research Institute in Pittsburgh.

The debate over monumentality prompted a symposium by the British *Architectural Review,* published in September 1948. Internationally acclaimed architects and critics, including Henry-Russell Hitchcock, Walter Gropius, Albert Roth, Gregor Paulsson, and Sigfried Giedion, were invited to participate.[18] Hitchcock attempted to define the terms *monument, monumental,* and *monumentality.* He defined the noun "monument" in both the traditional sense, as a tombstone or memorial statue, and the sense that any building of the past serves as a monument to that civilization. He defined the adjective "monumental" in terms of its physical and formal characteristics, such as durability, solidity, and scale. The most important characteristic in achieving a monumental effect, according to Hitchcock, was an emotional impact that conveyed a sense of dignity. Reiterating Giedion's argument, Hitchcock also warned of the pitfalls of pseudomonumentality—the imitation of historical forms to achieve a sense of the monumental—citing the National Gallery in Washington, D.C., as an example. The quality of monumentality, he concluded, had been abstracted from any traditional association with the monument and could be achieved only by assuming the characteristics of the monumental—characteristics that he located in the twentieth century in large-scale engineering projects such as dams, highways, and power stations. Hitchcock questioned whether modernist architecture, with its emphasis on transparency, was creating a realm of evanescent architecture that denied monumentality, and he noted that the "leaders of modern architecture . . . have

done little, even on paper, to develop a viable new monumentality."[19]

Gropius and Roth, on the other hand, identified monumentality with the transcendent—not in a religious sense, but within a "spirit of the age" context. "Monumentality," noted Roth, "is the transcendental, most inspired expression of the essence, the will, the greatness of an epoch." Gropius elaborated: "The old monument was the symbol for a static conception of this world, now overruled by a new one of relativity through changing energies."[20] In the end, there was no consensus as to what specific form or forms future monumental architecture might take. Giedion again linked monumentality to civic centers and spectacle, while Paulsson questioned whether any monumental forms could exist within a democratic system.

In 1948, none of those architects and critics were able to foresee the specific forms that modernist monumentality might assume, although most architectural critics seemed to recognize the need for monumentality in public architecture. The American public, on the other hand, thought in more general and traditional terms, still associating monumental architecture with a sense of pride, dignity, and identity. They reasoned that if the United States was indeed triumphant in World War II and the world superpower that it claimed to be, those facts somehow needed to be conveyed visually—not in an abstract language, but in one readily recognizable.

Eventually, those conflicting voices would create the discordant chorus of controversy that surrounded the Air Force Academy construction, as congressional critics debated many of the same issues with which the architectural community was wrestling. But while the debates within the architectural profession addressed specific issues and drew on an awareness of historical precedents to substantiate and reinforce their positions, the congressional debates were muddled and often lacked specific focus, addressing multiple concerns and serving hidden agendas.

CONGRESSIONAL DEBATE OVER THE ACADEMY DESIGN

July 1, 1955, the date by which construction of the academy was to start, marked the beginning of the 1956 congressional fiscal year. It was assumed by SOM and the air force hierarchy that military appropriations for the year would be finalized by then, with the May exhibition timed to provide the impetus for funding of the academy design. Instead, faced with mounting criticism of the design, Congress delayed project funding while those criticisms were addressed through the political process of committee and subcommittee hearings. The first hearing that provided insight into how those issues would be addressed occurred on Thursday, June 30, 1955, before the House of Representatives Subcommittee of the Committee on Appropriations, whose task it was to determine military construction appropriations for 1956. Members of the subcommittee included Representatives Mahon, Whitten, Deane, and Scrivner. Among those who appeared as witnesses for the air force were Ferry, Washbourne, and Erler, while John Merrill represented SOM.[21]

Following a brief description of the academy's major design components—the airfield, Cadet Area, and family housing—and SOM's responsibilities in overseeing those facets, the discussion turned to architectural design. Whitten initiated the discussion:

Whitten: Could I ask, roughly, what type of architecture will be involved here? Is it generally termed "western"? I mean, does it fit into the appearance of the area? . . .
Merrill: We believe the design will be modern in its character, but will be colorful and interesting.[22]

Mahon interrupted, commenting that he had read in the papers that the amount of glass to be used seemed extensive. Merrill tried to parry his criticism, stating that the amount of glass would be "considerably less" than indicated on the exhibition models, photographs of which had been presented at the hearing along with charts outlining the master plan. Congressman Deane, however, sought specifics in the form of pictures of the designs, stating, "I think it would help us, Mr. Chairman, if we had a picture, or offset, or something we could actually see. . . . Do you have a large picture, or blown-up picture?"[23] Merrill responded in the negative, stating they only had photographs of the model. Confusion over how to "read" those photographs was indicated several minutes later when Mahon mistook the cadet social center for the dormitory. These introductory remarks set the tone for the discussion. They indicate that congressional members did not really know what they were looking at in terms of the overall design and were frustrated in their attempts to address specifics.

Although some of the issues regarding design and materials were practical, such as the possibility of heat gain or loss resulting from the extensive glass facades, or the problem of snow loads on flat roofs, the underlying concern was that the design would be too "modern" and that the glass walls would be susceptible not only to heat loss, but to loss of meaning. Deane worried that the design might not be deemed satisfactory "50, 75, or 100 years from now." Again, Merrill tried to quell those anxieties by opening up the possibility for alterna-

tive materials: "If it [the exterior] is not windows, stone. We are thinking of native stones. There is a very good travertine, which is a warm, brown-colored stone. Then there is Colorado marble."[24] Still, the solution presented was too generic for the members of Congress:

Scrivner: The way it is now, we are buying a pig in a poke. We do not know what we are buying at all do we? . . .[25]

Deane: I think this is inadequately presented. I think that we should have some blown-up pictures. . . .
Ferry: There are no approved designs for any of the structures on this base. . . .
Mahon: You are requesting funds for buildings that have not been designed?
Ferry: That is correct, sir.[26]

Scrivner stated that he wanted to see the chapel design. He was informed by Merrill that it was irrelevant, since it was not part of this appropriation. Earlier, Mahon had been told the same regarding the social center, which he thought employed too much glass in its design. Scrivner asked for pictures of SOM's designs for the Great Lakes Naval Station for comparative purposes and was told they were not available either.

Obviously, members of the subcommittee did not want to assume responsibility for an architectural design that could be unfavorably criticized by the press and their constituencies. Merrill and the air force witnesses, on the other hand, wanted immediate approval so they could minimize the participation and interference of congressional members in the design process. To that end, Merrill invoked the authority of Becket, Saarinen, and Belluschi, the project consultants. He represented them to the subcommittee as "competitors" who had been selected to ensure a system of "checks and balances so that this job is not going to be determined by our own firm, but will require the approval of three architects located from coast to coast."[27] In truth, Belluschi hardly qualified as a "competitor." He had not asked to be considered for the academy project and was appointed as a consultant only after Wallace Harrison resigned. At the time of this testimony, he was still associated with the firm of SOM through the Portland office of Belluschi/SOM.

Toward the end of the June 30 hearing, the issue of meaning in architectural form was again addressed, and it again underscored the differences between the parties involved:

Whitten: I hate to see this [the academy design] turned over entirely to the architects and the Air Force. . . . It looks all right from a practical standpoint . . . but it does not have to me as a layman the things in it that are usually given consideration in public buildings. Frankly, looking at the picture it looks like it might be a new canning factory. . . . [I]t makes me wonder if somebody should not clear this with people who have some thought on the appropriateness of the appearance and the American type of building and things of that sort.[28]

Ferry: After we opened the show at the Colorado Springs Art Institute . . . we left it on exhibit there for a matter of a month. . . . We had 25,000 visitors look at that model, and the reactions were mixed . . . but generally . . . very enthusiastic in favor of it.

Scrivner: If they could not see any more than we have seen I do not know how.[29]

Mahon: Yes. They [the general public] want something good and decent and fine, just as the people have with the Supreme Court Building. . . . You can go to West Point, you can go to Duke University or you can go to a lot of places and see dignity and strength.[30]

Merrill: These buildings should be a national monument, but they should be an honest monument. This is primarily an engineering school. I am a graduate of M.I.T. . . . We would be opposed to trying to dress these buildings up in what we might call a traditional style. . . . It should certainly not be a fortress, like West Point. . . . There are three different Academies; a different time, a different purpose, and a different conception. West Point, which is primarily an Army school, is a fortress. The Naval Academy is the sort of nice, light touch of naval life, with the English Georgian and so on. The Air Academy should have its own distinctive characteristics. I think it can adapt the so-called modern style, if you want to call it that . . . and just as good, and cheaper, more economical in construction cost.[31]

While the congressional comments represented the more traditional concerns of the public sphere, Merrill's remarks reflected the controversy swirling within the architectural community over monumentality and modernism. Congress members sought a literal expression of monumentality, but Merrill's defense of the transparent construction was metaphorical. In explaining the project to the press the previous month, General Harmon, the academy's superintendent, had described the academy's goals as providing a college education, an officer's commission at "the West Point of the Air," and a grounding in aeronautical engineering, emphasizing the academy's complex mission.[32] It was within that context that Merrill responded. The "national monument" or "honest monument" of which he spoke was defined within the parameters of an engineering school and a military academy—specifically, an air academy. Honesty, as Merrill expressed it, meant construction with glass and steel and the visible expression of the structural grid. The slick forms of the academy architecture symbolized the new technological defense capabilities that superseded the outdated methods and traditions of the army and the navy. The references paralleled Eisenhower's discussion of a "New Look"

defense policy in late 1953, which de-emphasized conventional systems, concentrated instead on nuclear deployment systems, and enhanced the role of the air force.[33] Those associations were reinforced at the close of the hearing, when Ferry read a prepared statement by Harold Talbott, the secretary of the air force, in which he responded to the "adverse criticism" of the design:

> We want the Academy to be a living embodiment of the modernity of flying and to represent in its architectural concepts the national character of the Academy. It would be incongruous for a modern service Academy to match the exterior of West Point, with its medieval fortress–like appearance depicting the traditions of land warfare, or the ivy covered quadrangles of the early eastern colleges. We want our structures to be as efficient and flexible in their basic layout as the most modern projected aircraft, and possessing the dignity and enduring qualities which will create the cultural and spiritual atmosphere of a great educational institution.[34]

Congress's hesitation in approving the academy design was also an extension of a larger debate that revolved around the United States building programs overseas. During the postwar years, the United States had used building programs abroad to forge alliances and to fight Soviet communism. Since the early 1950s, however, criticism had been mounting against overseas embassies, consulates, and staff housing constructed under the auspices of the State Department's Foreign Buildings Office (FBO).[35] The attack was launched on several fronts, reflecting concerns about design suitability as it related to specific geographic and cultural locations, issues of favoritism in the selection of architects, and economic feasibility.

The issue of climate suitability had initially been raised regarding the Rio de Janeiro and Havana embassies, designed by the firm of Harrison and Abramovitz and constructed between 1948 and 1952. The buildings' designs incorporated large expanses of glass that proved unsuitable for the hot climates. In testimony before House Appropriations Subcommittees in 1953 and 1954, Nelson Kenworthy, an FBO consultant, charged that the firm had ignored the authority of the Brazilian building inspectors and created buildings in Havana that were "completely unsuitable" for the hot climate. In addition, he accused the FBO system of favoritism in its appointment of architects, noting that contracts were awarded without competition—a "racket that has gone on for years."[36]

By then, Leland King had assumed directorship of the FBO. Appointed in January 1952, King hired SOM to oversee the FBO's extensive building program in Germany. Gordon Bunshaft was placed in charge of the project, and he designed consulates for five German cities—Bremen, Düsseldorf, Frankfurt, Munich, and Stuttgart—as well as consular housing in Bremen. In its March 1953 issue, *Architectural Forum* published a photograph of the Bremen consulate in contrast to a Soviet Monument in Berlin. Glass designs, the article implied, created an open, friendly, and inviting look befitting a democracy. On the same page, the American embassy in Havana was contrasted with the Soviet embassy. The modernist vocabulary, the magazine claimed, was a "vehicle of our cultural leadership"—an effective tool to combat Soviet agendas, as represented by the official Soviet state architectural style of monumental classicism.[37]

By the time of the *Architectural Forum* article, however, the House Committee on Government Operations had established the Special Subcommittee Investigating the German Consulate/America House Program to begin an inquiry into the dealings of the FBO. Hearings began in February 1953 and led to King's dismissal by the summer's end. It was during that subcommittee's investigations that criticism of SOM's work arose, focusing on the staff apartments and consulate the firm designed in Bremen. Congressional critics cited the overall expense of the apartments, which were not only quite large but included a maid's room in each apartment. Members of Congress were also concerned about SOM's use of materials. They were perplexed as to why SOM had employed so much glass, rather than masonry, in the Bremen design. Bremen, located just thirty miles from the North Sea, was hardly a temperate climate, and the extensive use of glass maximized heating costs. To the end, King defended the modernist designs he advocated. When he was questioned about the overall high cost of SOM's German projects, he stated it was due to the architects' lack of experience with such projects. In a July 7, 1953, memo to Assistant Secretary of State Edward Wailes, King noted, "Even among the more conservative art circles, the modern 'style' is considered as well established as any style of the past. . . . [T]he Department should conform to this world-wide contemporary trend, in which the United States is the undisputed leader, if its buildings are to be truly representative of the progressive and characteristic way of American life."[38]

Nelson Kenworthy took over for King and in January 1954 established the Architectural Advisory Committee, comprised of the architects Pietro Belluschi, Ralph Walker, and Henry Shepley. The group was chaired by Colonel Harry A. McBride, who had been administrator of the National Gallery of Art from 1939 until 1953. In its March 1955 issue, *Architectural Record* reported the objectives of the committee: "(1) to represent American architecture abroad; (2) to adapt itself to local condi-

tions and cultures so deftly it is welcomed, not criticized, by its hosts."[39] Again, SOM's work came under scrutiny. In October 1954, Shepley reported that SOM's Munich consulate design had run into stiff local opposition from town leaders who were outraged that the design ignored the context of the surrounding historic architecture in Munich. Shepley complained, "The plans went against their traditions and policy, and Bunshaft would not make any concessions."[40] Although a design quite close to Bunshaft's original version was eventually approved, the project was delayed due to the controversy and the consulate was not completed until 1958. These issues were in the minds of legislators as they discussed the academy project on July 7, 1955.

Like the previous week's hearing, this one addressed the design's practicality and its ability to fulfill a symbolic function. But special interest groups also expressed their concerns at this meeting, giving the discussion a slightly different slant. Serving as their spokesmen were Henry Hope Reed and Frank Lloyd Wright.[41] Reed was a member of the Municipal Arts Society of New York, taught city planning at Yale University, and had recently coauthored a book with Christopher Tunnard entitled *The American Skyline*. He was an extremely conservative voice within the architectural community. Opposed to modernism in all its forms, Reed advocated a return to Beaux-Arts principles of the 1920s.[42] Citing examples of past edifices, he pleaded for an architectural style that would incorporate the decorative arts—"sculpture, mural painting, wrought-iron work, furniture, porcelain, wood carving and stained glass"—to provide a panorama of American history. That two House Appropriations Subcommittee members, Whitten and Deane, were in sympathy with Reed's ideas was reflected by their remarks when his testimony ended:

Whitten: Again, it [Reed's testimony] points out the total lack of it [the decorative arts to provide historical meaning] in the edifice and the pictures which we have seen here which the present architect apparently is trying to sell to the Department of the Air Force.
Deane: There appears to be a trend, a modernist trend, in America, to get away from the real fundamental ideas which have made this country great. . . .
Reed: I think it is a fashion.[43]

The next witness was Frank Lloyd Wright. Wright's disdain for SOM's academy design, and the approach to architecture that it implied, was well documented. He had been quoted in the press in May, calling the plans a "violation of nature" and claiming the academy would become known as "a factory for birdmen."[44] Extolling the virtues of his own organic approach to design, Wright criticized SOM's lack of response to the Colorado site. Wright's specific criticism of the design was vague, however, and his testimony consisted largely of character assassination of members of SOM and the three consultants to the project. Misrepresenting the academy competition, Wright noted that, out of seven hundred applicants, the list of competitors had been narrowed down to three, "two represented by . . . advertising agencies, in New York City, and myself, with no representation." He resigned from the competition, he said, when he realized its crassness. He referred to SOM as "commercial artists" with no talent. Asked about the consultants, he said of Becket, "I do not know him, but I know of him. I wish that something would happen to him soon. I would hate to see his things going as they are now." Of Saarinen, he stated, "His father wanted me to train him architecturally. That is[,] the young boy." Wright gave Saarinen's age as thirty-five or thirty-six when Saarinen was, in fact, nearly forty-five years old at the time. Of Belluschi, Wright said, "He is a teacher. He has done some very nice little houses, but he has no experience as a builder." Belluschi, of course, had actually been involved in a substantial number of projects spanning thirty years.[45] When asked what his own approach would be, Wright was evasive, stating that the chapel would be the crowning feature, with escalators running up the hill. Impatiently, he concluded, "I am not going to give the scheme away." He suggested the design be voted upon by every high school student in the United States, since they were the ones that would "have to live with it," and that funding be withheld indefinitely, pending other design considerations.[46]

Reed and Wright had both been encouraged by Representative John Fogarty to voice their complaints. Fogarty, it will be remembered, had expressed his disdain for the academy design before Congress on June 20. On the surface, his concerns seemed similar to those of other Congress members, defined in terms of practicality or meaning. But in its August 1955 issue, *Architectural Forum* carried the story of the backstage alliances that led Fogarty to launch his attack.[47] Prior to his election to Congress, Fogarty had been president of the Rhode Island Bricklayers Union. The union was a component of the Allied Masonry Council, whose members had launched a barrage of letters to their respective Congress representatives in opposition to the design. Reed had earlier written to Robert Denny (public-relations director for Henry J. Kauffmann and Associates, the advertising agency that handled the Allied Masonry Council) protesting the fact that SOM had received a New York Municipal Arts Society award for its Manufacturers Bank design. Denny contacted Fogarty, who urged Reed to contest

SOM's academy design before the House subcommittee. He also contacted Wright and met Wright at the Washington airport when he arrived to testify. Ironically Wright, who was vehemently opposed to the bureaucratic governmental process that SOM negotiated so well, became a pawn in that process.

Fogarty was not the only congressman who was contacted by the Allied Masonry Council. Numerous others had received complaints from the council and had sent letters to Talbott. Representative George Miller stated the design was "cold, stark, and bizarre . . . that of a world's fair." Senators Capehart and Jenner requested that the air force "include in the plans and specifications the word 'masonry' to afford that industry the opportunity to submit its bid for the use of these materials in the construction of the Air Force Academy." Representative Thomas Curtis included in his letter a copy of the official four-page "Fact Sheet on the Air Academy from the Allied Masonry Council," condemning the design.[48]

Several days later, on July 11, the Senate Subcommittee of the Committee on Appropriations heard testimony regarding the design. No members of SOM were in attendance, although several members of the Department of the Air Force were present.[49] Ferry spoke on Talbott's behalf, defending the selection of the architectural firm and the consultants. Reaction from the senators was anything but favorable. Senator Chavez commented that site consideration was a necessity, since a building that would do in New York would "look like the deuce in Colorado Springs." Senator Ellender added: "It is a great pity when you started you did not have these architects give you an idea of how it should be built and look over those plans and select the one that gave you the best idea."[50]

As a result of these hearings, on July 14, 1955, the House Appropriations Committee voted to deny further allocations to the project until the air force produced a more acceptable design. The next day, Representative Mahon was challenged in Congress by Representative Rogers of Colorado to explain the reasons for the delay. Mahon said that it had occurred because no definitive plans existed for a project that would cost the taxpayers $79 million, and that the proposed design, as it had been exhibited, was inappropriate: "It would appear to be an appropriate edifice for a modern factory."[51] Rogers reassured him that the design was being changed, with the substitution of stone for glass and a more conscious integration of the design with the landscape. Representative Chenowith, also from Colorado, added that the original chapel design had already been changed.

On July 15, leading members of the Allied Masonry Council and its subsidiary unions testified before the Senate Subcom-

mittee of the Committee on Appropriations.[52] Wright reap-
peared, again indicting the academy project:

> It would be a shame to turn the average ambition loose in
> that magnificent opportunity where buildings and scenery
> and the countryside could be made one and express some-
> thing noble, something worthy of our Nation, something you
> could call American architecture. . . . I think the thing is sort
> of a cliché. . . . It is not genuine modern architecture. It is a
> glassified box on stilts which is practiced abroad and has
> now become fanatic with certain of our commercial archi-
> tects. They are the ones that unfortunately succeed to Gov-
> ernment work. A man like myself would never be thought of
> in connection with a Government job.[53]

While Wright's criticism seemed to parallel that of Reed and
the members of Congress, a more sophisticated understanding
of architecture underlay his critique. He would have been as
appalled by Reed's proposal to provide a literal panoramic historical framework for the academy as he was with SOM's solution. His understanding of the American condition was filtered
through the writings of Emerson and Whitman and the architecture of Louis Sullivan, as he continually attempted to reconcile
an indigenous vernacular with a European vocabulary of forms.
In the process, he abstracted those polarities into a synthesis
of natural and geometrical order.[54] That abstract approach—in
which the architect looked to nature as the reference point for a
prospective architectural solution—would probably have
seemed as alien to congressional members as had SOM's solution. The *New York Herald,* in fact, realized the ironic nature of
Wright's testimony and published an editorial on July 14 entitled "Architecture and the Air Force Academy," stating, "But
Mr. Wright is not arguing against contemporary architecture; he
is arguing for his own particular style and concepts. It is mis-
chievous of him, and he must know it, to lend his support to
those who stand in every artistic consideration at the opposite
pole from himself."

Congress members also wanted an architectural style that
could contain and convey meanings both contemporary and
historic, but their understanding of architectural forms was obviously far less comprehensive than Wright's. They wanted an
architectural expression that would represent America's leadership role in the free world, recall a specifically American tradition, and embrace associations with its western site. But in attempting to visualize that architectural form, they reached an
impasse. They realized revival styles would be perceived as expensive and associated not only with a regressive political
agenda but, in the case of classicism, with totalitarian regimes.
Perhaps they thought Wright could provide a solution, but they

must have realized that his cantankerous nature and outspo-
ken disdain for government involvement in architectural
projects would have undermined the project. Under mounting
pressure, with newspapers such as the *Denver Post* and the
San Francisco Chronicle portraying the legislators as inept and
interfering critics, congressional members of the Senate Appropriations Subcommittee met again on July 18.[55]

SOM was represented at that hearing by its team's most
persuasive public-relations member—Nathaniel Owings. Academy project consultants Saarinen and Belluschi were present,
as were representatives from the Department of the Air Force,
including Talbott.[56] Talbott explained the parameters for the
site selection, architect selection, and consultant selection and
then turned the discussion over to Owings. After a prolonged
introduction that broached topics ranging from climate to athletic facilities, the subject of the design arose. Owings immediately addressed site considerations and materials: "There is a
certain amount of dramatic quality. . . . Let me have a picture of
the mountains again. We have back of us these great mountains. You see these shadows on the site plan. We propose as a
basis to tie this into Colorado, as you put it, to use that stone
as the retaining walls that are necessary to support this campus up here on the mesa. So the first thing we contribute in the
way of tying it into the area is the fact that we use native natural material to support the land on which we go."[57]

Moments later, he reassured advocates for the masonry industry: "This is the academic building. This academic building
with its great red stone face has less glass in it than the Department of Commerce Building in Washington D.C. It has been reduced to that point. . . . The materials we use there are entirely
a matter of selection on the basis of weather, durability, and
expense and color and attractiveness."[58] Finally, Owings
stressed the design's economic practicality: "Architecturally we
are in a modern age. Modern architecture as such has been
dictated by economics. If we tried to reproduce a Gothic or Colonial architecture, we would have to ask for almost double the
appropriation."[59]

Owings convinced the subcommittee members that there
had been an 80 to 90 percent reduction in the glass area since
the original designs had been displayed. Talbott concurred: "I
thought it was too modernistic and too much glass [*sic*]."[60]
Senator Flanders expressed his enthusiasm over the "new" design, realizing that a "Tudor or Georgian" style would have
been much more costly. Senator Ellender was also impressed
by the presentation but asked Owings for further assurance
about its cost: "If any other design had been submitted, as
some of us thought would be the case—perhaps a Colonial

style or something else—the Academy would have cost a good deal more, would it not?" Owings replied: "Absolutely."[61]

Judging by the congressmen's remarks, SOM was much better prepared for this series of hearings. The firm's earlier attempts to secure funding with minimal visual material had failed. The architects now made a more convincing presentation, although many of the changes shown in the "new" design were simply cosmetic—replacing areas of glass in the drawings with opaque stone material. Caught up in the enthusiasm for creating a "new" look for the academy, those at the hearing turned their discussion to the most trivial aspects of functionalism—comparative analysis of the distance to toilets at the various service academies. The conversation between Talbott and Senator Smith was recorded in the record of the hearing under the heading "West Point Showers and Toilets":

Talbott: General Twining just said something that was interesting. He said at West Point you have got to go down four flights of stairs to the shower and toilet.

Smith: That is why I was asking the question [about the distance to the toilets] since we are building something new.[62]

Having defused opposition to the point that toilet distance was the standard for modernity, the subcommittee gave the "new" design its support.

The next day, July 19, the full Committee on Appropriations convened. For that key hearing, SOM was represented by Skidmore, Owings, John Merrill, and Hartmann. E. P. Purves, executive director of the American Institute of Architects, was there to lend authority to a statement that would be delivered on behalf of the architecture profession. Representatives for the air force included Talbott and Ferry.[63] Talbott again summarized the processes of selecting the site and the architects. His synopsis was somewhat inaccurate, in that he stated that SOM was the first choice and the next three in order (Harrison, Saarinen, and Becket) were chosen as advisors. As previously noted, Becket was not even a finalist in the selection process. Talbott then introduced Purves and read a prepared statement from the AIA in support of SOM.[64] The statement consisted of six short paragraphs, the heart of which read:

The architects and the architect consultants selected by the Secretary of the Air Force are among the most distinguished of American practitioners. Their experience is extensive, their reputations are worldwide and the buildings and projects to their credit are among the most significant productions of the American professionals. It is understandable that any structure or work of art will find itself the target of criticism, sometimes voiced without the knowledge of the

problems involved. Design is best accomplished by men who are trained and experienced. There is no question of the experience and ability of the professionals engaged by the Department of the Air Force.[65]

Talbott then underscored the sincerity of the testimony by emphasizing that it was unsolicited, and that he himself "did not know what the American Institute of Architects was." Talbott's memory was obviously selective, since the statement had been written in early July and sent to John Merrill, who then forwarded a copy of it to Talbott's office.[66]

With his way prepared, Owings again testified on behalf of SOM. Using aerial and site photographs, charts, and drawings, he explained the design process and how SOM had addressed the site. Then, with diagrams and drawings, he meticulously walked the committee members through the functional aspects of the design from the vantage point of the cadet, noting that the most controversial element of the design—the chapel—would not be finalized until the end. The explanation dealt with minute functional details such as where in their rooms the cadets would place their galoshes and where in the classrooms they would hang their hats—offered as proof that not a single detail of the overall design had escaped the attention of SOM.

Owings then compared SOM's incorporation of the latest technologies in the academy design to the technological innovations of past architects, such as the anonymous Gothic designers. But he again underscored the practicality of his firm's modernist solution: "What we do here today is, in the consensus of our four consultants and ourselves, not only the best approach, but the only possible approach to the problem, because modern architecture is not an aim, it is a product of the economics of the age." Gothic architecture, he added, would cost twice as much as "the so-called contemporary design." Finally, he addressed the issue of the site: "How do you tie that contemporary design into the terrain, into the site, and give it a soul? . . . We have tied those red stone mountains in by taking the red stones and building the retaining walls. . . . [T]hat gives you the sense of the quality of sturdy permanence of the mountains around you."[67]

Owings's argument was intended to convince Congress that SOM's modernist vocabulary was not only the correct choice, but it was the only choice—a product of its time. But one committee member remained dissatisfied. Noting that the "new" design was essentially the same as the old, Whitten complained: "So far as the record is concerned . . . the pictures which you have published and which were presented to us before, and the pictures you have today—there is no substantial difference in general appearance?" Ferry responded: "The character of the buildings is substantially of the same type."[68] In spite of Whitten's comments, other members of the subcommittee termed the new design a "compromise" between the "antiquated past and modern present." The terms of that "compromise" were revealed later in the hearing, when the discussion came to landscaping.

Miller: Is there any place for ivy?
Merrill: Absolutely. As one of the great architects said, ivy is one of the architect's best friends.
Owings: Yes; that is one of the nicest things you can have around these things. It really warms it up.[69]

The hearing concluded with Mahon's stating that he thought the presentation was "a thousand percent superior" to other presentations. As a result, the Senate voted to restore $79,527,000 in funding for the academy construction several days later, on July 23, 1955. A Conference Committee was called, and the House compromised on a $20 million allocation by the month's end.

With the funding approval, Congress tacitly acknowledged its support for SOM's modernist design solution. Although the design was controversial, criticism would undoubtedly have occurred no matter what firm had been selected. The controversies resulted from the expectation that the academy design would embody the reality of postwar America in a simplistic, all-embracing solution, which was impossible within the context of a democratic and complex society. Those issues were only compounded by the public nature of the commission, which raised the specter of taxpayers' and voters' concerns over the funding of a multimillion-dollar fiasco. Ultimately, the problems the academy design had to address were simply overwhelming in nature. Were the academy's symbolic forms to be interpreted and embedded with meaning by citizens at home or by citizens abroad? Should its forms incorporate a nostalgic search for a pre-atomic age or express an enthusiastic belief in a technological future? Should the overriding factors of construction be economic or propagandistic? If propagandistic, what agenda, architecturally or politically, would be supported? And in what form should the transcendent or moral values that defined this country in the cold war era be realized?

THE SEARCH FOR MEANING IN THE COLD WAR ERA

Ongoing debates within the architectural community echoed many of the concerns of Congress. Many architects praised the design and criticized politicians for intervening in an area in which they had no expertise. The board of directors of the AIA issued a statement supporting the architects in its June 30 newsletter. As mentioned, the AIA's executive director, E. P. Purves, appeared before the Subcommittee of the House Committee on Appropriations, and both Purves and George Bain Cummings, the AIA president, appeared before the Senate Appropriations Committee.[70] Architectural magazines such as *Architectural Record, Architectural Forum,* and *Progressive Architecture* expressed support for SOM, as did numerous architects who, even if they differed in design philosophy, deplored governmental intervention in the architectural realm. Newspapers such as the *Denver Post* (July 13), the *New York Herald Tribune* (July 14), the *San Francisco Chronicle* (July 14), and the *Boston Herald* (July 15) expressed the same sentiments in their editorials.

But not everyone agreed. Wright continued to plead his case for an alternative solution. In comments on the outcome of the academy debate, made several days after Congress had restored funding, he expressed his dismay: "The design was of the sort to be expected of an efficiency expert selecting efficiency-architects. . . . The Skidmore, Owings and Merrill design puts on our record the shame of an already dated cliché: imported Swiss via South America [a reference to Le Corbusier and his projects]. . . . The imitative design slanders the strength and beauty of the American spirit. In abstract but realistic terms it is the perfect picture of the beauteous mountain-maid betrayed by the city slicker."[71]

Specifically, Wright's attack was against modernism as it had been presented and formally defined at the 1932 MoMA exhibition. While emphasizing modernism's formal concerns had enabled Alfred Barr, Henry-Russell Hitchcock, and Philip Johnson to divorce the architecture from its socialist roots, the disassociation from a specific social and political realm also allowed the International style to be presented as a style teleologically determined by technological imperatives, free from individual inspiration. It was, as Hitchcock and Johnson had written, a style that "did not spring from a single source but came into being generally." It was a "contemporary style . . . unified and inclusive, not fragmentary and contradictory."[72]

In exploring the issue of this "international style," in the early 1990s Richard Pommer and Christian Otto identified the roots of the term "international" within explicitly socialist contexts that preceded World War I. With the formation of the Third Internationale of 1919 and the negative reaction to nationalistic fervor following World War I, the term assumed universal as well as socialist overtones.[73] Although the 1932 MoMA *Modern Architecture* exhibition marked an attempt to eliminate the social and ideological content from the term "international," vocal critics representing contrasting points in the political spectrum still associated modernist architecture with Bolshevism. Hitler unleashed a diatribe against modernism as a Bolshevist phenomenon in his book *Mein Kampf* (first published in 1925), reiterating the condemnations expressed by other German writers who criticized the architecture of Le Corbusier and the Bauhaus.[74] In American publications there were similar charges. The July 1933 issue of *Living Age,* for example, carried "Bolshevized Architecture," a translation of an article by a French critic who attacked modernist architecture.[75] In response, historians such as Nikolaus Pevsner attempted to make modernism more palatable and acceptable to the agendas of Western democracies by underscoring its historical continuity within an Anglo-Saxon tradition. In his 1936 publication *Pioneers of the Modern Movement,* Pevsner established a lineage from William Morris to Walter Gropius, and included American architects (specifically, those with close Chicago ties) such as William Le Baron Jenney, Henry Hobson Richardson, Louis Sullivan, and Frank Lloyd Wright, as well as the firms of Holabird and Roche, and Burnham and Root.[76]

In February 1948 the Museum of Modern Art held a symposium entitled "What Is Happening to Modern Architecture?" Barr opened the conference by implicitly framing modernism within the context of Western democracies, in opposition to totalitarian regimes: "We may mention in passing the bitter hostility of Hitler and his National Socialist architects to the International Style. . . . But parallel to the German reaction has been the Soviet revival of the stylistic chaos and pomposities of the nineteenth century in the name of proletariat taste and socialist realism."[77] The symposium was organized in response to Lewis Mumford's comments in the October 11, 1947, issue of the *New Yorker.* In that editorial, Mumford cited the "natural reaction against a sterile and abstract modernism" as reason for "the continued spread, to every part of the country, of that native and humane form of modernism one might call the Bay Area style, a free yet unobtrusive expression of the terrain, the climate, and the way of life on the Coast."[78] Mumford himself had initially been a proponent of functional modernism, but in texts such as *Sticks and Stones* (1924), *The Golden Day* (1926), and *The Brown Decades* (1931), he emphasized the efficacy of incorporating regional traditions into architectural planning. After the bombing of Hiroshima, his suspicion and fear of the applications of technology led him to contest more stridently the

mechanistic metaphors of modernists such as Le Corbusier and Mies van der Rohe and the formalist approach of writers such as Hitchcock and Johnson. In their place he posited a humanist approach to architecture.[79]

Mumford's critics at the 1948 MoMA symposium included Barr, Hitchcock, and Johnson, who argued that Mumford had overemphasized the dogmatic tendencies of the International style. Barr, for example, stressed that the International style, as it had been differentiated in 1932, had never been intended as a rigid definition of form, and that the style had emerged only as its proponents had carried out architectural experiments throughout the world. He further pointed out the problematic issues of adopting a domestic vocabulary for larger projects, specifically addressing William Wurster's work—work that Mumford had singled out as being exemplary of the Bay Area style. Barr noted that although Wurster employed a "Cottage Style" in his domestic work, he had difficulty translating that domestic vocabulary to a larger scale. As a result, Wurster's large-scale work was "a pretty orthodox version of the International Style."[80]

Hitchcock spoke next, observing that discussion of a Bay Area style, an architectural vocabulary most appropriate for detached housing, was less important than other architectural issues. A more pertinent concern, Hitchcock felt, was the lack of expressive range in modern architecture. An exception, he noted, was the work of Wright—"the Michelangelo of the twentieth century." Wright, he concluded, could indicate "that he is less of an enemy of the International Style than he claims to be, and that there are many possibilities of expression within the frame of reference of modern architecture."[81]

Ultimately, the MoMA symposium underscored uniquely American contradictions and polarities that had existed since colonial times: the search for a synthesis between a vernacular tradition in architecture and the model of a European classical ideal; the role of individual expression within a democratic framework in contrast to the increased anonymity of the individual, imposed by a technological and industrialized society; and the opposition and definition of the roles of nature and culture within society. In reality, at the time of the MoMA symposium there were not only various approaches to "modernism" but various "regionalist" approaches, and myriad overlapping of the two. Above all, the symposium underscored those complexities and the multiple possibilities for architecture and modernism during the cold war era, as architects anxiously searched for forms that would respond to that cultural and political climate.[82] Those issues continued to be articulated in the architectural press during the early 1950s. Nearly every publication carried an article or commentary that attempted to redefine modernism within the context of the International style or a regionalist approach, or attempted to find a synthesis between the two. In 1951, for example, Hitchcock published an article entitled "The International Style—Twenty Years After" that retracted many of the dogmatic statements he had made regarding the International style in the 1932 exhibition and publication. Many of the parameters he earlier defined, he admitted, were arbitrary and had led to sterile and imitative work by lesser architects.[83]

Parallel to those discussions were arguments about what constituted a humanist approach to architectural form. Rudolf Wittkower's *Architectural Principals in the Age of Humanism,* published in 1949, had contributed to a rethinking of the term "humanism." As a result of that publication, the term came to be associated with the transcendent, geometric forms of the Italian Renaissance, as exemplified by architects such as Palladio. It was in that form that "humanism" would align itself with the International style.[84] Regionalism developed as a critique of this "Palladian humanism" by emphasizing a design approach that considered specifics of site and society.[85] These polarities of meaning in defining "humanism" may be directly applied to the academy design. The problem that dichotomous argument posed was whether humankind's relationship to architecture occurred within a context of transcendent form or within the context of social and regional parameters that unfolded historically. The conditions of the argument were summarized in 1954 by Sigfried Giedion, in his book *Space, Time, and Architecture.*

Giedion differentiated between two types of architectural "facts"—transitory and constituent. The former he compared to the "short-lived brilliance of a fireworks display," and he described them as accidental manifestations—"fashions" of an era. Constituent facts, on the other hand, occurred throughout history. By their inevitable appearance, they identify the underlying rules of architecture. He wrote:

> The history of architecture could be treated by sketching, in very bold strokes, all the great variety of movements and the masses of fact connected with them. But in attempting to determine the extent and nature of our period's consciousness of itself, it is more helpful to examine . . . cross sections of decisive stages in the history of architecture. . . . A few facts seen clearly enough may lead to something more important than the isolated facts themselves: the inner structure of architecture at the stage of growth which it has reached in our time.[86]

The difference between the two approaches is best clarified by a comparison to linguistic theory, which was adopted and applied to architectural polemics by modernist proponents. In his 1915 publication *Course in General Linguistics,* Ferdinand de Saussure (a Swiss linguist and countryman of Giedion) argued that language be analyzed both in terms of its historical development and as a system of sounds that constructs itself in the present. The former he termed diachronic, the latter, synchronic. Diachronic development, for Saussure, was evolutionary and fortuitous, wholly unintentional and accidental. Synchronic development, on the other hand, was a static system of language, manifested as a series of formal relationships that achieved meaning through its arrangement apart from history. The separate nature of the two systems precluded the possibility of using one to gain insight into the nature of the other. Illustrating his thesis with reference to a chess game, Saussure argued: "One who has followed the entire match has no advantage over the curious party who comes at a critical moment to inspect the state of the game; to describe this arrangement, it is perfectly useless to recall what had just happened ten seconds previously."[87] Saussure used a biological analogy, comparing the diachronic mode to a longitudinal slice of a plant stem and the synchronic mode to transverse or cross-sectional slices. He concluded by emphasizing the superiority of the synchronic method over the diachronic in examining language.

Applying these arguments to the academy design debate, SOM architects employed technological metaphors as a constituent fact of architecture, synchronically comparing their design solution to that of past (Gothic) architects and modern aircraft. By associating the architecture of the other academies with outmoded traditions of warfare and technology, they reinforced their arguments. Conversely, the members of Congress sought meaning in a diachronic sense. They wanted to know how the design would evoke and continue past cultural traditions, reflect a uniquely American experience, or relate to its western site. In a final attempt to assure that meaning, in tragicomic desperation, the Congressmen sought to include ivy in the landscape component of the academy design—an addition, by the way, that was never realized.[88] Their search for meaning, however, would not end there. Although Congress's decision to restore limited funding to the academy project marked a victory for SOM, it was only a partial win. The debates over architectural meanings at the academy, ultimately affecting its funding and design, would continue until the decade's end. Meanwhile, construction began.

THE ACADEMY'S CONSTRUCTION

Although the Senate voted on July 23, 1955, to restore over $79 million dollars to the supplemental appropriations for academy construction, on July 30 a conference committee reduced the amount to $20 million dollars, reflecting continued concerns over the design and the desire to maintain a tight monitoring system as the construction progressed. Construction began after the reduced amount was allocated, although bureaucratic and political processes continued to affect the project. The architects from Skidmore, Owings, and Merrill managed to buffer themselves somewhat from academy personnel by making design decisions in small committee meetings attended by persons who supported them. But they still had to deal regularly with funding constraints and often had to justify their designs in congressional hearings.

CONSTRUCTION MANAGEMENT: CONTROL AND CONTENTION

The parties involved in making the decisions regarding the academy's design and construction included the firm of SOM, the secretary of the air force, the secretary's architectural consultants, the Air Force Academy Construction Agency (AFACA), and, upon occasion, other military personnel. Those parties ultimately answered to Congress and were also subject to scrutiny by the press and general public.

An SOM organizational chart for the academy project, published in 1956, differs slightly from the chart the firm had submitted when applying for the project. The new chart indicates that Owings, head of the San Francisco office, was partner in charge of the project. Directly answerable to him was another partner, John Merrill, of SOM's Chicago office, who more closely supervised the project. Hartmann, also from the Chicago office, was the partner in charge of administrative direction for the project. Bunshaft, working out of the New York office, was SOM's partner in charge of design, and beneath him was Netsch, director of design, who had been promoted to full partner following the May 1955 exhibition and who worked out of the Chicago office.[1] Bunshaft later described the organization as follows: "The team that went to work on that job consisted of Nat and Skid as kind of supreme dealers at very high levels, John Merrill as the working administrative partner on the job, and myself as the overall old master designer overlooking and guiding, as best I could, the young Netsch. . . . Bill Hartmann was to look in every once in a while, but he used to attend major meetings and that's about all. That was essentially our team; in other words, five partners [although Bunshaft cited six] from all offices."[2]

In a May 1956 memo, Netsch provided additional insight into SOM's organizational structure for the academy project:

> The initial program was prepared in Washington with John Hoops, Ralph Youngren and myself working directly with the then forming Air Force Academy Construction Agency. . . . As a result of the master plan itself, the design group was divided into eight major sections. . . . John Kirkpatrick and George Wickstead headed the group primarily involved with the preparation and research necessary for the master plan. Stan Gladych, Otto Stark, and Walter Metschke assisted primarily in developing the individual site plans for the Academy Area. The building groups were divided into four major components—Academic Area, Housing Area, Service and Community Facilities[,] and the Airfield. With the exception of the airfield . . . design teams have been formed within the four major groups. . . . Basically, the organization is now functioning based upon Gordon Bunshaft acting as design critic with myself directly in charge of the design of the project. Ralph Youngren, assistant to Chief of Design—with Bob Ward, Ralph Youngren, John Hoops, George Wickstead, Stan Allan, Otto Stark, and Al Lockett heading up the individual groups.[3]

In later interviews, Netsch recalled that he was specifically responsible for the design of the following Cadet Area buildings: the administration building; the social center; and the chapel. Ralph Youngren led the design team for the academic building; William Rouzie, the cadet quarters team, and Gertrude Peterhaus, the dining hall team.[4]

Netsch also outlined the procedure by which the designs were developed in the same memo. The Air Force Academy Construction Agency prepared design directives on each of the buildings or units of the project. Design presentations by SOM were first made to the academy consultants (officially referred to as the consultants to the secretary of the air force) Saarinen,

Belluschi, Becket, and Larson (Roy Larson, of the firm Harbeson, Hough, Livingston, and Larson, was added as a consultant in early 1956). Formal presentations were then made to the secretary of the air force and his staff. After approval of the conceptual aspects of the design, design sketches were submitted to the AFACA and the Air Force Academy. Definitive drawings and project drawings followed. All those drawings were executed in the Chicago office.

SOM's meetings with the academy consultants were meetings of professional colleagues. These encounters would have contrasted sharply with the presentations of the designs to Congress, or even to the AFACA. As noted earlier, Belluschi, although dean of the School of Architecture and Planning at MIT, was still involved with SOM through the Portland, Oregon, office of Belluschi/SOM. He was also working with Skidmore and the New York SOM office on the design of a new YWCA building in Pittsburgh, and in 1952 he had designed a house for Skidmore in Florida, which was being completed. Although Belluschi often employed a modernist vocabulary in his own corporate projects, such as the Equitable Building in Portland (figure 39), he was reluctant to use stylistic labels in describing his work. That Belluschi's approach to architecture could embrace the modernist academy design is indicated by comments he wrote supporting the design in *Architectural Record*. He observed that it would not "make sense to carve out the Rocky Mountains as a New Egyptian Valley of the Kings to house the Air Academy so as to give it the flavor of the region. On this particular project one may question the appropriateness of using vast amounts of glass, but the juxtaposition of crisp, clean, business-like structures on a mountain landscape can be justified by sound esthetics—but more so by the strictly disciplined around-the-clock life which 2500 cadets must live while being educated and trained in the waging of aerial warfare."[5]

The relationship between Belluschi and Saarinen was close. Belluschi was an advocate and defender of Saarinen's MIT work of the 1950s. In 1953 Saarinen married Aline Louchheim, who, as the art critic for the *New York Times,* had specifically cited Belluschi's work as exemplary.[6] There was a great deal of respect for the ideas of Belluschi and Saarinen on the part of SOM designers, and the two men functioned as an extension of the SOM design team. By 1958, in fact, Bunshaft, Belluschi, and Saarinen were all involved with the Lincoln Center project, coordinating their activities.[7]

Becket and Larson seem to have been less important voices in these meetings. Welton Becket and Associates was based in Los Angeles, where Becket was the supervising archi-

Figure 39. Equitable Building, Portland, Oregon. Pietro Belluschi, 1948. Photograph by Ezra Stoller, © ESTO.

tect for the UCLA campus.[8] Certainly he was not as respected in the architectural community as were Belluschi or Saarinen, and the SOM team undoubtedly knew his firm had not been a finalist for the academy design. His comments during these meetings were often ignored or contradicted by others in attendance. Roy Larson's office had also been a finalist for the academy project, in association with the firms of Harrison and Abramovitz, and Gugler, Kimball, and Husted. Larson's firm had collaborated with the latter firm in preparing the 1953–54 preliminary sketches for the academy. As with Becket, Larson's comments at the consultant meetings were of secondary importance. However, although minutes of the meetings between SOM and the consultants are cursory, there are no memos or letters to indicate that any of these meetings were fraught with tension or animosity.

On the other hand, despite Netsch's comment that SOM worked in unison with the AFACA, there was from the outset an acrimonious relationship between that agency and SOM. As noted earlier, the agency's mission was "to direct the planning, designing, and construction of an Air Force Academy."[9] A promotional "Fact Sheet" written in 1955 emphasized that since the academy project was the first such project undertaken solely by the United States Air Force, without supervision by either the United States Army Corps of Engineers or the navy's Bureau of Yards and Docks, special care was taken in selecting the agency's staff. That staff was comprised of seventy military people and civilians with backgrounds in construction and engineering.[10] Animosity between the AFACA and SOM began shortly after the appointment of Albert Stoltz as director of the agency, on January 25, 1955. Stoltz replaced Colonel Leo J. Erler, who had known members of SOM in his capacity as the air force's director of installations in Tokyo between 1949 and 1952. The relationship between Erler and the firm was a good one. He had helped SOM in its bid to get the academy contract. Erler supported decisions made between SOM, the consultants, and the secretary of the air force, but after his replacement by Stoltz, the AFACA tried to take a more active role in the design process, which SOM personnel resented.

Complaints from Stoltz reveal a widening gulf between the architects and the AFACA. Major General Robert Burns, assistant vice chief of staff, issued an official authorization on May 13, 1955, that placed the responsibility for the academy design, including "architectural theme or style," under the joint authority of SOM and the AFACA. Under those guidelines, Stoltz supposedly had the power to "approve site plans, sketch drawings, definitive and final contract drawings, and definitive and

final contract specifications." Although John Ferry, as special assistant for installations, resubmitted a copy of the order to SOM in September of the same year, SOM continued to claim full responsibility for the project.[11] From SOM's point of view, the AFACA was simply one more bureaucratic body to which the firm had to respond, and it often circumvented the agency. In a letter to Stoltz in February 1956, Carroll Tyler, SOM's general manager in charge of operations in Colorado Springs, addressed the AFACA involvement:

> While it can be agreed that the Architect-Engineer has not always complied fully with the directives, particularly in regard to staying within the scope and costs, it can be agreed further that the Air Force Academy Construction Agency's comments on our submittals have been unduly lengthy and detailed on items which, in many instances, could have been better and more economically resolved by conferences and which in many cases have resulted in the necessity for redesign. As a result design costs to the Architect-Engineers in the last 18 months have materially exceeded our estimated design cost as included in the contract.[12]

The letter went on to outline procedures that SOM would follow in the future. Under those guidelines, SOM and the AFACA would confer on all stages of the design and would work together on interpreting the design directives handed down from the agency. SOM would then make design submittals which would be approved "at appropriate stages" by the agency. Modifications to those submittals could result in SOM's submitting a claim for additional reimbursement. In theory, this outline seemed to establish a teamwork approach, with SOM and the AFACA sharing in the design process, while providing SOM recourse in the case of costly design modifications.

Stoltz, however, continued to complain bitterly that SOM went over the agency's head, responding directly to the Office of the Secretary of the Air Force.[13] On September 25, 1956, Stoltz sent a memo to General Washbourne complaining of the cost of using concrete and metal panels rather than masonry in putting up structures in the Service and Supply Area. He added, "As you know, SOM has a propensity for ignoring design criteria and instructions. . . . They have an equal propensity for designing structures from the outside in, based upon preconceived architectural concepts." He concluded that "based on this knowledge . . . we should review the position of SOM's unlimited license to design completely in accordance with their own desires and without conformance to economical practices."[14] Washbourne replied in a memorandum that the AFACA should be formally charged with the authority "to see that the Secretary's decisions and Congressional directives on this project are carried out."[15] In the same memo, however, Washbourne noted that the agency's demand to meet deadlines "has generated intense pressure upon S-O-M [sic], who have very humanly sought to escape this pressure by promoting a direct relationship with the Secretary and his consultants." The relationship between SOM and Stoltz became strained to the point that in October 1956, when Stoltz was contacted by Culver Military Academy in Indiana to recommend an architect to design its auditorium, he responded, "In no case can I recommend Skidmore, Owings and Merrill." Heading the list of firms Stoltz recommended for the job was Welton Becket and Associates.[16]

In October 1958 Stoltz requested a final performance rating of SOM by the academy's Engineering and Operations Divisions. The people in the Operations Division concurred with Stoltz. They replied that the continual tardiness of SOM in reviewing plans was a result of the firm's refusal to man the job in Colorado Springs, referring important decisions instead to the Chicago office. Even after the firm agreed to a local office, the report continued, the personnel sent were unqualified for the job.[17] The firm's lack of cooperation was summarized as follows: "We emphasize that the apparent prime factor governing SOM's operation is the insistence that the client's (USAF) interests be subordinated to those of the company."[18] The performance rating concluded, "Neither of us would recommend that SOM be used for any future Government work." Stoltz's subsequent evaluation of SOM was scathing. He stated, "As I have indicated previously . . . I consider organization and management to be the greatest weakness of this architect-engineer. I cannot help but feel that had it not been for the efforts of this Agency, the results obtained would have been inferior, almost completely uncoordinated, far more costly, and would have subjected the Air Force to great criticism."[19]

PRELIMINARY CONSTRUCTION AND DESIGN CONCERNS

The original timetable for the academy construction, set at an August 1954 meeting with personnel from the air force, the Air Force Academy, and SOM, stipulated that by June 1, 1958, the Cadet Area be sufficiently completed to accommodate 900 cadets. The most important date in the minds of academy personnel at that meeting was May 1959, when the first academy class would graduate.[20] It was also assumed that by 1960, the academy would be able to accommodate an additional 1,500 cadets

for a total enrollment of 2,400.[21] By October 1954, the 1958 target goal had been modified, with all parties agreeing that by late summer or fall 1957 the cadets would be able to move to the permanent academy site.[22] The fall 1957 date was reported by the press after the May 1955 exhibition of the design and confirmed by General Washbourne, who testified in a June 30, 1955, congressional hearing that "in 1956 we would require funds to cover the construction of those facilities necessary to open the Academy with a part of the programmed number of cadets in fall 1957."[23] In the interim, the academy was to be located in a temporary facility at Lowry Air Force Base in Denver.

The first reviews of SOM's academy design sketches took place in the Chicago offices of SOM on March 11 and 12, 1955, with representatives of the AFACA and the academy consultants in attendance. In a letter to Bunshaft, Owings expressed annoyance that Ferry had invited the consultants without the approval of SOM. Owings immediately sent out letters to each of them, downplaying the presentation and stating that it was to be "very preliminary . . not a final presentation or even a real preliminary presentation but simply an attempt on our part to expose the Secretary to our thinking on the uncrystalized stage."[24] In contrast, Owings expressed concern to Bunshaft that the meeting was "pretty critical" and asked him to fly in from New York to help with the presentation.[25] The day before, SOM had received a letter from Director Stoltz of the AFACA, giving reason for the urgency: "I would expect, as a result of your presentation, basic decisions as to the [proposed architectural] style can be made at that time." He went on to write that a subsequent meeting would be scheduled (it was originally set for May 3, but later pushed up to April 25), at which time a final presentation would be made to Secretary of the Air Force Talbott, who "would then be in a position of making public . . . his decision as to the architectural style."[26]

The AFACA's response to the preliminary presentation was less than enthusiastic. At the beginning of its two-page report, the agency representatives noted the following: "We feel that a disregard for regional environmental factors exists in the designs we reviewed. The natural characteristics of the physical site seem to be subordinated to the architecture. In conjunction with this, a lack of consideration of the elements of nature seems to be expressed in the design of the buildings." Comments in the report indicate that the concerns were primarily pragmatic. Specifically, the report stated that the design ignored the natural contours of the site, which would lead to a greater expenditure for retaining walls and earth moving. It also commented that there was an excessive use of glass in the design, which created a sense of monotony, and ignored the extreme weather conditions of the region. There were, for example, no provisions for wind breaks for the proposed open middle deck of the Cadet Building, and the intended glass-roofed galleries ignored the probability of hailstorms that were common to the region. The glass would also create glare and, since there was no form of sun control, facilitate heat gain. The memo also focused on overall functional concerns; for example, too much room was devoted to circulation, and too large an area in the cadet rooms was taken up by wardrobe space. The use of columns in the dining hall interior was questioned "on the basis of blocking views of the poop deck," and the report criticized the separation of the Jewish chapel from the academy chapel.[27]

There was another conference on March 17 and 18 at the SOM Chicago office, with Stoltz and Talbott attending. Stoltz responded to that presentation several weeks later in a brief letter that was generally favorable regarding the Cadet Area design. But he was still very critical of the extensive use of glass, urging the introduction of opaque material—preferably "materials native to Colorado and adjacent areas."[28] A follow-up letter from Stoltz to SOM dated April 4, 1955, complained that the problems outlined in his March report were still not being addressed. He reiterated the concern with "functional layouts [that] conform to a preconceived architectural style." Urging the adoption of sunshading and a decrease in the expanses of glass, he requested "that expeditious action be taken with the above comments." He further noted that the agency would be providing alternative plans for the cadet rooms, which the AFACA also thought were poorly designed.[29]

A second presentation of the design was made on April 25, again in SOM's Chicago office. Stoltz's follow-up letter to that presentation was more detailed and reflected his irritation with SOM in ignoring the AFACA suggestions. He began his list of criticisms by reiterating his concern that the use of glass was excessive in all areas, including housing, and stipulated that the skylights originally intended for the academic building be eliminated. Again, he asked that the open middle floor of the cadet quarters (SOM termed it "an open arcade") be enclosed, citing the possibility of an accumulation of snow, dirt, or debris. In response to Stoltz's recommendation that Colorado stone be used as facing material, SOM had proposed the use of New England granite. Stoltz objected, citing cost considerations. Other objections related to such matters as the placement of the cadet hospital (Stoltz wanted it closer to the Cadet Area) and the presence of interior columns in the dining hall.[30]

The initial public presentation several weeks later in Colorado Springs seems to have only partially addressed those criticisms, perhaps due to time constraints. In the press packet, for example, mention was still made of the "open arcade" at the center level of the Cadet Building. The extensive use of glass continued to be a source of criticism.

The general site plan (or master plan), as displayed at that May exhibition, was basically an extension of Husted's analysis of the previous year.[31] To what degree Husted specifically influenced the overall academy plan or its architectural design is not recorded. The June 1955 issue of *Progressive Architecture* noted that Husted served as "Special Consultant to the Air Force on sites and master plans of air bases." In fact, Husted was a special consultant to the AFACA during this time, although it is not known how often he met with that agency or what the nature of his feedback to them was. Like Husted's plan, SOM's master plan was organized around four functional areas: an airfield; housing for the academy staff and families, including provisions for schools for children of those families; a community center for the residential areas; and the Cadet Area (figure 40). The terrain dictated that the airfield be located to the east, where the area was flatter, in order to facilitate takeoffs and landings. Two housing areas were located in adjacent valleys on the site, with the community center located on the mesa between them. The Cadet Area was located on the most prominent ridge. Adjacent to that area were athletic fields and a parade and drill ground.

By the time of construction, the architectural program for the Cadet Area required that it accommodate approximately 2,640 cadets, with the possibility of expansion to accommodate up to 5,000, and that it include the following buildings: the cadet quarters; a classroom-library building (the academic building); the dining hall; the administration building; the social center; and the chapel. The original design featured three ascending steps: the parade ground was the lowest level; the first trio of cadet buildings (the cadet quarters, the academic building, and the dining hall), the second; and the more public facilities on the Court of Honor plaza (the social hall, the administration building, and the academy chapel), the third. The levels were intended to be joined by masonry ramps in order to accommodate formations of marching cadets (automobiles were prohibited within the Cadet Area). Retaining walls defined the areas.

The cadet quarters, located on the north side of the Cadet Area, consisted of one rectangular building and one nearly square building, separated by an open area. At the May 1955 exhibition, these structures appeared as modernist slabs of re-

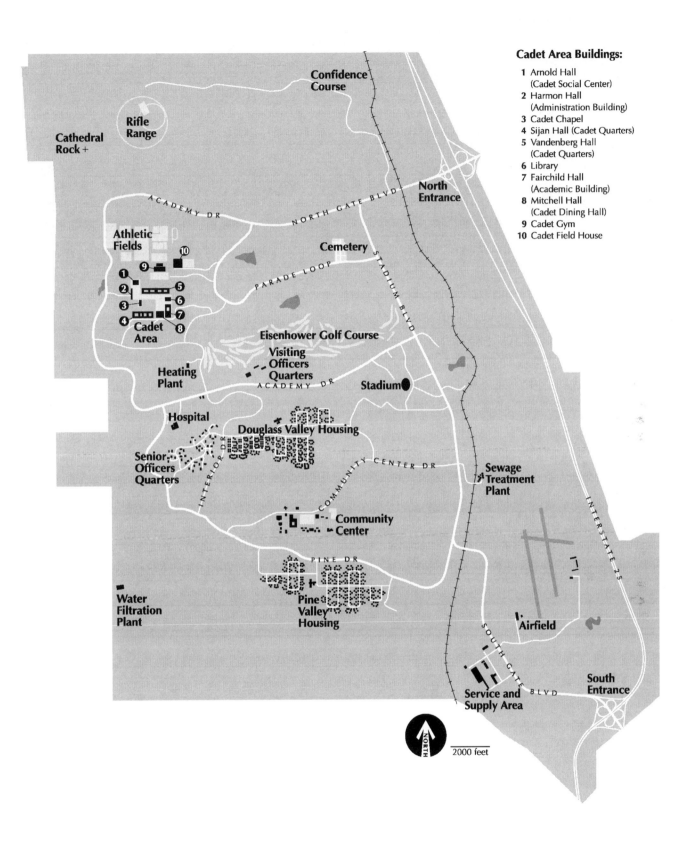

Cadet Area Buildings:

1 Arnold Hall
   (Cadet Social Center)
2 Harmon Hall
   (Administration Building)
3 Cadet Chapel
4 Sijan Hall (Cadet Quarters)
5 Vandenberg Hall
   (Cadet Quarters)
6 Library
7 Fairchild Hall
   (Academic Building)
8 Mitchell Hall
   (Cadet Dining Hall)
9 Cadet Gym
10 Cadet Field House

Figure 40. United States Air Force Academy Site Plan, 1984. Redrawn by Dennis McClendon, 1994.

inforced concrete, steel, and glass with enclosed courts. The June 1955 issue of *Architectural Forum* noted that the intent was to achieve an "Oxford intimacy of contained courts and gardens." The article reported that the initial studies for these quarters considered a number of smaller buildings, "but the sloping made a good arrangement impossible and hindered future expansion." At a right angle to the cadet quarters was the academic building, originally designed as a single rectangular building of reinforced concrete, steel, and gray glare-resistant glass. It was actually three connected buildings (the library, the humanities building, and the science building) with enclosed courts located on the east end of the Cadet Area. The dining hall was placed on the southeast corner of the Cadet Area, adjacent to the sciences section of the academic building.[32]

On the western end of the Cadet Area site was the Court of Honor, a ceremonial plaza accessible to both the cadets and the public. It was bounded on the north side by the social center, on the west by the administration building, and on the south by the chapel, which was elevated on its own podium. The chapel was originally oriented on an east-west axis on the dominant knoll overlooking the Cadet Area. The June 1955 issue of *Architectural Forum* stated the chapel was to accommodate Protestant services at one end, Catholic in the other, and Jewish in the center (on a mezzanine level). The building was described in that publication as a "long, tall steel framed structure roofed in intersecting planes of marble" and in the June issue of *Architectural Record* as a "space frame of thin strips of aluminum filled in with narrow slabs of marble."[33] Viewers at the May 1955 exhibition would have seen, in both the model and the renderings, an opaque accordion-like folded structure raised on a podium and overlooking the entire Cadet Area (see figures 22, 23, and 34). The retaining wall supporting the podium appeared gigantic on the model, towering over the adjacent trees.

Several additional buildings adjacent to the Cadet Area were indicated in the "Master Plan" published in *Architectural Forum*'s June issue: a hospital (later moved to a different location) located in a valley south of the dining hall; a superintendent's house (also moved to a different location) situated on a hill overlooking the parade ground; and the physical education building (or gymnasium, as it was sometimes referred to) and athletic arena, located on a plateau north of the cadet quarters and on a perpendicular to that complex. The arena was intended to be a glass structure with a conical concrete seating area for 7,500 spectators. It was not included in the initial construction, and the physical education building was later reoriented parallel to the cadet quarters.[34]

The massing of the major buildings of the Cadet Area was intended to create a dynamic rhythm, reinforced by the overall asymmetrical arrangement of the major components and by the interplay between their negative and positive spaces (the dining hall, for example, was aligned with the void in the cadet quarters). General Harmon was particularly critical of the asymmetrical plan, proposing a symmetrical schematic layout in its place. In response, Stoltz explained SOM's rational: "Normally a rugged site is more suited to an asymmetrical scheme than to a symmetrical scheme of development because of the inherent site imbalance. Contemporary architecture has embraced wholeheartedly asymmetrical balance. . . . For years [SOM] has been recognized as a leading exponent of contemporary architecture and this fact was well known at the time the Architect-Engineer for the Air Force Academy was under consideration."[35] The plan's asymmetry was reminiscent of that in early De Stijl paintings, an association that had been with modernist architecture by Henry-Russell Hitchcock in his 1948 publication *Painting toward Architecture*.[36] During the academy's subsequent design phases, this formal interplay between solids and voids would become more pronounced, with the reorientation of the chapel on a north-south axis, the movement of the social hall further north, and the placement of the physical education building on axis with the void in the cadet quarters.

Once preliminary funding for the academy was approved by Congress, contracts went out for essentials, such as the construction of roads, utilities, and water facilities. How to provide for the academy's water needs, estimated at five million gallons per day, had been a concern since the Colorado Springs site was chosen. As reported at the October 4, 1954, meeting, the largest supply of water, bringing an estimated 5,200 million gallons a year to the academy and Colorado Springs, was to be provided by the Blue River system, located on the western side of the continental divide.[37] By December 1955, a tunnel had been constructed through the Rampart Range to accomplish that goal.[38] The location of the single runway in the flat southeast area of the site had been resolved at a meeting between air force and SOM personnel on October 4, 1954.[39] To address the problem of diurnal wind shifts, the runway had to be slightly reoriented, which not only involved relocating U.S. Highway 85-87 and the Atchison, Topeka, and Santa Fe Railway line, but reconfiguring Kettle and Pine Creeks.[40] Mountain States Construction Company was awarded a contract for $1,177,350 to relocate the highway and divert the creeks. The issue of flight training itself had been debated since early discussions of an air academy. The official statement on flight training at the academy had finally been issued on June 2, 1954, by Colonel T. H. Holbrook: "All graduates of the Air Academy will be qualified as aircraft observers. All students will be qualified as navigator-bombardiers; failure to complete aircraft observer training at the Air Academy will mean elimination from the Academy. Air Academy students will be given familiarization with light plane flying as pilots, but will not be qualified as Air Force pilots upon graduation. Thus, all Air Academy graduates will be aircraft observers; a large percentage will go on to pilot training, but failure to obtain a pilots' rating will not affect the Academy graduate's commission."[41] The airfield, therefore, was intended for limited cadet flight instruction, flight demonstrations, and general use.

In June 1955, SOM representatives met with Talbott and the academy consultants to discuss congressional and public reaction to the design, and it was agreed that certain aspects of the Cadet Area would be reexamined. Attention was focused on the area's west end, where the chapel was located.[42] Those concerns continued to be addressed into the fall, with the balance of accountability again shifting for SOM as a storm of controversy engulfed Talbott. The Senate Permanent Investigations Subcommittee had accused Talbott of misusing his position as secretary of the air force to solicit business for a firm in which he was a partner, and he resigned as secretary in August 1955.[43] Donald A. Quarles replaced the embattled Talbott—a position he would retain until April 1957.

On October 1, 1955, SOM again presented the academy site plan and design to various members of the air force, the academy staff, and the academy consultants.[44] After the presentation, SOM personnel withdrew, and the consultants and air force representatives gave their opinions of the design. Approval was given to proceed on the cadet quarters, the dining hall, and the academic building, but it was agreed that full-scale mockups of a dormitory room and the exterior walls of the academy building would be built so that the use and effect of glass and construction materials in general could be more effectively studied. The consultants again voiced concern that the west end of the Cadet Area design (including the Court of Honor) was unsatisfactory. They concentrated their attention on the chapel location and orientation and the extensive use of retaining walls surrounding it. The social hall was also criticized, and SOM agreed to a complete new design for that building. Saarinen emphasized the need for a landscape consultant on the project, particularly to deal with the Court of Honor area.

The extensive retaining walls required to create the three stepped levels that comprised the Cadet Area, ascending from

the parade grounds to the chapel, were also discussed. Ferry questioned the expenditure for the construction of the walls, but the consultants defended it on the basis of the "monumentality" the walls lent to the complex. Becket suggested the architects follow Wright's advice and integrate the architecture with the site by using native brown rock for the walls. Belluschi, however, disagreed and stated that the walls should relate to the buildings and not to the site. The firm of T. F. Schols, Inc., was contracted to do the site grading and to construct the retaining walls. Approximately 10,000 lineal feet of walls—walls that reached as high as thirty-six feet—were built. In some cases those walls were supported by fifty-foot manmade earthen embankments (see figure 2). The cost of grading Lehman Mesa into a series of terraces and the construction of the required retaining walls exceeded $2.3 million dollars.[45]

THE CADET QUARTERS, DINING HALL, AND ACADEMIC BUILDING

The cadet quarters—later named Vandenberg Hall, for former Air Force Chief of Staff General Hoyt S. Vandenberg—was one of the first Cadet Area structures designed by SOM (figures 41–43). Fronting the four-acre formation quadrangle, the quarters consist of a rectangular building and a square building, constructed with concrete flat-slab spans, steel columns, and glass walls, separated by an open area. The cadet quarters are six storeys in height, although from the so-called Terrazzo, or pedestrian, level within the Cadet Area they appear to be only three storeys high because they are abutted against the north side of the mesa. From a distance, below and outside the pedestrian area, the building's height creates the monumental presence that Congress and the air force sought. The Terrazzo level of the quarters, actually the fourth storey, had originally been designed as "an open arcade," similar to the first storey. The other levels contained the cadet rooms. There were originally 1,320 two-man rooms included in the complex (some of the rooms later accommodated three cadets). The rooms each had a sink, with shared showers and baths. The press packet for the May 1955 exhibition described the functional layout of the building as follows: "The basic layout of the cadet quarters is based upon the organizational grouping of the cadets into six groups each comprising four squadrons . . . each group to be located around a quadrangle and to be limited to two adjacent floors."[46]

Bunshaft credited Netsch with the design: "He came up with a beautiful idea of stepping down the hill with the build-

Figure 41. Cadet quarters (Vandenberg Hall). Photograph by Clarence Coil. Stewarts Photographers and Custom Lab. Courtesy Pikes Peak Library District.

ing. It was really a six-storey building; on the ground level of the high part, you looked right through the building. That acted as a walkway and garden for the upper three floors and was the roof of the lower three floors. It was a very nice scheme, and it was Walter's."[47] The original design took the cadets into consideration. When they stood in formation in inclement weather, they could do so in the shelter of the open level, and no cadet had to ascend or descend more than two storeys to his room. The quarters included recreation facilities, such as hobby areas for various clubs, a cadet store, and barber and tailor shops. The design reflected the advice regarding air force dormitories that was printed in a 1952 *Architectural Record* article: "Another problem, in half-war half-peace times, is to encourage re-enlistment, and this is largely a matter of giving the men decent living accommodations."[48]

Construction was based on seven-foot modules. Walter Netsch later stated, "Falling back on my Japanese experience of the tatami oriented world the module of 7' x 7' was selected, and multiples or divisions of this proportion were used. This meant that within any structure system the solids and voids would relate." Multiplied four times, the module created the standardized beam size and structural bay; doubled, it created the width of the cadet room. The module also determined fenestration and facade detailing. It would, Netsch stated, reinforce a geometry that "would contrast with nature's more complex character."[49] The geometric window division, with narrow vertical sashes (which slide open) flanking a fixed central pane, is, in fact, as least partially indebted to turn-of-the-century Chicago fenestration.[50] Each of these units is further articulated by an opaque band below the window, divided into halves by a vertical mullion. Structural bays are further defined by the supporting pilotis at the ground level at two-room intervals.

Netsch had firsthand experience with Japanese architecture and tatami proportions (whose actual dimensions are 6' by 3'). During the Korean War he had worked for SOM in Okinawa (then a possession of the United States) and Japan, designing military air bases. In addition, there had been a pervasive influence of Japanese architecture on Chicago architects

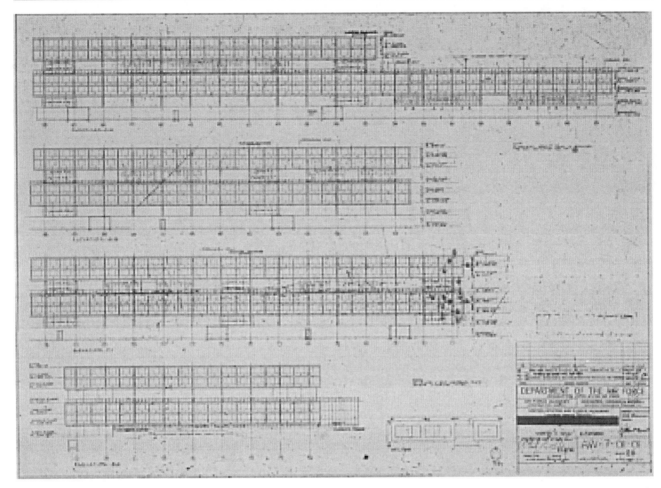

Figure 42. Cadet quarters (Vandenberg Hall), north and west elevations. Courtesy Skidmore, Owings, and Merrill LLP.

since the city's 1893 World's Columbian Exposition. Frank Lloyd Wright, for example, frequently discussed the impact that Japanese architecture had on his approach to design, and he mentioned the tatami mats and the function they served as the unit of standardization in Japanese domestic architecture. Wright's point was that Japanese living was conditioned by an ideal that Westerners would do well to emulate—not literally, but in a spiritual and ceremonial sense.[51]

Netsch's employment of tatami mat proportions, on the other hand, was primarily used to reinforce a Cubist-like use of solids and voids within the context of modernist modular design and the grid. Le Corbusier, for example, had emphasized the economic advantages of modular design in a chapter on the "Mass-Production Houses" in his 1923 *Vers une architecture*. In his discussion of mass-produced artisan housing, Le Corbusier also used a seven-foot module, creating a 21'-by-21'

space.[52] Using abstracted classical models, he associated those proportional systems with prefabrication and technology. In 1932, discussing the International style, Henry-Russell Hitchcock and Philip Johnson championed standardized units and contemporary methods of construction.[53] Walter Gropius, advocating mass-produced units produced according to standardized plans, grounded his synchronic argument in technological solutions to architectural design. He wrote that "the 'modules' of the Greeks, the 'triangulation' of the Gothic builders give evidence that in the past also optical keys have existed, serving as common denominators for the working teams of early builders."[54] Sigfried Giedion had also written at length about the relationship between new potentialities in construction brought about by mass production. On the practical level, previous air force design criteria, as outlined in the January 1952 issue of *Architectural Record,* suggested modular con-

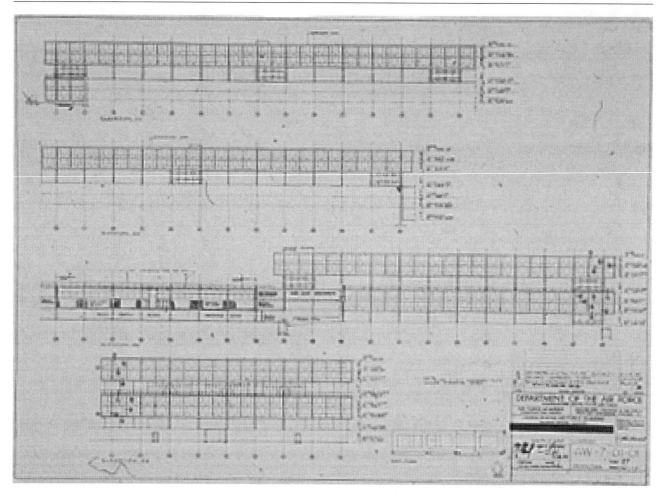

Figure 43. Cadet quarters (Vandenberg Hall), south and east elevations. Courtesy Skidmore, Owings, and Merrill LLP.

struction based on a grid system for all its buildings (the modular size they suggested for a dormitory building was thirteen feet, with other buildings' modular sizes varying from twelve to sixteen feet).[55] More closely related to the academy design, and surely more relevant, were Bunshaft's designs for the United States Consulate in Düsseldorf, completed in 1955, and the United States Consular Housing in Bremen, constructed in 1954 (figure 44). In the latter, sixteen apartments contained in a pair of three-storey buildings were designed using a modular grid and a modernist vocabulary. The staircase details—seen through four vertical expanses of glass—are nearly identical to those of the cadet quarters at the Air Force Academy. While Netsch's experience in Japan may have provided a poetic explanation for the academy design, his use of a grid proportional system was also informed by his education at MIT and a modernist aesthetic.

The problem with heat gain resulting from the great expanse of south-facing glass in the cadet quarters, which were not air-conditioned, had been addressed by SOM in preparation for the October 1, 1955, design presentation meeting. In an SOM memo to Netsch dated September 30 and headed "Room temperatures—Summer—South Exposure," a scenario was presented in which exterior temperatures were 85 to 90 degrees. With "shades drawn," the following interior room temperatures were projected:

1. With all windows closed—96° at noon rising to 100° in mid-afternoon;
2. With top ventilating section open—88° at noon rising to 93° in mid-afternoon;
3. Air Exhaust is now contemplated at 80 cf per minute. This small quantity will have negligible effect on room temperature.[56]

Figure 44. United States Consular Housing, Bremen, Germany. Skidmore, Owings, and Merrill (Gordon Bunshaft, designer), 1954. Photograph by Morley Baer.

In response, SOM's Robertson Ward enlisted the help of the Libbey-Owens Ford and Pittsburgh Plate Glass companies to develop tinted glass that would reduce transmittance to 35 percent and cut the solar gain. SOM had hired Ward, who had also worked with SOM on some of its wartime projects, to deal specifically with many of the technological areas of construction required in the academy design.[57]

The full-size mockup of a dormitory room requested at that October 1 meeting was presented to the consultants and members of the Air Force on April 16, 1956, in Colorado Springs. Owings, Bunshaft, and Netsch were among those representing SOM. All four academy consultants were present, while the air force representatives included Quarles, Harmon, and Stoltz. The display consisted of a complete cadet room interior, as well as material samples that could be used for the buildings' exterior treatment and for surfacing the paved areas and retaining walls. The cadet room mockup, built at a cost of approximately nine thousand dollars, allowed the consultants

and the air force representatives to observe not only the effect of lighting and fenestration, but also such details as the effect of different wall panelings, the location of electrical outlets, and how the room would be furnished and arranged.[58]

The task of furnishing the rooms was the responsibility of Walter Dorwin Teague Associates, which had been hired by the academy in February 1956 to oversee the interior design at the academy. In choosing an industrial design firm, an academy board (whose names are unrecorded) had narrowed its selection to five firms. In voting for a firm, points were awarded on the basis of 1 point for first place, 2 for second, and so on. Teague Associates received 6 points; J. Gordon Carr Associates, 14 points; Raymond Loewy Associates, 17 points; Dave Chapman Company, 25 points; and Cushing and Nevell, 28 points.[59] The firm's budget, as reported in the April 1956 issue of *Industrial Design,* was $70 million.[60]

Teague's background, like SOM's, included commissions at the 1939 New York World's Fair, where he played a major role in both architect selection and design. At that fair, he designed interiors for Eastman Kodak (for whom he had designed the Bantam Special camera in 1936), United States Steel Subsidiaries (including its futuristic diorama), the DuPont Building, and the Ford Motor Company Building.[61] His other projects had included the design of Pullman cars and Texaco service stations. Shortly after receiving the academy commission, his firm was contracted to design the interiors for the Boeing 707.[62] Teague's optimism regarding machine technology was boundless. He had written in 1934 that a universal modern machine aesthetic would "create itself . . . out of the preferences and the prejudices of this age,"[63] and that its principles underlay "the structure of this universe and the structure of our perceiving minds."[64] He later clarified those ideas in his book *Design This Day:* "As modern engineering has advanced in mastery, designing for purely functional needs alone, it has created examples of perfected order that meet all the high standards of Sullivan and Wright. . . . In the superlative rightness of certain modern airplanes . . . nothing has been admitted which did not contribute to efficiency, materials and processes. . . . As a result these things approach a classical, abstract beauty of form which advances towards perfection with each new advance in functional efficiency."[65] Teague made no attempt to hide the fact that, in his industrial designs, functionalism was abstracted into formal qualities that metaphorically stood for technological efficiency. The opening epigraph for *Design This Day* was a quotation from Plato's *Philebus,* dealing with the eternal and absolute beauty inherent in forms. Earlier, with rhetoric that echoed that of Le Corbusier's *Vers une architecture,* Teague had declared that the modernist approach to industrial design would be "familiar in Athens: the beauty of precision, of exact relationships, of rhythmical proportions."[66]

SOM had objected to the decision to employ an interior design consultant. In a letter to Ferry in November 1955, John Merrill wrote, "The seriousness of this situation cannot be overemphasized, both from the standpoint of the final design of the buildings, of the construction cost problem and our time schedule. The proposed procedure in connection with the major buildings is unprecedented in our experience and would be a tremendous handicap to us in discharging the responsibilities to which we are now committed."[67] In response, Ferry advised that the wording in the "Statement of Work" be changed to read: "The industrial designer and engineering contractor to the Air Force Academy will design, list, etc., all furnishings and equipment to properly meet the needs of the Academy and will

prepare his design so that they are compatible with the interior designs developed by the Construction Agency's architect."[68] Upon Teague's appointment, Ferry wrote a reassuring letter to the office of the secretary of the air force stating, "He [Teague] knows the Skidmore, Owings and Merrill people and they have agreed that this firm will be satisfactory for this work and that SOM can work well and in harmony with them."[69] Netsch, however, complained bitterly about the quality of Teague Associates' work. In a letter to Owings in June 1956, Netsch stated, "Both Gordon [Bunshaft] and I were extremely disappointed in the design quality of the material selected by his [Teague's] office." He further noted that Teague's firm seemed to have a $70 million budget with no system of checks and balances, and he suggested another consulting group be formed to oversee the work. Netsch concluded, "It is unfortunate he is responsible only to the Academy with its, of necessity, changing personnel who are not trained to question design submitted [*sic*]."[70] Owings responded the following day, recommending "we simply give the Academy a stiff criticism of Teague's work."[71]

At the April 1956 presentation of the mockup, the secretary and his consultants decided that a dull aluminum and white marble facing would be used for the buildings' exteriors.[72] Aluminum as a construction material had been used extensively in the aircraft industry, and its employment on the academy buildings alluded to that function. SOM, a firm that was in the forefront in the development of anodized aluminum, used that technology because anodizing prevented discoloration of the metal and the end product was said to be durable—lasting for decades without replacement. The firm addressed the problems of leakage associated with curtain-wall construction by developing an extrusion process for the aluminum. The molten metal was forced through a mold, allowing complex fabrication of single components to hold the glass and to shed water.[73] Quarles also asked that native materials be considered for the retaining walls and paved areas, and he authorized SOM to spend an additional $10,000 for the construction of a second display to include those materials.[74]

At that second presentation, on July 28, 1956, Secretary Quarles and his consultants agreed that the cadet quarters unit, as furnished by Teague Associates, was acceptable. After inspecting over twenty samples of materials, presented in a display 42 feet wide and 21 feet high, they also decided that the academy retaining walls would be surfaced with rough-textured gray granite panels to blend with the site. The granite would be procured on the basis of competitive bids.[75] Eventually, a Minnesota firm was hired to provide the granite, and a Georgia firm provided the marble used in the paving and buildings.[76] The vast areas of pavement (over 200,000 square yards) were to be comprised of cement with embedded aggregate, called "terrazzo," from nearby Canon City. The monotony of the paving areas was broken by dividing the expanse into 28' modules demarcated by strips of marble, which also reinforced the 7' modules of the buildings.[77]

The stark planes of glass and stone facing that formed the facades of various academy structures, including the cadet quarters, were given color by mosaic tiles. The idea to use mosaic tiles at the academy may be related to visits that members of the academy and SOM made to the University of Mexico. In June 1953, air force officials had visited the University of Mexico campus, and in September 1954 several SOM representatives, including Netsch, Bunshaft, and Owings, also toured the campus. The SOM contingent noticed and commented upon the use of mosaics and murals to decorate the walls of the austerely modernist buildings. But at the University of Mexico campus the mosaics were didactic, or at least illustrative, while at the academy they formed color planes on the geometric facades. The technique was reminiscent of the De Stijl architect Gerrit Rietveld's application of exterior color to his 1924 Schroeder House in Utrecht.

Netsch had originally proposed that green and blue mosaic tiles be used at the academy, to harmonize with the landscape. But Bunshaft suggested primary colors (Netsch referred to them as "Bauhaus colors"), and those colors were eventually chosen.[78] The choice of Italian glass mosaic tile, manufactured in Murano, rather than glazed ceramic tile, was controversial for several reasons: among them, the decision allowed SOM to omit the "buy American clause" from its specifications, and American-manufactured ceramic tile was less expensive. SOM and the AFACA justified the choice based primarily on superior color quality. Netsch explained that the small tesserae "were selected from Venetian mosaics for their fine size, elegant color match ability, and most importantly for their texture. As these small bits vary in thickness they give a wonderful texture that gives sparkle to the broad colored wall surfaces on which they are applied."[79] Less-expensive ceramic tile was originally intended to be used inside the academy buildings, but the Murano glass tiles were eventually carried into the interiors as well.[80]

Work also began at this time on the dining hall and the academic building. The dining hall (later named Mitchell Hall,

for Brigadier General "Billy" Mitchell, a pioneer of military aviation and an early advocate of air power) had a unique program. Seating capacity was required for three thousand cadets, all of whom would arrive together in formation and be seated and served at once (figures 45 and 46). Cadets were allotted 25 minutes for breakfast, 25 minutes for lunch, and 30 minutes for dinner. That schedule required numerous entryways into the hall to facilitate rapid seating, and an open space unobstructed by internal supports.[81] Netsch recalled the original dining hall plan in a 1958 interview:

> We developed a fancy and quite technologically exciting system of putting all the kitchen services on the floor below and using elevators to carry heated service carts up. This produced a splendid amenity in that the men would eat in an unencumbered dining hall beautifully enclosed by glass all around. Well, of course, if there were a power failure it could happen that the elevators would not work and that the cadets might miss a meal or have to achieve it in some confusion. We thought the risks slight. . . . But we lost the argument. The final main heating and serving areas as well as the dishwashing will be on the main floor and so the cadets will not eat in a glass-enclosed pavilion.[82]

In an interoffice memorandum of November 1955, Netsch discussed the decision to eliminate the original two-storey system: "General Harmon has . . . gone on record that a one storey dining hall is the only system that will work." Netsch complained that the issue was an example of "the complicated liaison existing within the Air Force itself, the Agency [AFACA], the Academy, the Secretary's Staff as well as the internal complexities and empire building within the Academy. General Harmon has used Mr. Ferry's concern about the suspension of electrical service to the elevators as a means for re-opening the dining hall question."[83]

As constructed, glass walls enclose the east, south, and west sides, while a masonry wall completes the north side. Masonry walls also surround the kitchen and service areas on the interior, to hide those functions. A service floor beneath the dining area provides storage space and loading docks. In the original design, as seen at the May 1955 exhibition and shown in George Rudolph's renderings, the roof was divided into nine equal units by means of intersecting trusses. In the final design, 308-foot-long trusses were constructed, spanning an interior unobstructed space of 266 feet. The prefabricated roof system was assembled on the ground (figures 47 and 48). On January 6, 1958, the entire roof, weighing 1,150 tons, was lifted

Figure 45. Dining hall (Mitchell Hall). Photograph by Clarence Coil. Stewarts Photographers and Custom Lab. Courtesy Pikes Peak Library District.

over 24 feet onto sixteen columns in just six hours. Twenty-four hydraulic jacks were used, in a construction technique usually applied to concrete lift-slab construction. Structural calculations were aided by the use of a recently developed University of Illinois computer system, one of the first times computer technology was used for structural analysis. Photographs of the truss design were reproduced in magazines throughout the country, underscoring the idea that the latest applications of high technology were being used in the academy's construction.[84] While high technology was celebrated, women's equality suffered a setback. The head of SOM's dining hall design team was Gertrude Peterhaus, who later recalled that, as a woman, she was "prevented from participating in design presentations to the client" and was "excluded from the site" on the day the unique roof truss she had designed for the struc-

ture was raised into place.[85] Construction of the dining hall was virtually completed, at a cost of $4 million, by the time the cadets moved to the campus in August 1958.

The academic building (later named Fairchild Hall, in memory of General Muir S. Fairchild, first commander of the Air University) also met "minimum essential requirements" (meaning that classes could be held in the building) by August 1958. It was 98 percent completed by November of that year. At a construction cost of over $22 million, it was the largest single academy contract awarded.[86] Ralph Youngren, who also assisted Netsch on the Court of Honor buildings, headed the design team for the academic building. One of the largest academic buildings in the country, it includes a humanities area; a science area; laboratories; the library; the cadet dispensary and dental clinic; and the commandant's offices. It was one of

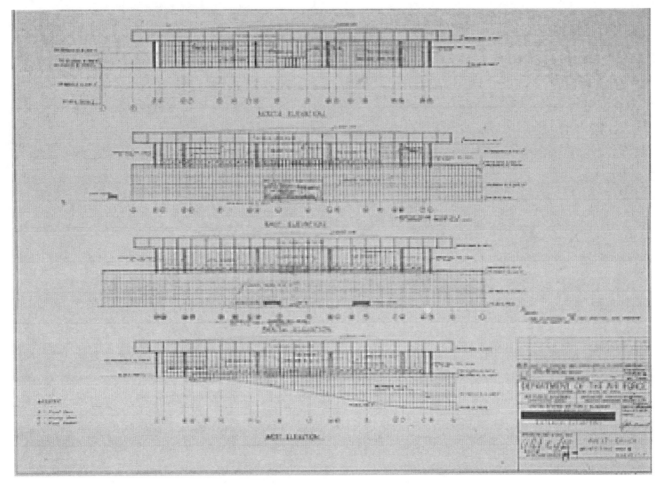

Figure 46. Dining hall (Mitchell Hall), exterior elevations. Courtesy Skidmore, Owings, and Merrill LLP.

only two buildings at the academy (the other being the administration building) designed to be completely air-conditioned. Like the cadet quarters, the building is divided into two sections, with an enclosed courtyard between, but here four of the six storeys of the building rise above the Terrazzo level (figures 49–51). Instead of being abutted against the mesa, it is free standing and connected to the Terrazzo level by bridges on the third level. Upon crossing the bridges, the cadets may either ascend to the classrooms or descend to the laboratories. Again, the profile of the building from outside the Cadet Area, elevated on the mesa, is intended to create an effect of monumentality.

Included in the academic building design are two 250-seat lecture halls, two 450-seat lecture halls, one 1,000-seat lecture hall, and nearly 200 classrooms. Academy officials had de-

cided that cadets would be distracted by exterior views, so the classrooms (on the fourth and fifth floors) were designed without windows. Consequently, the white marble facing of the exterior creates an awkward, top-heavy appearance, in comparison to that of the library wing or the cadet quarters. Because cadets are required to work at chalkboards during class, the program for the classrooms also called for chalkboards on all four walls (ninety-six lineal feet of chalkboards per room).[87] Over six miles of corridors, many with glass walls, are contained in the academic building—color-coded for the cadets' convenience. SOM said of the design: "These elements combine into a building where the structure is expressed in aluminum for ease of maintenance and to express the age in which the cadet lives, glass so that the cadet can take advantage of the environment of the academy site as he moves through the

Figure 47. Dining hall (Mitchell Hall) construction. Photograph by Clarence Coil, c. 1958. Stewarts Photographers and Custom Lab. Courtesy Pikes Peak Library District.

Figure 48. Dining hall (Mitchell Hall) construction. Photograph by Clarence Coil, c. 1958. Stewarts Photographers and Custom Lab. Courtesy Pikes Peak Library District.

Figure 49. Academic building (Fairchild Hall). Photograph by Clarence Coil. Stewarts Photographers and Custom Lab. Courtesy Pikes Peak Library District.

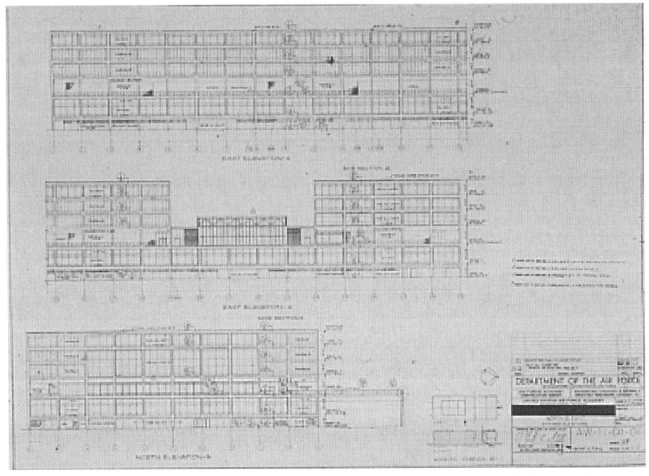

Figure 50. Academic building (Fairchild Hall), north and east exterior elevations. Courtesy Skidmore, Owings, and Merrill LLP.

building, and masonry which shows the conditioned classroom where his training occurs."[88] It was decided that the offices of the commandant of cadets would be located in the west end of the library, with windows overlooking the formation area and campus. The faculty and administrative offices, located on the top floor, also have exterior facing windows. The dispensary and dental clinic is located halfway between the cadet quarters and the dining hall, with easy access from the classrooms.

The library is on the north end of the academic building, closest to the cadet quarters and convenient to the classrooms. Located above the Terrazzo level, the library was intended to be articulated as a separate building—an effect that has been compromised by the unfortunate 1970s addition of a reading room in the void between the two parts of the academic building. On the north and south ends of the library,

the corner two bays on the top three floors are faced with white marble. Although the fenestration echoes that of the classroom section, the manner in which the facing is used does not, creating an awkward transition between the two parts of the building. The library's most distinctive feature is a monumental helical staircase, again designed with the help of a computer, leading from the lobby to the main reading rooms (figure 52). The entire wall behind the staircase was originally intended to be glass, which would have made the gesture all the more spectacular. The wall adjacent to the staircase on the third floor is gold mosaic, the only mosaic of that color at the academy.

Lieutenant Colonel Arthur Larsen, director of the library, discussed the library in an interview conducted during its construction. Larsen complained that the air force hierarchy re-

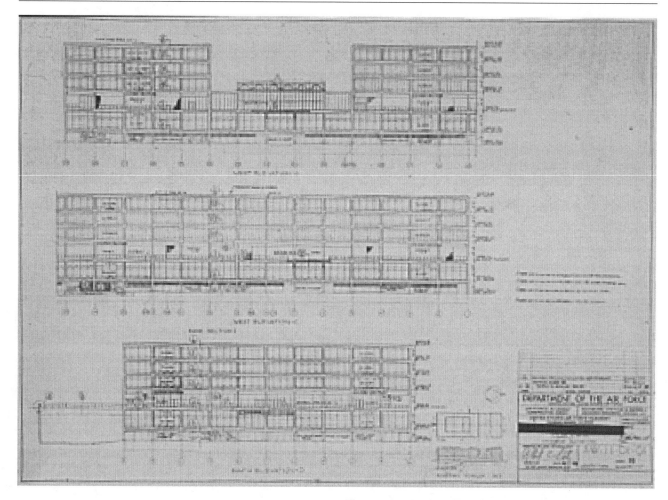

Figure 51. Academic building (Fairchild Hall), south and west exterior elevations. Courtesy Skidmore, Owings, and Merrill LLP.

garded the library as a luxury rather than an integral component of an academic institution and that as a result, he had little input in its design. He recalled that a standing operating procedure was developed during the academy construction to protect the architects from unnecessary intervention by academy personnel. Meetings had to be requested and coordinated with the AFACA. Larsen also complained that those meetings were difficult to schedule because SOM's supervision of the design was headquartered in Chicago, even though the firm had set up an office in Colorado Springs. As a result, during the design phase for the library, Larsen met only four times with the architects. The first meeting was for submission of general specifications. The next two meetings took place without advance notice, to review drafts of the plan. The last was con-

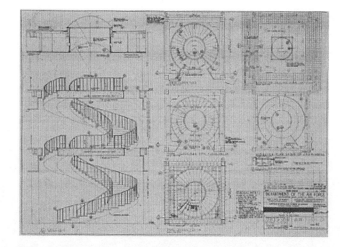

Figure 52. Academic building (Fairchild Hall), library stair, plans and section. Courtesy Skidmore, Owings, and Merrill LLP.

ducted in Chicago at the urgent insistence of Larsen. "Unfortunately," Larsen lamented, "because of the lack of freedom of contact, we were never able to have incorporated in the plans an entirely acceptable library plan, and the present plan, in my opinion, represents much more a compromise of our requirements in favor of architectural design than any modification of architectural design to meet the operating needs of the institution." Regarding the library's defects, Larsen stated, "First and foremost is the fact that the administrative space has been cut 4,000 feet below what we stated were the minimum requirements of the library staff. This has meant a hodge-podge of arrangement, utilizing for administrative purposes areas which were originally intended for storage, or areas that are essentially public. . . . There are other defects, all within the definition of space arrangement, which require the library to adapt its functions to conform to architectural design."[89]

THE COURT OF HONOR AND ACADEMY LANDSCAPING

While the three buildings discussed above were approved at the October 1955 meeting, the structures located within the Court of Honor proved to be much more controversial. They formed the public plaza that overlooked the rest of the Cadet Area and would be accessible to the general public. The structures included the cadet social center, the administration building, and the chapel. From the first public exhibition of the plans for the academy, the harshest criticism was leveled at that element of the design. At the October 1, 1955, meeting, the academy consultants and air force representatives asked that the entire area be restudied. The social center had to be redesigned, as did the administration building (the latter building was originally intended to house the commandant's offices, which were later moved to the library). The Court of Honor area in general was criticized for its excessive amount of paved areas and its lack of landscaping.[90] The chapel remained the most criticized element of the entire academy design.

Both the social center and the administrative center were scheduled for completion in 1958.[91] The social center (later named Arnold Hall in honor of General Henry H. "Hap" Arnold, commander of the Army Air Forces in World War II) was originally intended to include two sunken gardens, ballrooms, bowling alleys, a 2,900-seat theater-auditorium, and a snack bar. The auditorium and ballroom shared one air-conditioning system, since it was assumed that they would be used at separate times.[92] The enclosed garden courts were to articulate circulation, and the main auditorium was to be located within one of them. Gallery corridors in the auditorium were intended for art exhibitions, and also to provide views of the gardens.

At the May 1955 exhibition, the design for the social center appeared in several forms. George Rudolph portrayed it in one of his renderings as a pristine three-storey glass box. It was elevated on pilotis that extended through the interior as structural supports separated from the glass curtain wall, which was articulated with vertical mullions (see figure 34). The model and a different Rudolph rendering, on the other hand, displayed a three-storey building with glazed exterior and a projecting concrete slab roof, supported by pilotis (see figures 22 and 23).[93] Cantilevered sun-control plates separated the lower level (intended exclusively for the cadets) from the upper two storeys (open to the public) and created a horizontal emphasis. In that regard, the building's general appearance was similar to that of the Laboratory Sciences Building at the United States Naval Postgraduate School in Monterey, designed by Netsch between 1952 and 1955, although the social center was essentially a square building, while the Monterey building is an elongated rectangle (see figure 13).[94] In response to congressional criticism, the social center was eventually redesigned with marble facing on two sides, although glazing was retained on the entire west side, facing the Rampart Range, and on the north facade, facing the landmark Cathedral Rock (figures 53 and 54).

The main entry to the social hall is one level below the Court of Honor on the west side of the building. The exterior terrazzo material is brought into the interior in polished form, complete with the defining marble bands that form seven-foot grids on the exterior. Mounting a flight of steps, one comes to a balcony and the auditorium entrance. From the balcony, through the glass facade, is a view of the spectacular Rampart Range. On either end of the balcony, spiral staircases wind down to the ground level. The auditorium was designed to seat the entire cadet population at once. Its walls are covered in a wire-mesh material that extends from floor to ceiling, echoing the references to technology that appear elsewhere at the academy. To the north of the auditorium, one descends from the entry foyer to lounge areas that overlook a two-storey ballroom. The ballroom is accessed by a pair of spiral staircases at either end, allowing for ceremonial entrances into the space. The parquet floor is comprised of light and dark woods, with the light wood emulating the marble bands on the terrazzo

Figure 53. Cadet social center (Arnold Hall). Photograph by Clarence Coil. Stewarts Photographers and Custom Lab. Courtesy Pikes Peak Library District.

pavement and marking out the omnipresent seven-foot grids. A glass wall allows views from the ballroom along the Rampart Range and opens onto an exterior terrace.

In contrast to the nearly square design of the social center, the three-storey administration building (later named Harmon Hall for Lieutenant General Hubert Harmon, first superintendent of the academy) was a long thin rectangle. It too appeared in several forms at the May 1955 exhibition. In one of Rudolph's renderings (see figure 34), the administration building appeared as an opaque fragment to the west of the social center. In the model (see figure 22), it was raised on supporting pilotis. It was lower in height than the social center but echoed its design in the use of projecting horizontal plates. Its exterior design was similar to Bunshaft's United States Consulate in Düsseldorf, completed in 1955. There, however, the emphasis was horizontal, with an exterior facing below the windows providing a continuous banding effect, whereas at the academy there is no facing below the windows, and the horizontal and vertical elements more clearly articulate both the bays and the storeys.[95]

Like the academic building, the administration building

was constructed using a structural steel frame, with aluminum curtain walls, coated tempered glass, and marble facing. Alcoa's most recent advances in the field of aluminum construction were utilized in the design of both buildings. One-piece extrusions, up to two feet wide, were used to cover structural columns, creating the sharp-cornered, flat-surfaced profiles that SOM desired.[96] The elevated design, which was retained, affords both public access under the building at plaza level and views to the lower Cadet Area, functioning as "a symbolic gateway into the Cadet Area" (figures 55 and 56).[97] Corridors run the building's length on the second and third floors, with lobbies, elevators, and stair cores on the essentially open ground floor. Marble facing on both ends of the building match that of the social center, although the juxtaposition between the two is awkward. The former seems to hover above the ground on its pilotis, while the social center appears heavy in contrast—essentially an earthbound box. The administration building contained offices for the superintendent and his staff, as well as general facilities for records. The building was later redesigned to include a 9,000-square-foot printing plant.

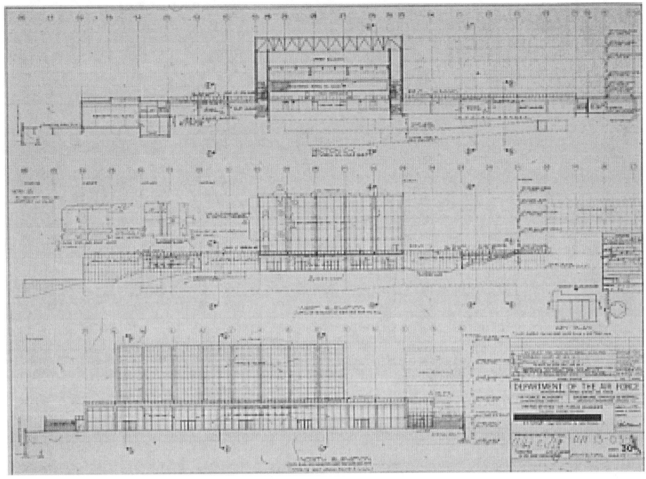

Figure 54. Cadet social center (Arnold Hall), exterior elevations and sections. Courtesy Skidmore, Owings, and Merrill LLP.

As a result of Saarinen's recommendation for a landscape consultant at the meeting on October 1, 1955, SOM hired Dan Kiley as a component of its design team. Kiley's background was impressive. After graduating from the Harvard Graduate School of Design, he and Saarinen had won first prize in the 1948 Jefferson Memorial National Competition for St. Louis. In 1953 he had worked with Belluschi on the Mondawmin shopping center project in Baltimore.[98] Kiley was also known to the military hierarchy. He had served in the United States Corps of Engineers during the war, and at the end of World War II he lived in Paris as a designer in the Office of Strategic Services. In that capacity, he was the recipient of the Office of the United States/Chief of Council/Legion of Merit for his design of the courtrooms for the Nuremberg trials. While in Paris, Kiley was deeply influenced by the seventeenth-century Baroque French

gardens designed by Le Nôtre. As a result, he took exception to the biomorphic forms favored by some of his colleagues, such as Garrett Eckbo and James Rose. The manner in which Kiley perceived the relationship between the cadets, the academy, and nature has been explained by the landscape architect Jory Johnson: "The forms come from the dynamics of the cadet's life—geometrical and disciplined. . . . [T]he freshman cadets . . . walk only on the marble strips that define the 28-foot modules of the Terrazzo Level terrace. This 'marching module' geometrically interlocks with the 7-foot module on which the buildings are based. This carefully proportioned architecture and the landscape architecture frame and clarify the cadet's relationship to the physical, transcendent truths of the Rampart Range."[99]

Kiley's design for the 700-foot-long Academy Air Garden

Figure 55. Administration building (Harmon Hall). Photograph by Clarence Coil. Stewarts Photographers and Custom Lab. Courtesy, Pikes Peak Library District.

was parallel to and west of the academic building (figures 57 and 58). It was comprised of a series of rectangular pools, some of which were placed perpendicular to others to break up the straight lines formed by the marble strips that defined the 28-foot modules in the large Terrazzo area. Holly hedges were planted beside them. As Kiley explained, instead of marching in a straight line through it, the cadets were required by the design to do a "side-step" around the pools: "Movement is ever-continuous and elusive, like a maze," he said. Comparing it to a walk in the natural environment, he continued, "You might squeeze through some small maple trees, pick your way across a rushing stream. . . . It's always moving and changing spatially. . . . What I did with the Air Garden was create a man-made scene having those spatial qualities."[100] The design, however, is strictly geometric and lacks the random qualities of nature. It is more like a three-dimensional manifestation of a De Stijl painting. The original bid for the construction of the Air Gardens was approximately $400,000. In a memorandum dated June 5,

1958, the office of the secretary of the air force asked SOM to eliminate certain aspects of the original design, including marble benches and paving, and to "decrease the quality of trees" in order to reduce the cost. The adjusted construction cost was projected at $318,527.[101] Unfortunately, continual problems with leakage led to the decision to drain the pools of the Air Gardens, and during the 1970s they were filled in.

Kiley's original concept for the cadet quarters courtyards was an exception to his geometric approach. The courtyards, which were protected by the buildings, were designed as free-flowing, biomorphic forms, and they contrasted with the stark geometric planes of the dormitory (figure 59). Never realized, they were to include "lush plantings and small pools that would seem to flow underneath the dorms from one courtyard to the next." Kiley was later critical of his intended departure from a geometric format. In a 1992 interview he stated, "I would never do this now. There should be a contrast, but this is a little much."[102]

Kiley's concept for landscaping the Court of Honor, on

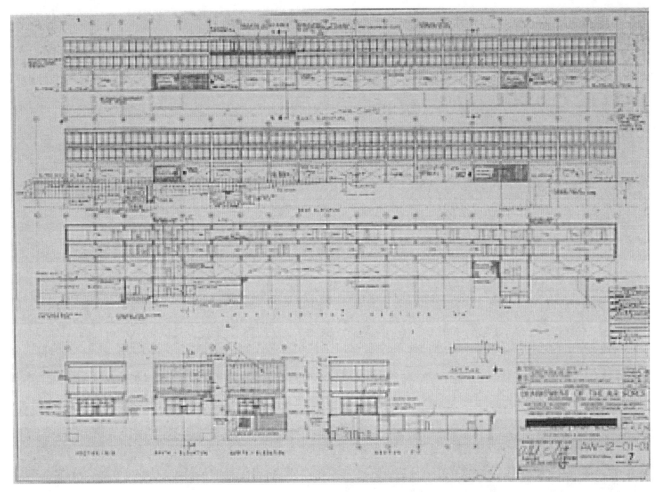

Figure 56. Administration building (Harmon Hall), elevations and sections. Courtesy Skidmore, Owings, and Merrill LLP.

which the administration building and social center were located, was to create a geometric grid of small deciduous trees and Douglas firs that would gradually become more organic in design toward the perimeter, where it would blend with the surrounding trees. The concept was in keeping with Kiley's overall approach to landscape, in which man imposes order on nature. Much of the design was never executed. Explaining Kiley's overall concept of landscape design at the academy, Johnson detected a hierarchical plan: "At the Cadet Area, nature is experienced as measures of control on a continuum from the ordered geometry of the Air Garden, the controlled 'art forms' of the courtyards, to the minimal management of the larger site."[103] But in public and private meetings between SOM, the consultants, and air force personnel, the only hierar-

chical divisions that were discussed were the lower cadet zone and the upper public area. As the landscaping was realized, there is a sharp distinction between the natural and the manmade elements. That effect was heightened by the addition in the 1960s of another cadet quarters (not part of SOM's original plan) on the south side of the Cadet Area, which effectively closed off the natural site, although critics had noted the landscaping deficiencies prior to that addition. Indicative of this was Henry-Russell Hitchcock's introduction to *Architecture of Skidmore, Owings and Merrill, 1950–1962,* written in 1961:

> At the Air Force Academy the weakest aspect is the deficiency of planting. The fault is not SOM's but that of a penurious Congress, which was ready to spend many millions on a group of buildings that may well be unneeded

Figure 57. Air Garden. Photograph by Clarence Coil, c. 1958. Stewarts Photographers and Custom Lab. Courtesy Pikes Peak Library District.

Figure 58. Air Garden. Photograph by Clarence Coil, c. 1958. Stewarts Photographers and Custom Lab. Courtesy Pikes Peak Library District.

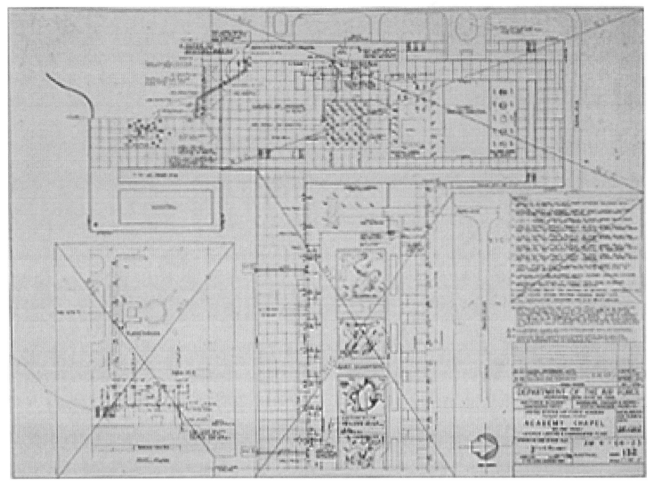

Figure 59. Academy chapel, walkway paving. This gives an indication of the original Cadet Quarters quadrangle garden plans. Courtesy Skidmore, Owings, and Merrill LLP.

within a decade, and yet refused the relatively small sums that would have made possible the filling of the courts with foliage, the completion of the water-garden approach to the dining hall in the central plaza with a quincunx of full-grown trees, and the general wedding of the tremendous man-made organism to its superb natural setting by the general inclusion of a great deal of large-scale plant material.[104]

Whether Kiley's unrealized landscape plan for the public area would have integrated the areas more effectively is difficult to determine.

The Cadet Area, minus the chapel, was reportedly over 90 percent completed as the cadets moved to the Colorado Springs site and their newly constructed cadet quarters in August 1958. The comic-strip character Steve Canyon was depicted visiting the site in the August 3, 1958, issue of the *Chicago Sun-Times*. *Newsweek* also depicted Canyon and his cousin Poteet visiting the academy in a comic strip that ran in its August 18, 1958, issue. In the comic strip, Poteet remarked, "I feel downright futuristic, lookin' at this spankin'-new Air Force Academy." The caption beneath read, "Air Force Academy: Big but minus a heritage." That missing sense of heritage had already become a major issue of contention and debate, as it focused on the one essential ingredient lacking in the Cadet Area—the chapel.

"IN GOD WE TRUST"

The Academy Chapel

While the academy chapel design had been a lightning rod for criticism since it was first displayed in the May 1955 exhibition, few people at the time seemed concerned that the centerpiece for the academy plan was a religious edifice, or that it posed any challenge to the separation of church and state. On the contrary, the presence of a highly visible religious structure at the academy reflected postwar American culture in the context of several congressional acts of the early 1950s.

On February 10, 1954, Senator Homer Ferguson introduced a motion to amend the American pledge of allegiance, unchanged since 1892, inserting the words "under God" into the text. The motion passed Congress, and it was signed into law by Eisenhower on Flag Day, June 14, 1954.[1] The phrase "In God We Trust" was not adopted as the official national motto until 1956, but at Eisenhower's 1953 inauguration parade, the parade of floats representing the forty-eight states was led by a "float to God" with that phrase appearing upon its base. Several Supreme Court rulings had preceded these events, the most relevant for the Air Force Academy being the 1952 *Zorach v. Clauson* decision. That case addressed the issue of permitting release time from regular classes in the public schools for the purpose of religious instruction. Citing the instances of West Point and Annapolis, which required chapel attendance, the justices decided to allow for such time.[2]

Informing those events were the cold war and McCarthyism. Although McCarthy ceased to be a dominant force during the Eisenhower administration, the perception of godless Communism created a climate in which democracy and religion became synonymous. In a period in which the possibility of atomic war cast a long shadow, religion came to symbolize traditional values in a changing world, even as the institution itself became less spiritually charged. By 1955, with the demise of McCarthy, the death of Stalin, and the end of the Korean War, religious fervor had receded but was still a potent symbolic force. Will Herberg, in his book *Protestant—Catholic—Jew,* commented that religion had become "religiousness without religion"—a way of simply "belonging." But he also observed that "being a Protestant, a Catholic, or a Jew is understood as the specific way, and increasingly perhaps the only way, of being an American and locating oneself in American society."[3]

There was, in addition, the precedent of the other two military academies. At each, the chapel was a focal point of the design and overlooked the campus area. The prominent chapel at the Naval Academy, designed by Ernest Flagg in 1905, was modeled after Jules Hardouin-Mansart's church of Les Invalides in Paris (c. 1680) and employed a French Baroque vocabulary. It was flanked by the cadet quarters and Academy Group.[4] Flagg employed a Hennebique system of construction for the chapel's large domical vault and support system. The innovative technique was so noteworthy that photographs of the chapel were published in the February 4, 1905, issue of *Scientific American,* which reported that the structure "represents the most elaborate form of framework of this kind that has yet been attempted in the United States."[5] Cram, Goodhue, and Ferguson located its picturesque Gothic chapel at West Point on a promontory overlooking that academy. Designed in 1910, it romantically recalled medieval and monastic religious traditions in architecture.[6] During the early 1940s, *Life* magazine had depicted worship services at both West Point and Annapolis. When the Annapolis chapel was pictured in the October 28, 1940, issue of *Life,* an article by Walter Lippman entitled "Weapon of Freedom" appeared opposite the photograph; the following year, the Episcopal service at West Point was illustrated in a *Life* magazine article entitled "The Spirit of West Point."[7] Thus, for a combination of reasons, the church as a symbolic presence carried enough ideological weight to require its location as the focus of the academy design. The question now confronting Skidmore, Owings, and Merrill was, What form would it take?

Arguments for more traditional church designs had been presented within the architectural press in articles such as the one that appeared in the December 1953 issue of *Architectural Record.* The author, Reinhold Niebuhr, dean of Union Theological Seminary, noted that "Gothic vaulting and the church spire are fitting symbolic expressions of the yearning of the religious spirit" and declared that America had two great religious traditions in architecture. He thought Belluschi's religious architecture exemplified this, stating that it combined "the virtues of Gothic with the simplicity of the New England meeting house."[8]

Yet Belluschi, in a 1949 issue of *Architectural Forum,* had written that Gothic design was prohibitively expensive, and that a contemporary solution—an alternative to Gothic and colonial—was needed.[9] His "contemporary solution" was in opposition to revivalist ecclesiastical designs.

For modernists, however, the issue of religious architecture remained complicated. They had to justify the use of a formally abstract vocabulary while designing building types that had strong associations with the past and were expected to take on an appropriately monumental form. One possibility was to employ new materials, allowing a technological interpretation of a religious structure that could then be synchronically associated with structural innovations such as Gothic construction or Brunelleschi's cathedral dome in Florence. An alternative approach was to create an architecturally transcendent form. Mies van der Rohe, for example, expressed his belief that rationalism in architecture symbolized transcendent order through the square form of his chapel at the Illinois Institute of Technology (1949–52). Another possibility was to experiment with historical precedents. The brick cylindrical form used by Saarinen in his 1955 MIT chapel design, for example, recalled early Christian baptisteries. Finally, there was the choice of designing churches with dramatic sculptural forms, an example of which was Le Corbusier's Notre-Dame-du-Haut in Ronchamps (1950–54).[10]

The architects of SOM were certainly aware of those possibilities when, on February 28, 1955, the chapel's program was first discussed in an academy design meeting. In addition to representatives from the air force hierarchy, those in attendance included Major General Carpenter, chief of chaplains for the air force, and Netsch and Youngren, representing SOM. Upon discussion, it was decided that a single chapel, housing the three major religions, would be the best solution for the academy chapel. The Protestant part of the chapel was to seat 1,600, with a choir loft accommodating an additional 150 men. The Catholic section was to seat 600, with a choir loft accommodating an additional 50 men. A 100-seat Jewish synagogue was to be provided as a separate small chapel within the Protestant area. This proposal modified a suggestion from the previous summer, signed by Carpenter, in which a two-chapel solution was suggested, with each chapel accommodating 600 men.[11] The minutes of the meeting explained the demographic factors behind the change: "Experience factors in the percentage of cadets in each faith were discussed. It was agreed that the following factors would be the most reasonable to apply to the Cadet Wing: 25% Catholic; 72% Protestant; and 3% Jewish."[12]

At the May 1955 exhibition, the single-chapel solution, de-

signed by Walter Netsch, appeared in the model and drawings. That Netsch was the major designer for the chapel was a
fact that SOM publicly acknowledged—one of the first times
an individual's name was associated with an SOM project.[13] In
its original form, Netsch's design combined a sculptural and
geometric form (see figures 22 and 23). Despite later denials
by SOM and Secretary of the Air Force Talbott, it was intended
to be a folded-plate concrete construction with a freestanding
carillon. In subsequent testimony before the Air Force Contract
Appeals Panel, Netsch stated that the design was "a folded
plate chapel containing two chapels on the grade level, one
for the Catholic services, one for the Protestant services, and a
Jewish chapel on the mezzanine."[14] Albert Lockett remembered being sent to Denver to learn about the folded-plate
construction technique, while Netsch recalled that it was
SOM's Carl Kohler who folded the cardboard model that was
displayed at that exhibition.[15] The building's triangular transverse section continued to be a defining feature throughout
the evolution of its design.

There were precedents for both the folded-plate construction and its triangular section. Marcel Breuer's 1954 design for
a church at St. John's Abbey, a Benedictine monastery in
Collegeville, Minnesota, had used folded concrete plates along
the side of the building to provide structural stability and create a sculptural presence. Breuer explained that the cantilevered concrete slab was "a form as characteristic of our time as
the dome was in the sixteenth century."[16] At approximately the
same time, a series of churches had been constructed that
were defined not by steeples, but by their use of equilateral tri-
angles. The February 1954 issue of Architectural Forum pictured
two of the prizewinning church designs, each defined by an A-
frame structure, which had been selected by the National Joint
Conference on Church Design. The article rejected Gothic and
colonial styles, stating that the "A-frame construction provided
a vertical motif lifting the worshippers above the squat proportions of the conventional mission church."[17] The justification
for the triangular form also had precedence in the nineteenth-
century writings of Eugène-Emmanuel Viollet-le-Duc. In his entry entitled "Style: The Manifestation of an Ideal Based on a
Principle," in volume 8 of his Dictionnaire, he proposed that architectural style be derived from natural crystalline forms. Triangular rhombohedron structures, he noted, were "an a priori
law" from which nature never deviated. The dynamic oblique,
manifested in nature and systematically applied in French
Gothic architecture, was the cornerstone of his structurally rational theory of architecture. This ideal geometry linked historic

forms to the positivistic outlook of the nineteenth century, and
the natural to the manmade.[18] For Viollet-le-Duc, the triangular
form, as applied to religious architecture, exceeded trinitarian
associations and symbolized not only man, who before God
was at his simplest, but the timeless and transcendent forms
of nature. For Netsch and SOM, the Chapel's siting and design
represented synthesis. First of all, it was a synthesis of two major traditions of architecture—the classical and the Gothic. The
architects' constant references to the Cadet Area as an acropolis established a classical reference and, prominently located
on its podium, the chapel thus evoked classical types.[19] The
classical references were combined with allusions to Gothic
structural innovations. Second, the design represented an attempt to synthesize the approaches of the artist/architect with
those of the engineer, resulting in the integration of a uniquely
expressive sculptural creation with a functionally rationalist
technological solution.

As noted previously, criticism of the initial chapel design
was severe and was probably the primary reason Congress
withheld funding on the academy project. The chapel, symbolizing the most traditional American values, carried the burden
of defining and identifying the academy as a national monument—an expression of this country's postwar civilization.
While many critics could be swayed on issues of classroom or
dormitory design, they were stubbornly opinionated on the
subject of church design. Churches, they felt, were defined by
characteristic architectural elements—steeples or spires, a
pitched roof, and vertical walls. Traditionalists regarded SOM's
proposed design as a caricature or an eccentric aberration per-
petrated in the name of modern art. Fanning the flames of the
debate was Frank Lloyd Wright, who attacked the overall academy design, specifically the chapel. Wright acerbically noted
that the chapel design should be studied for ten years and
then thrown away.[20] On the other hand, Wright's granddaugh-
ter, Elizabeth Wright Ingraham, an architect in Colorado
Springs, favorably responded to the dynamic nature of the
chapel design, stating it was the only structure which "aspires
to an ideal."[21] Owings said of the original design, "The published versions showed a model of a chapel in the location we
propose to place it. . . . [T]his design, which was serious on our
part, has found many adherents."[22] Indeed, the Colorado
Springs Free Press ran a headline during the weekend that
SOM's first exhibition of the design opened to the public,
which read, "Most Churchmen Questioned on Academy Chapel
Like It."[23] In contrast, the Denver Post, in a special report on the
design, reported: "Although a dominant structure, the Cadet

Chapel appeared to be in a radical style. Louis Skidmore, senior partner in the architectural firm of Skidmore, Owings and Merrill & Associates, said the model was 'only a block of wood—that isn't the final design.'"[24] Recalling the details of the response to the chapel design at the May 1955 exhibition, Netsch later wrote:

> After weeks of a grueling schedule and many sleepless nights the exhibit was a great success, except for the design of the chapel. I had thought it a disaster and hid in the back room in tears. Nat Owings, the project's manager for SOM, came over and said, "What's wrong with you? Everything has been approved but the chapel and you can always do another one!" . . . Nat advised that I had better go to Europe for inspiration, that the next chapel design would meet with controversy and would probably be the focus of a congressional investigation. Unfortunately, he was right.[25]

The following month, at a June 30, 1955, congressional hearing, John Merrill sidestepped the issue of the chapel design, stating that it was not part of that appropriation. General Washbourne commented on the design only by comparing it to the smaller community chapel, explaining that the latter would be "a permanent building, but it would not be the monumental type of building that would go in the cadet area."[26] At a July 11 hearing, confronted with criticism of the academy chapel design by Senator Thye, John Ferry responded, "Senator, I can assure you that nothing like that chapel that was shown in the original picture will be constructed."[27] At an appropriations hearing a week later, Talbott dismissed the design entirely: "There is no design. . . . They had no design and they put something in and it grabbed everyone's eye."[28] At the same hearing Owings, when asked if the "wigwam" chapel design shown at the exhibition would be constructed, replied, "It has been removed from the model and from consideration."[29] The "wigwam" analogy had been applied to the design since the initial academy exhibition. It had first been made by Senator Robertson, who commented to the press after the May exhibition that the chapel design looked like "an assembly of wigwams." The July 22, 1955, issue of U.S. News and World Report also used the comparison, printing a photograph of the model with the caption, "Skirt or Wigwam."[30] Ironically, Wright was designing the Beth Shalom synagogue in Elkins Park, Pennsylvania, at the same time, which, he noted, would have a pyramidal dome, "along the lines of an Indian teepee."[31]

As criticism of the original chapel design mounted, SOM and the academy consultants were forced specifically to address the problem. In a conversation with Bunshaft on June 23,

1955, Ferry went so far as to suggest the building's design: "the chapel, used as a working model of the Air Force Air Academy, is to be removed and a new model chapel substituted before the model is put on exhibit at Lowry Field in connection with the opening of the Air Academy 9, 10, and 11 of July. The new chapel shall be of the greatest simplicity, but should fall in conventional lines usually associated with a Christian church. The new model chapel should have a pitched roof and some sort of steeple, while the building itself should have vertical walls."[32] For Ferry and other critics, the architectural design elements that signified religion had been reduced to the equivalent of a child's drawing, representing a type similar to the New England meetinghouses of the eighteenth century. John Merrill, responding to Ferry's remarks, asserted, "I do know it will not be New England in its final concept. The New England chapel was a small meeting-house and its pattern could not be adapted to a building to accommodate 1500 persons. It would look like a 10-foot high hot dog."[33]

The original folded-plate chapel design was replaced in early July with a less radical "tentative" design, presented in photographs by the national press. The Colorado Springs Gazette Telegraph reported, "The new model conforms more to conventional American ideas of a place of worship and is complete with steeple and stained glass windows." The chapel now appeared as a triangular section that was isosceles in form rather than equilateral, and the folded-plate elements had disappeared, or were at least less pronounced. In the article, Merrill noted that the model was not the final design model for the chapel, and that it "may not resemble in the least the final concept."[34]

At an October 1, 1955, meeting between the academy consultants (Saarinen, Belluschi, and Becket), air force representatives, and representatives of SOM (including Owings, J. Merrill, Netsch, and Bunshaft), it was agreed that the chapel location and design were problematic, and that before the rest of the Court of Honor complex could be designed, a chapel solution had to be found. Academy Superintendent Harmon had earlier insisted the building plan be cruciform, but he was informed by air force chaplains that Jewish agencies would "strenuously object" to such a design.[35] It soon became apparent that the ultimate design solution for the chapel would have to be delayed, but that the problem of its location should be addressed immediately so that construction could begin on the other buildings in the Court of Honor area. Saarinen felt the placement of the chapel on such a prominent podium isolated it from the rest of the Cadet Area.[36] A revised plan, in which the chapel was moved onto the Court of Honor, was presented on January 31, 1956, in Chicago, at a meeting between the academy consultants (a group that now included Roy Larson), SOM representatives Owings, John Merrill, Netsch, and Bunshaft, and several members of the air force staff. The plan again met with disapproval, particularly from Saarinen, and SOM was given three weeks to prepare another solution.[37]

Netsch and Bunshaft later credited Saarinen and Belluschi with contributing most to the overall academy plan and specifically to the chapel design.[38] Saarinen had just completed the Kresge Chapel at MIT the previous year, while Belluschi, recognized as one of America's foremost ecclesiastical architects, had designed several churches in association with SOM between 1951 and 1956.[39] Although Bunshaft stated that he and Netsch initially opposed Saarinen's suggestions for relocating the chapel, Netsch admitted that Saarinen's ideas regarding the chapel placement and design were warranted. In a 1958 interview with John Burchard, Netsch recalled, "In the beginning we took a sort of medieval approach to its location in the community and I think we were wrong. The Mont-Saint-Michel aspect would have been wrong. Cadets are not monks and there was no reason why they should be made to climb 125 feet to go to church. So I am glad the first proposal was rejected."[40]

On February 29, in Chicago, a revised plan was shown, with the chapel turned 90 degrees, orienting it north-south rather than east-west, the orientation that had existed since the May exhibition (figures 60 and 61). Secretary of the Air Force Quarles was present, as were members of SOM and staff members from the AFACA, including Stoltz. The placement was approved, but the new chapel design, which was never publicly released, generated additional controversy and criticism. In a letter to Washbourne, dated March 9, 1956, Stoltz noted that Quarles did not approve of the new design and that the secretary had asked SOM to develop four or five different models for the chapel. Stoltz himself wrote, "I consider the new model to be more extreme and less acceptable than the previous model." He added: "At the recent Chicago meeting, SOM designers indicated that they feel that the public must be conditioned to what they, the designers, consider best. I do not concur in this thinking. I do think that the design must be in the modern contemporary style, consistent with the other buildings, but the Chapel design must tend towards neutral rather than radical concept. Otherwise, I feel, we shall be involved in continual public controversy which shall serve only to delay the completion of the Chapel." Stoltz's comments

were undoubtedly based on the experiences of the previous summer, when Congress had delayed construction at the academy while debating design issues. Stoltz proposed a competition be held "among a select and limited number of recognized church architects" to select a design, with SOM then being required to retain that competitor as a consultant.[41] In response, Netsch included four chapel models at the next congressional presentation of the entire academy project. The presentation, at which Netsch and Bunshaft represented SOM, took place on March 27–29, 1956. In a memo dated March 2, 1956, Netsch requested $15,579.85 to cover the cost of the chapel models (a cost of just $150 out of the total amount), site photographs, six 30" by 40" color renderings by George Rudolph, and floor plans and models for the cadet quarters, the dining hall, the academic building, the social hall, and the administration building.[42]

The following week, Lieutenant Colonel Noonan sent a letter to General Washbourne, stating that he had consulted with Edmund Purves, executive director of the AIA, and Walter Taylor, chairman of the Commission on Architecture for the National Council of Churches. He asked Taylor to submit the fifteen best church plans in the United States so that he could forward them to the AFACA. Noonan, however, would hardly have found support for Stoltz's proposal from Purves or Taylor. Purves and the AIA had supported SOM in congressional hearings the previous summer, and Taylor was director of the AIA's Department of Education and Research. Taylor had written an article for *Church Management* in October 1954 advocating modern church design, and he sent it to Noonan along with a letter stating that none of the fifteen designs that leading clergy, architects, and architectural magazines found most appealing were "in any of the 'styles' of romantic classicism." He concluded, "It demonstrates a realization that the recent habit of copying architectural styles of a remote past is an anomaly of the nineteenth century and that the real architectural tradition of the church for eighteen centuries was to be 'modern,' i.e.[,] of its own time." The essay, with its critique of nineteenth-century architecture, was informed by modernist dogma. Both the magazine article and the statement were forwarded to Washbourne.[43]

A congressional hearing on May 15, 1956, again dealt with the academy construction progress and cost to date. The air force requested an additional appropriation of nearly $83 million, bringing the total appropriation amount to $118 million of the originally budgeted $126 million for the academy. When questioned about the remaining $8 million, Stoltz responded

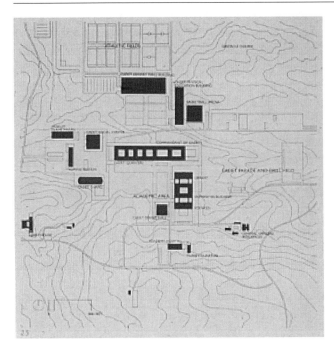

Figure 60. United States Air Force Academy Cadet Area master plan, 1955. Courtesy Skidmore, Owings, and Merrill LLP.

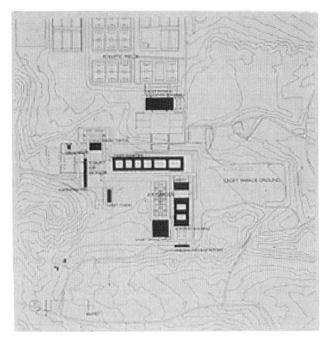

Figure 61. United States Air Force Academy Revised Cadet Area master plan, 1959. Courtesy Skidmore, Owings, and Merrill LLP.

that most of it would cover the chapel construction, anticipating that the balance would be needed by October 1, 1957.[44] Meanwhile, the chapel design itself had still not been resolved. Since the February 29 design meeting, it had appeared in all press releases as simply a block of wood. A press release in late April, for example, showed the block occupying its new position on the Court of Honor on a north-south axis and noted that the design would be finalized in the "next few months."[45] Undoubtedly, design decisions were affected by the fact that the chapel's overall program was still unresolved. On June 1, 1955, a design directive had been issued that called for two cadet chapels—an academy chapel that was to serve Protestant and Jewish denominations and would seat approximately 1,600, and a cadet chapel that would be used for Catholic services and would seat 600.[46] On October 18, 1955, another design directive had been issued, calling for a single interdenominational chapel, with balcony and choir, that would accommodate 1,550 persons.[47]

In a five-page memorandum dated June 9, 1956, Brigadier General Robert Stillman, commandant of cadets, addressed the problem.[48] Despite the previous directives, Stillman stated that three alternatives still existed for the chapel program: one nondenominational chapel; three separate facilities; or one structure housing three chapels (Protestant, Catholic and Jew-

ish). He immediately ruled out the first alternative, stating that "one large non-denominational chapel would result in a real lack of religious atmosphere." At the time, however, nonsectarian military chapels were actually the norm. In its January 1952 study of building types, *Architectural Record* had noted that "Chapels for airmen are, of course, non-sectarian, [and] will serve equally well for any religious group."[49] Nonsectarian chapels in the military had become so commonplace, in fact, that Drew Pearson, writing an editorial in 1957 for the *Washington Post,* noted the unfairness of a system in which standard worship services of the most general nature were intended to suit the needs of all denominations.[50]

In discussing the second option, Stillman compared the situation at the Air Force Academy to those at West Point and Annapolis, and he found marked differences. At West Point, he noted, there were essentially three facilities. The Archdiocese of New York built a Catholic chapel there at its own expense, and Jewish services were held at the Cemetery Chapel. At the Naval Academy, on the other hand, preexisting facilities for Catholic and Jewish services were located in the city of Annapolis itself, within several blocks of the academy. In recommending the third solution—housing the three chapels in one facility—Stillman noted that, due to liturgical demands, the separation of the three chapels would be absolutely necessary.

He proposed seating accommodations for 1,200 Protestants, 600 Catholics, and 80 Jews. Based on projected weekly attendance figures of 2,842, 922, and 76, respectively, for each denomination, he noted that a minimum of three Protestant and two Catholic services would be required per week. A drawback with that plan, he stated, would be the problem of circulation and congestion between the multiple Protestant and Catholic services. In closing, Stillman recommended that any plans be submitted to the chief of air force chaplains and the academy chaplains, "to assure practicality of the chapel facilities in addition to architectural beauty."

On December 27, 1956, yet another design directive was issued, calling for a Protestant chapel of 900 seats, a Catholic chapel of 500 seats, and a Jewish chapel of 100 seats, all to be located within one building.[51] Netsch undertook the chapel design within the constraints of a proposed $4 million budget, but on February 1, 1957, that directive was superseded by design directive FY 1957, #6-B, which cut the budget to $2,550,000.[52] Ironically, a *Colorado Springs Free Press* story published in March gave some idea of how the chapel design appeared in January. The headline read "Air Academy Chapel May Look Like a Row of Teepees After All," and the paper reported that the sketches for the chapel included in a current MoMA exhibition showed a triangular structure with a saw-tooth vertical design that looked similar to the original 1955 design.[53] That MoMA exhibition—entitled *Buildings for Business and Government*—had actually opened in New York in early February and included drawings and a model of the entire academy. The chapel in the model was represented simply as a transparent triangular form, while the sketches, which had been sent to the museum in January, did not reflect changes resulting from the February 1 budget cut.[54] By the time of the *Colorado Springs Free Press* story, the chapel design had changed.

Responding to the February budget cut, Netsch and Bunshaft presented three alternatives for a chapel design at a meeting on March 12, 1957. Numerous air force and academy personnel, including Quarles, Stoltz, and three air force chaplains, attended that meeting. The proposed designs were: a single nondenominational chapel; a two-level building with a Protestant chapel at the upper level, and the Catholic and Jewish chapels at the terrace level; and three chapels at the same level. The two-level design was the one preferred by SOM. After discussion, it was agreed that it was the best solution. Of the consultants present, Belluschi and Larson commended the design, while Becket expressed concern that the aluminum roof might be a source of noise problems in rain or hail storms, and

that the problem of expansion and leakage in the roof should be studied. Meeting minutes noted that the "inspirational quality was well-liked and that S.O.M. should pursue the design of the Chapel as shown." Quarles requested that SOM stay within a $3 million budget and that the design be shown to and approved by Congress before being released to the public.[55] Optimistic that a solution was at hand, Quarles issued a press release on the same day wherein he proclaimed, "In another six weeks I'll be able to describe the chapel more fully to you."[56] SOM's two-level design seems to have been inspired by several sources. Bunshaft attributed it to his familiarity with the church of St. Francis in Assisi. He stated, "I remembered that in the Church of St. Francis in Assisi, the upper church, you come in from the main approach and it is a very big church, very handsome, and down below is another church, sort of crypt-like. . . . The basic idea of two levels, I guess, you might say was mine, or you might say, the architect who did St. Francis of Assisi."[57] Netsch, having been sent to Europe by SOM for three weeks in 1955 to study church designs, recalled that Ste.-Chapelle in Paris, with its Gothic upper level and "medieval" lower level, also provided inspiration for the two-level design.[58]

It was at this point in the design process that the chapel's distinctive system of construction was adopted. Netsch recalled "scribbling away" at the design at lunch one day, when an engineer on the project asked, "Do you know what you are drawing? Those are tetrahedrons."[59] The initial presentation of the tetrahedron design seems to have taken place at the March 12 meeting, although there was no specific reference to it. The tubular steel technology that would be required to construct the tetrahedrons had been explored by the military for airplane hangars (figures 62–66). While the use of that technology, as well as the proposal to clad the exterior in aluminum, would later reinforce the technological metaphors applied to the academy, they were solutions that evolved during the design process. Netsch later recalled that one of the original design proposals for the chapel used onyx as an exterior cladding.[60] Between the tetrahedrons, which were spaced two feet apart, Netsch intended one-inch-thick panels of stained glass. The new design was a refinement, rather than a rejection, of Netsch's earlier design.[61] That at least some critics were aware of that fact was reflected by comments made in Congress. Congressman Whitten, for example, noted that "3 years later they have come up with substantially the same appearing building that they had in the first instance."[62]

At a Pentagon meeting on May 15, 1957, color renderings and a model of the chapel in section was presented to the

Figure 62. Academy chapel. Photograph by Clarence Coil, c. 1963. Stewarts Photographers and Custom Lab. Courtesy Pikes Peak Library District.

academy consultants, the secretary of the air force, and other staff members of the air force and the Air Force Academy. Earlier in the month, Quarles had been appointed assistant secretary of defense, and James H. Douglas, who was instrumental in landing SOM the academy commission, replaced Quarles as secretary of the air force.[63] In the minutes to that meeting, it was noted that "Mr. Douglas and the consultants expressed themselves as being extremely enthusiastic about the design of the chapel."[64] There were, however, concerns. SOM informed the gathering that its estimate for the chapel had risen to $3.5 million, not including contingencies, fees, or equipment. In response, Douglas proposed a nondenominational main chapel, with a Jewish chapel in the basement, but it was determined the savings would not be great enough to warrant such a radical design change. Ferry expressed continuing concern about leakage at the many transitions between the metal tetrahedrons and the glass inserts, but Bunshaft informed him that neoprene seals would solve the problem.

By early June, Netsch had begun designing an edifice that included an upper level that would seat up to 1,200 Protes-

tants, with separate Catholic and Jewish chapels in the lower level with seating capacities of up to 550 and 100 persons, respectively (Netsch's seating capacities seemed to have been optimal, and perhaps included guests, since the capacity indicated in the most recent directive was 1,500 total). He also contacted Walter Holtkamp, the organ designer for Saarinen's MIT Chapel and Kresge Auditorium (projects on which Belluschi had served as an advisor), to design organs for the academy's Protestant and Catholic chapels.[65] When the request for funding came up in a congressional hearing on July 1, 1957, Douglas gave a projected cost of $3 million. Douglas also requested an additional $21 million above the original $126 million allocated for the entire academy project, noting that the original allocation had been based on 1953 construction costs, which had risen. Although that increase was denied, Netsch believed that construction on the chapel was to proceed.[66] On July 11, in a hearing before the same subcommittee, Colonel Noonan again quoted the $3 million figure and gave the total capacity as 1,500 persons.[67] At the Senate Appropriation Hearings the following month, Noonan gave the same figures and justified the

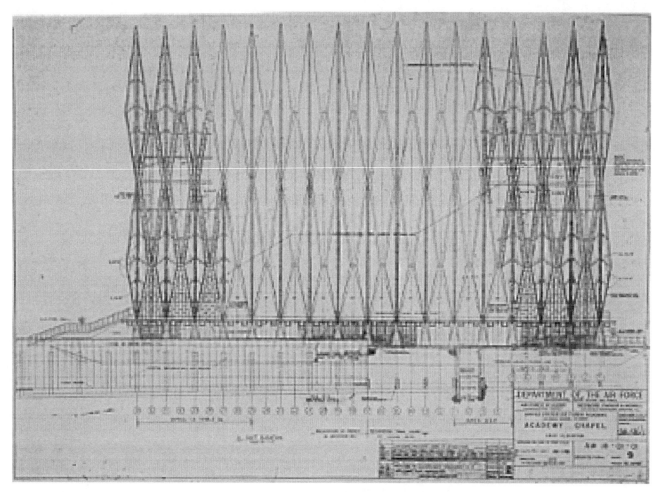

Figure 63. Academy chapel, east elevation. Courtesy Skidmore, Owings, and Merrill LLP.

$3 million in cost by stating, "It isn't really a chapel, in size and structure, but a cathedral."[68] By that time, SOM had received an official memo (dated July, 31, 1957) from Stoltz and the AFACA. The agency had earlier inquired as to why the firm was delaying its design for the chapel, and it had been informed by the SOM architects that they were awaiting approval by Congress. In the July 31 memo, Stoltz impatiently countered, "This is to advise you that the sketch plan has been shown to the Congress and that you are to proceed with the design without further delay."[69]

Apparently, Stoltz was premature in his advice, because on August 6, by a vote of 102 to 53, the House of Representatives voted to delay construction of the academy chapel. Out of a total military construction appropriation of approximately $1.5 billion that was approved by the House, it was the $3 million appropriation for the chapel that met with the most resistance.

Excerpts from the debate indicate that the problems of meaning (along with the teepee analogies) had resurfaced with a vengeance. For example, Congressman Scrivner commented: "Three million dollars should build a cathedral. . . . [O]ne spire is good, but why should there be a polished aluminum cathedral with 19 spires? This design and material is completely incompatible with the greatest beauty of all . . . the natural grandeur of the Rocky Mountains."[70] Moments later, Scrivner called the design a "19-spire polished aluminum monstrosity . . . that will look like a row of polished teepees upon the side of the mountains."[71] Scrivner's remarks prompted a heated debate, with one advocate, Congressman Flood, attempting to justify the design through regional associations: "Now, I can assure you that when the 19 spires that were spoken of so lightly rise to the heavens of the Rockies . . . and when you see the teeth of the white-capped Rockies match the spires of this beautiful

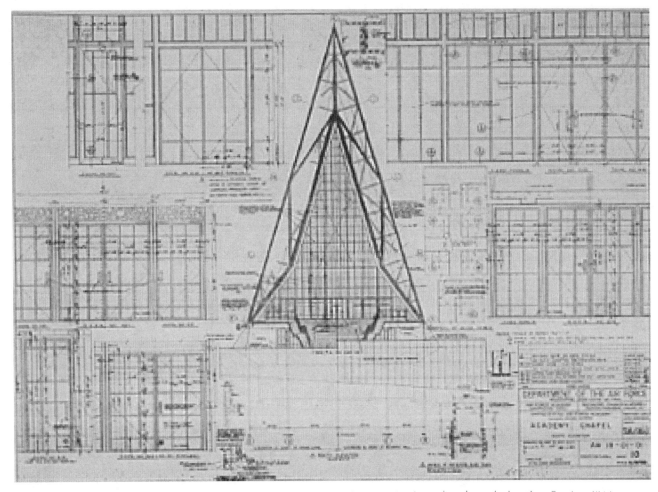

Figure 64. Academy chapel, south elevation. Courtesy Skidmore, Owings, and Merrill LLP.

chapel . . . every requirement of your esthetic senses will be met to the fullest, and I believe these lines of pure Gothic majesty—not cubism—will meet the requirements."[72] Others, such as Congressman Siemenski, justified the design by its technological or hypothetical symbolic associations: "Do we know how many religions there are in the world? I know in the Hawaiian Islands there are 19, and if we must symbolize the 19 spires, perhaps everyone who serves the colors will find in that chapel his pathway to heaven. As for aluminum, the boys fight and die in aluminum planes. . . . They can worship in aluminum if they can die in it, can they not?"[73]

The issue of the number of spires, and just what they symbolized, concerned several members of Congress:

Rhodes: I am curious about the number 19. Why should there be 19 spires instead of 20 or 15 or 14?

Mahon: I am no engineer or architect, but I do not question the 19. It is a goodly number. . . .

Rhodes: Does the gentleman have anything against the number 20 or against the number 18?

Mahon: It would be alright as long as the spires point heavenward, and are symbolic of this great country and our progress upward and ever onward.

Mahon even recited a somewhat maudlin poem in the chapel's defense:

Some American girl at some future time may write . . .
I saw the spires of the Air Academy as I was passing by,
The 19 spires of the Air Academy against the pearl-gray sky,
My heart was with the Air Force men who went abroad to
    die.[74]

Unmoved, Whitten reiterated Scrivner's criticism, stating that

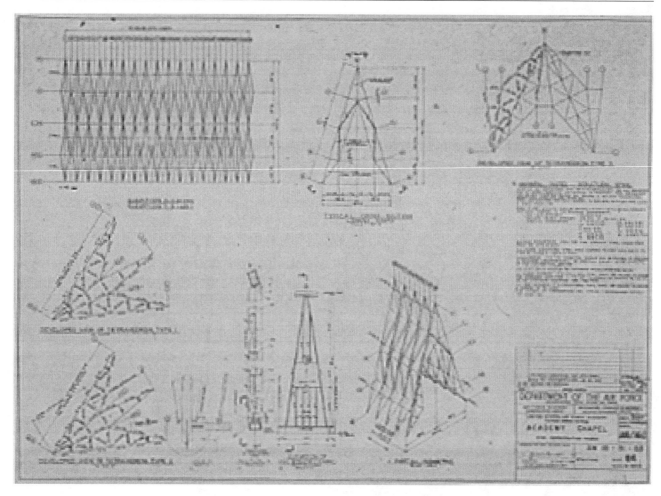

Figure 65. Academy chapel, steel superstructure framing. Courtesy Skidmore, Owings, and Merrill LLP.

the design "looks like a rectangular accordion that is stretched out on the floor. . . . [It] is peculiar." He added, "This planned chapel is a monstrosity that would look in place in a Disneyland picture."[75] Whitten would not have been aware of the ironic nature of his comment, for Walt Disney and his wife had accompanied Welton Becket during the March 1957 review of the academy chapel design.[76] In the end, despite Mahon's argument that "the best architects in America" had worked on the chapel design, the House voted to withhold funds until the design was altered.[77]

The next day (August 7, 1957) the House resumed its discussion of the chapel design. This time a model of the chapel was available for viewing in the Speaker's lobby. Scrivner again attacked the design, and Mahon defended it, adding to his testimony statements by Secretary of the Air Force Douglas in sup-

port of the design. Representative Hardy felt the design was essentially the same as the original design. Congressman Gary questioned whether Congress had the authority or time to approve the design of every government building erected. His remark prompted Congresswoman Bolton to ask if SOM was also responsible for some of the embassy designs throughout the world, using the criticism that had been leveled against those designs as proof that Congress did indeed need to monitor architectural design for government edifices. Dooley responded to Bolton's criticism with yet another technological metaphor: "Is it not a fact that the chapel is supposed to represent flight in architecture. . . . The flying buttresses of a cathedral are replaced by the ailerons of the planes wings and the bow of the plane pointing skyward are the spires. I like it."[78] In the end, concerned that the academy would open without a religious

Figure 66. Academy chapel tetrahedrons. Photograph by Clarence Coil, c. 1960. Stewarts Photographers and Custom Lab. Courtesy Pikes Peak Library District.

structure and that public outcry would be severe, the House reversed its decision of the previous day, voting 147 to 83 to restore the $3 million in funding to the project.

But the controversy was far from over. On September 11, 1957, at a meeting with the air force vice chief of staff, the design was again found unacceptable. On September 13 Stolz issued an order on behalf of the AFACA suspending all design work on the project until further notice.[79] A week later, Stoltz sent a letter to the SOM Chicago office stating that the suspension was lifted and design work was to continue, but that "under no circumstances, shall the construction cost for this structure exceed $2,608,700."[80]

Publicly defending and promoting their chapel design, the air force and SOM arranged an exhibition and forum at MIT during the first week of November. Foster Furculo, governor of Massachusetts; John B. Hynes, mayor of Boston; Nathan Pusey, president of Harvard University; Jose Luis Sert, dean of the Harvard Graduate School of Design; six prominent religious leaders; and members of the press were invited to attend. Pietro Belluschi defended the design in his capacity as the principal speaker.[81] The clergymen's response to the design was favorable. Rabbi Aryeh Lev, chairman of the National Jewish Welfare Board, was "completely satisfied" with it, espe-

cially praising an approach that included all three faiths in one chapel. Reverend Edward Fry, executive director for church architecture of the National Council of Churches, observed that "it is as daring as the early development of Gothic in the churches. I could worship here." The Very Reverend Joseph Marbach, Cardinal Spellman's assistant in the Military Ordinate appointed by the president, praised it for its "farsightedness." Walter Taylor, who earlier in the year had supported the design in his capacity as chairman of the Commission on Architecture for the National Council of Churches, adamantly noted, "No man has a right to decide whether God approves or disapproves a house of worship. I feel it is in the best religious tradition that this new style of church architecture be developed."[82]

Belluschi was not the only academy consultant to defend the chapel design publicly. Saarinen also actively supported it, noting its relationship to both the site and the other Cadet Area architecture, its monumental quality, and its metaphorical implications. In a press release the previous month he had stated:

I think the chapel is very beautiful. It is well located in relation to the other buildings, and can be seen from all sides. The form is strong and simple as it had to be with the mountains behind. The basic shape is a pointed roof like hands held upward in prayer. There are pinnacles at the top which give it a relation to Gothic spires. The main thing is to capture that indefinable spirit that makes a chapel a religious building and different from any other. This is achieved by the shape of the building and the way the light is used.[83]

That December, comments by the consultants Becket and Larson appeared in *Architectural Record*. Both reinforced the notion that the design suited the environment and was also an appropriate symbol for a technological school. Becket wrote, "Architecture should harmonize, if possible, with geographic surroundings and the pinnacles symbolize architecturally the sharp mountains which serve as the Academy's background. For young men trained for modern aircraft and missiles, use of aluminum as the basic exterior material is far more fitting than would be a more traditional chapel or dark and heavy stone or ponderous, earthy materials."[84] Accompanying the comments was a photograph of the model with nineteen spires.

The November 6, 1957, press release in conjunction with the MIT exhibit specifically mentioned those spires, stating, "Features of the striking design are 19 soaring aluminum spires."[85] But by November 11, Netsch had redesigned the chapel, reducing the tetrahedron double spires on the exterior to seventeen. The change resulted in an overall reduction of the interior space and was a response to budgetary restrictions—a practical change that was facilitated by the lack of any specific numerical symbolism attached to the spires. The structural system was also simplified at that time, and other amenities, such as air-conditioning and an elevator, were eliminated. Netsch sent a five-page letter to Noonan, estimating the revised design could be constructed for $2,850,000, and on December 24, 1957, Congress approved that sum for the chapel construction. It had been almost exactly a year since the December 27, 1956, issuance of Design Directive FY 1957, #6, which had set the Chapel construction budget at $4 million.

All this confusion contributed not only to delays, but to costly design modifications. In a letter to the Pentagon's special assistant for installations, dated December 27, 1957, SOM asked for a fee increase of $215,121 (boosting the original fee of $75,866 to $290,987) to cover all the design changes for the chapel project.[86] The request, as might be expected, elicited an adversarial response from Stoltz and the AFACA. In a memorandum to General A. M. Milton, Stoltz stated, "It is obvious that the A-E [architect-engineer] has chosen to pursue a highly controversial design concept for the Chapel. While such an approach is understandable and consistent with policies of the

firm, the Air Force should, in no manner, be expected to pay excessive design costs, if any, generated by the action of the A-E to vary so widely from normally accepted design practices for a structure of this type."[87]

The design and budget for the chapel continued to be debated throughout 1958. In summarizing the year's activities, SOM cited thirty-three separate chapel-related design directives, criteria instructions, submittals, reviews, and approvals.[88] In February, the bell tower that was to be sited next to the chapel was deemed unnecessary.[89] By March, definitive design drawings had been submitted to the AFACA, which it approved, advising SOM to proceed with the development of the design. But meanwhile SOM, in a memo dated March 6, reestimated the total cost for the chapel at over $3.6 million, stating that "serious repercussions might develop from going on record that the building as presented can be done for anything like $2,849,220."[90] In April, the *Denver Post* reported that the entire project was again in jeopardy due to renewed congressional attacks by Senator Chavez of New Mexico and Senator Miller of California. Reviewing the design, Miller stated, "I said before it looks like an accordion and even though I voted for the appropriation I still think it looks like an accordion. I believe a house of God should have certain traditional things about its design. This design is, I think, a travesty on religion." Chavez predicted the design would be changed again, noting that until construction begins, "there are a lot of possibilities for design changes. Actually a chapel isn't essential to academy activities. The cadets can commune in silent prayer anywhere on this beautiful campus."[91] During the summer of 1958, review meetings between SOM and the AFACA continued, as minor details of the chapel design were presented and approved. As a result of those changes, another meeting with the consultants was required. On October 14, 1958, SOM representatives Owings, Hartmann, Netsch, Train, and Youngren met with academy consultants Belluschi, Larson, and Becket and air force representatives Douglas and Ferry to discuss estimates and alternatives for the chapel design "so that the drawings can be completed and go to bid."[92] Thinking the design process had finally come to completion, a reporter at the *Rocky Mountain News,* in the December 14, 1958, issue, stated that invitations to bid the chapel construction would go out on January 2, 1959, and the project would be completed by the summer of 1960.[93]

As if those problems were not enough, the chapel design was also criticized within the SOM hierarchy. Netsch reported that at one point some of the architects within the firm lodged a protest against his design that was deflected only after Bunshaft's intervention.[94] In May 1958, Owings had suggested eliminating the large north and south windows that were an integral part of Netsch's design. Owings thought the windows established too much of a vertical emphasis, which was the exact effect Netsch had sought. Frustrated, Netsch wrote Bunshaft for his advice and support, and the proposed change was averted.[95]

As the design process dragged on, construction estimates rose and delays continued. On February 19, 1959, construction bids came in totaling $3.7 million, necessitating the job be bid again.[96] In August 1959, revised bids came in, totaling approximately $3.3 million. When informed of the cost, Congress members again balked and suggested the glass between the tetrahedrons be eliminated. They felt the change would "simplify the structure, reduce the complication of the joint, eliminate possible future leaks and would probably mean that it could be built within the $3,000,000."[97] Netsch responded immediately, stating that savings realized at the expense of such a radical design change would be minimal, and that the cost "would never compensate for the loss in character and the change in concept or additional design costs."[98] The design and the $3,385,136 cost (including $3,237,298 for the chapel, and additional utilities and paving costs) were finally approved by Congress in late August 1959. Construction on the chapel did not begin until August 28, 1959, after the Santa Fe firm of Robert E. McKee, Inc., was awarded the construction contract.[99]

Kenneth Naslund and Andrew Brown were SOM's structural engineers for the chapel. The chapel's structural skeleton, fabricated of welded steel pipe, was prefabricated in Missouri and transported to the Colorado site via railroad. Eventually, over 100 of the tetrahedrons were used, each 75 feet long and weighing 5 tons (figure 67).[100] When constructed, the tetrahedrons rose over 150 feet from their granite abutments. Plaster panels with aluminum surrounds covered the exposed structure on the interior (figure 68), while embossed aluminum panels were used to clad the exterior.[101] The complex and extensive use of joints and the vast amount of aluminum cladding, which was subject to expansion and contraction in the Colorado climate, allowed leakage from the earliest phases of the chapel construction, although that may have occurred in part because flashing was eliminated, as a result of budget cuts.

Netsch later explained his overall concept for the chapel design. He explained that the Protestants, being in the majority, were to worship upstairs in the largest area (figure 68). That interior space, rising to 150 feet and illuminated by one-foot-

wide strips of stained glass, would be the showcase of the academy for the visiting public. Netsch stated, "I made an enclosure that embodies the concept of light and space . . . endowed with lofty grandeur."[102] His application of stained glass panels reinforced the effect. As he noted, "The colors change from darker blues to reds to gold as the altar is approached and at the junctions of the tetrahedrons star bursts occur."[103] Originally, Netsch had intended that the stained glass have Matisse-like images of scenes from the Old and New Testament, but budget cuts required revisions to that program.[104]

The liturgical furnishings for the Protestant chapel were designed by Harold E. Wagoner. Netsch did not approve of the overt references to propellers and jet technology in the pew ends, or to the dagger-like design of the cross, but he was overruled by the Council of Churches, which provided financing for the furnishings.[105] Luman Martin Winter executed the fourteen-foot-high Venetian glass mosaic reredos. The floor of the Protestant chapel is composed of the same polished terrazzo material used to pave the exterior plazas, while the window wells are stepped down approximately one foot from the floor level and paved with a light-reflective white terrazzo. The organs in the Protestant and Catholic chapels, designed by Walter Holtkamp, were built by M. P. Moller Company, of Hagerstown, Maryland. The acoustical consultants, retained by SOM for the project, were Bolt, Beranck, and Newman.

The Roman Catholic chapel and the Jewish chapel are located on the lower level. The former is approached by two sets of steps from the south, while the Jewish chapel has separate entrances at the east and west sides. The July 27, 1962, issue of *Time* magazine, describing the academy chapel, said, "The Catholic chapel, with its gentle arches and stonework, suggests the architecture and masonry of the Romanesque cathedral.[106] Essentially rectangular, the chapel has exterior walls constructed of precast concrete panels with stained glass inserts that provide illumination. Winter executed the 18'-by-45' Venetian glass mosaic reredos in the Catholic chapel, as well as the nickel silver crucifix. The reredos includes figures of Our Lady of the Skies and a Guardian Angel flanking a dove that symbolized the Holy Spirit (figure 69). Soft light filters into the area through the amber stained glass panels that define the area.

Frank Greenhaus was the interior supervising architect for the Jewish chapel. It is spatially defined by a surrounding circular wooden screen, with inserts of white opalescent glass (figure 70). Free from structural supports, the chapel was meant to suggest the "ancient tents of the wandering Tribes of

Figure 67. Academy chapel construction. Photograph by Clarence Coil, c. 1961. Stewarts Photographers and Custom Lab. Courtesy Pikes Peak Library District.

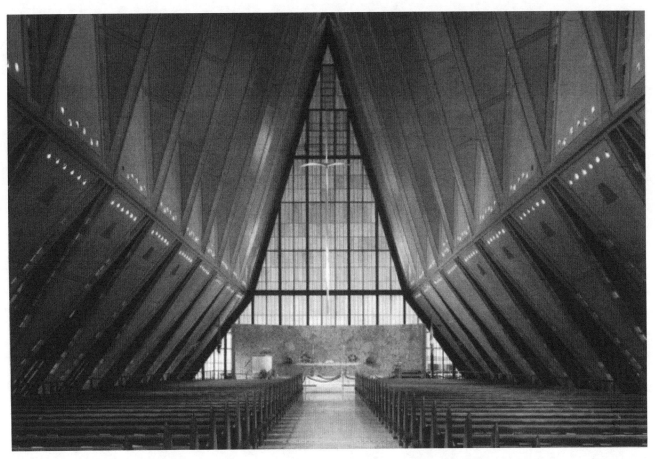

Figure 68. Academy chapel, interior of Protestant chapel. Photograph by Clarence Coil. Stewarts Photographers and Custom Lab. Courtesy Pikes Peak Library District.

Figure 69. Academy chapel, interior of Catholic chapel. Photograph by Clarence Coil. Stewarts Photographers and Custom Lab. Courtesy Pikes Peak Library District.

Figure 70. Academy chapel, interior of Jewish chapel. Photograph by Clarence Coil. Stewarts Photographers and Custom Lab. Courtesy Pikes Peak Library District.

Israel . . . a non-structural space."[107] Its furnishings were financed by the National Jewish Welfare Board, while its foyer floor was paved with Jerusalem brownstone, donated by the Israeli Defense Forces. Originally the interior of the Jewish chapel was intended to be lit with a continuous neon light strip that defined the circumference of the room (fluorescent lights now provide that function). The violet, green, and blue glass panels on the east and west walls of the foyer heightened the soft glow of that chapel. In addition to the Catholic and Jewish chapels, an All Faiths room, devoid of specific religious symbolism, was designed for the lower level. Netsch has stated that it was his own upbringing as a Christian Scientist that led to the inclusion of that room in the chapel design.[108]

Even as the chapel rose, criticism continued. Ignoring the religious climate of the mid-1950s, Allan Temko, in the December 1962 issue of *Architectural Forum,* questioned why a chapel, rather than a library, was the focal point of the design. Alluding to the chapel design as "our first militant monument to Mass Cult," he directed the brunt of his criticism against the "knock kneed and pigeon toed" interior of the Protestant level, with its "cloying" stained glass and its altar furnishings that "belong to the realm of Hollywood Biblical films." He stated:

> Surely a more positive distinction could have been drawn, in valid architectonic terms, between these ancient yet still vigorous cults, if only the architects had not denied the potential grandeur of their task, as they denied the actual grandeur of the surrounding country. . . . This ideal was reached more than half a century ago in Frank Lloyd Wright's

Unity Temple of 1906. It is the vital home of a living American religion, emphasizing the essential oneness of things, as well as their ineffable mystery; a form at once unique yet universal, of its own time yet ultimately timeless.

Temko was disappointed with the solutions realized by modernist architects whom he felt had failed to meet the challenge of creating spiritually inspiring work "in a rationalistic, technico-scientific age."[109] His criticism of the academy, with its references to the potential grandeur of the task and the grandeur of the surrounding country, continued the critique of modernist architecture, which questioned its ability to create monumental forms or relate to its specific site.

The academy chapel was finally completed in the summer of 1963 and dedicated on September 22, 1963, a year after Louis Skidmore's death.[110] By that time, Robert Venturi had begun writing his critique of modernism, which would later be published under the title *Complexity and Contradiction in Architecture*.[111] John F. Kennedy had replaced Eisenhower as president, and his references to the "New Frontier" had extended into outer space the frontier associations evoked by SOM. Meanwhile, in January 1960, SOM had filed suit to receive additional compensation for its work. Referring to the complex bureaucratic and political channels they had to negotiate to realize the academy chapel design, the architects summarized their frustrations over the processes that informed this final phase of their academy design:

> First of all, there was a problem in getting the air force representatives to settle upon a design. . . . [A] second problem arose from the numerous changes and revisions that were suggested to the architect engineer. . . . [A] third problem entwined with the first two arose from the circumstances of the number of people who had to be satisfied on all design matters. . . . [T]hose people included the representatives of and the Secretary of the Air Force, consultants to the Secretary, the chaplains who were to utilize the chapel, officers of the air force and of course the Air Force Academy, as well as subcommittees of congress and various public groups.[112]

THE CONSTRUCTION OF THE ACADEMY: PHOTOGRAPHIC SPACES AND CRITICAL SPACES

It has been noted that photographic images played a key role in reinforcing the various myths that SOM employed in promoting the academy design. Throughout the construction of the academy, SOM continued to employ photographic images to publicize its concepts and complement its architectural

agenda. Those images served as the primary means by which most of the general public, as well as other architects, critics, and potential clients, experienced the academy project, so it was essential that the images form a cohesive narrative of the project from start to finish.

SOM hired many photographers to document its work, but for the academy project it relied most on the Chicago firm of Hedrich-Blessing.[113] That firm's history is strikingly similar to SOM's. Founded in 1929, Hedrich-Blessing had first gained renown through its dramatic photographs of the 1933 Chicago Exposition. Although Hank Blessing had left the firm by that time, Ken Hedrich had retained the hyphenated name. It was Hedrich's dramatic black-and-white photographs that captured the sublime aspects of the 1933 fair, an effect that duplicated the metaphorical descriptions Skidmore and Owings provided to the press.

Like the firm of Skidmore and Owings, Hedrich-Blessing had a nucleus of family associations, with Ken Hedrich hiring two of his brothers. Hedrich-Blessing also adopted a team approach, with various partners specializing in specific aspects of architectural photography. After MoMA's 1932 modern architecture exhibition, the photographic sensibility of Hedrich-Blessing changed to complement that modernist vision. Images of entire buildings, captured with wide-angle lenses and framed in symmetrical compositions, gave way to images that were selectively cropped and that achieved their dramatic content not through spectacular lighting effects, but through the dynamic and abstract positioning of architectural fragments. Juxtapositions of positive and negative space and a concentration on geometric shapes expressed the formal tendencies codified by the MoMA exhibition. The purpose of those images was not simply to convey architectural functions, but to interpret through a two-dimensional image the artistic intent of the architects, creating in the process an equivalent experience for the viewer. By the 1940s, SOM had begun employing the firm to provide images of its work for national publications.[114]

The most widely distributed images of the Air Force Academy were those of the completed buildings of the Cadet Area, photographed by Bill Hedrich in 1959—the same year the chapel construction commenced. Mostly exterior photographs, the images emphasized the interpenetration of interior and exterior space, the expression of volume rather than mass, and the regularity of the organizing grid while avoiding axially symmetrical compositions. A timeless aspect was conveyed by divorcing the architecture from the specificity of nature and seasons. A rationally controlled environment was depicted, in which the transparent photographic window framed and revealed the transparent planes of the academy's architecture. Human figures sometimes served as counterpoint to the geometric purity of the architecture (figure 71). The images optimistically revealed a "perfect city," uncomplicated and pristine, in which the individual was subordinated to the ordering grid. Like the architecture itself, the images masked the complexities of 1950s culture with a seamless illusion of technological achievement. Structural elements, such as the library's helical staircase (figure 72), the cantilevered roof of the dining hall (figure 73), or the interior staircases of the cadet quarters (figure 74), which hover in the void of their own structural grids, were favorite themes for Hedrich.

Images provided by the Colorado Springs firm of Stewarts often supplemented the photographs by Hedrich-Blessing that appeared in the press. Stewarts meticulously recorded the construction of the academy for the architects, contractors, and subcontractors. Clarence Coil provided ground photographs for the firm, while Cloyd Brunson took aerial photographs (see figure 1).[115] Many of those images recorded the technological aspects of the construction in striking fashion. A 1961 Coil photograph, for example, depicted one of the seventy-five-foot-long chapel tetrahedrons arriving, prefabricated, by rail at the academy site (see figure 66). The photographic field is perfectly divided between sky and ground. The tetrahedron's inverted triangular profile extends nearly to the edge of the photographic image, while its upper side forms a parallel to the image's horizontal frame. Other photographs documented the raising of the dining hall roof (see figures 47 and 48) and the chapel construction (see figure 67). Stewarts's photographs appeared not only in national publications that discussed the academy design, but in advertisements published by contractors, subcontractors, and product manufacturers.[116]

Two articles published by major American architectural magazines in June 1959, the month of the academy's dedication, underscored the role of photography in reinforcing the critical dialogue that accompanied the academy's construction. *Architectural Forum* entitled its article "The Air-age Acropolis." A Stewarts photograph, picturing ranks of cadets parading up the ramps behind Fairchild Hall, appeared across the top half of the page, while a smaller Stewarts photograph of the academy, showing the building complex situated on its podium and framed against the background of the Rampart Range, appeared to the right (see figure 2). The caption at the bottom of the page triumphantly proclaimed: "On a base to rival the grandest pedestals of antiquity stands the nation's first

monument in the modern style—the new Air Force Academy."[117] The *Architectural Record* article, entitled "U.S. Air Force Academy," included a two-page spread featuring a Hedrich-Blessing photograph across the top two-thirds of the pages. It was taken facing the Rampart Range, with the clean lines of Fairchild Hall and the cadet quarters establishing a horizontal emphasis. Beneath the image was the following text:

> The questions suggested by the great photograph above go to the heart of today's architectural controversies on stylistic matters. As the Air Force Academy is dedicated this month, architects will be asking some of these questions and answering them in ways as sharply divergent as the ways of current architecture. Are the buildings appropriate to their site[?] . . . The architects have said that respect for an incomparably beautiful and highly assertive setting was their first principle in developing the architectural concept; but followers of Mies and of Wright, and some critics less easily classifiable, are likely to have differing views about the result. Are the buildings an appropriate expression of their purpose? Do they have the character suitable to the great national monument they will in fact be? Or—this questioning will run—do they signify merely the latest expression of what some observers have chosen to call an SOM style; perhaps crisper and handsomer than usual, but nonetheless expression of a corporate esthetic rather than of intrinsic purpose?[118]

The *Architectural Forum* caption unquestioningly accepted the modernist solution to the academy design. The "modern style" was synchronically associated with the great classical monuments of the past and had itself succeeded in attaining the status of a modern monument. The *Architectural Record* caption, however, revealed that the debate over the academy's design had hardly been resolved, despite the sensitive presentation of the photographic image. In questioning the design's appropriateness to its site, the article underscored the rift that was widening between modernist advocates and their critics. Whether those steel-and-glass edifices could contain and express a monumental presence was only part of that debate. The issue of how the project would be read (by both contemporary critics and posterity) was contained most tellingly in the final sentence of the *Architectural Record* caption. If we apply a Sausseurean reading to the project, the academy complex, or more specifically the cadet area, is the signifier. The problem is the identity of the signified. On the one hand, if what the academy signifies is "a corporate esthetic"—one dictated by the parameters of functionalism but, one would assume, defined by notions of popular culture and advertising—the signifier repre-

Figure 71. Cadet quarters (Vandenberg Hall) and academic building (Fairchild Hall). Photograph by Bill Hedrich, 1959. Courtesy Chicago Historic Society, Hedrich-Blessing #HB-22362-A.

Figure 72. Academic building (Fairchild Hall), library staircase. Photograph by Bill Hedrich, 1959. Courtesy Chicago Historic Society, Hedrich-Blessing #HB-22362-I2.

Figure 73. Dining hall (Mitchell Hall). Photograph by Bill Hedrich, 1959. Courtesy Chicago Historic Society, Hedrich-Blessing #HB-22362-Q.

sents a bastardization of the modernist agenda and will ultimately be criticized and ignored. If a bureaucratic or corporate esthetic is one possibility for the signified, however, whose agenda is served or whose needs are signified by an expression of "intrinsic purpose"? Is it an undisclosed mandate of modernist advocates, some sort of symbolic meaning within the context of the cold war, or the functional requirements of the cadets themselves? The article's subsequent text and images (primarily photographs by Hedrich-Blessing) offer the answer, as structural and technological aspects of the various buildings are discussed more thoroughly than their functions. Within the context of the images and text, modernism—expressed primarily in terms of its technological applications—is

the signified. Thus the text assumes that the academy buildings will be read as signifiers of a commercial enterprise (and dismissed), or as a signifier of modernism (and celebrated). No overlap of the two is, or will be, possible.

Ironically, the academy's critics, including historians, did overlap the two. SOM was cast as the purveyor of a generic corporate style, one whose work lacked individual identity, and its design solutions were folded into a more general critique of modernism. In addition, the academy was seen to embody the impersonal nature of governmental bureaucracy and the regulatory nature of military life and institutions—an analogy often included in a technology-based perception of modernism deemed inhumane. Thus analyzed, the project was summarily

Figure 74. Cadet quarters (Vandenberg Hall). Photograph by Bill
Hedrich, 1959. Courtesy Chicago Historic Society, Hedrich-Blessing
#HB-22362-G.

dismissed. In contrast to those assumptions, this case study has revealed the complex and contradictory issues that informed both the academy project and the project of modernism itself. As one of the largest projects ever undertaken by this country's government, the academy merits documentation. But its underlying importance goes far beyond its size and scope, providing a model that challenges the assumptions that block insightful analysis of architectural forms. It is in that capacity—within a diachronic continuum of history that replaces the synchronic structures of proponents and critics alike—that the United States Air Force Academy contributes to an understanding of architectural form and meaning during the cold war era.

Epilogue

THE UNITED STATES AIR FORCE ACADEMY
Additions and Extensions

While SOM could control the photographic representations of the academy, complete control over the final design was something the firm never achieved. The bureaucratic and political processes the architects had initially embraced became a liability that would result in litigation, with SOM blaming those processes for excessive expenditures and overruns and the military placing the blame on the firm's a priori approach to architecture. In January 1960, SOM went before the Armed Services Board of Contract Appeals to seek additional compensation of over $200,000 for expenditures incurred during the chapel design process. The firm was awarded approximately $147,000 of that sum.[1] A June 15, 1962 memorandum indicated that SOM made additional claims of $28,901 and $858,602 for extra design costs on other buildings in the academic complex.[2] In his autobiography, Owings maintained that SOM's loss on the project totaled $1 million.[3] The *Colorado Gazette Telegraph,* on the other hand, claimed in its March 13, 1964, issue that the air force was spending close to $500,000 a year to correct construction deficiencies at the academy and was considering suing SOM for $2.7 million.[4]

The original design of the academy remains, in large part, apparent beneath the additions of later years. Those later additions began almost immediately after the chapel dedication. A major expansion plan for the cadet area was begun in 1964. It included the construction of Sijan Hall—other cadet quarters—on the south side of the site (figure 75). Designed by the firms Leo Daly and HD&R, and constructed between 1966 and 1968, it transformed SOM's dynamic, open-sided design into a more static rectangular scheme. A year prior to that construction, the same firms extended the academic building to the south end of the dining hall, further undermining the plan's original dynamic intent and creating the quadrangle effect the design now assumes. Meanwhile, the firm of Sverdrup and Parcel was contracted to design a cadet fieldhouse—a design that does not begin to match the proportions of SOM's original cadet physical education building. Finally, from 1982 to 1983, a truss-roofed reading room was added to the library in place of the courtyard void SOM had originally intended for the complex, further solidifying the design's east side. In his autobiography, Owings lamented these deviations from the original plan, noting, "When an expansion plan was launched, SOM was not invited to submit its qualifications as a possible architect-engineer to do the work; and I was too proud to ask." At the time, Owings released an indignant statement to the press that read in part: "The government doesn't have the right to destroy the integrity of a national monument."[5] Owings's remarks, however, have led Duane Boyle, the current command architect at the academy, to suggest that the situation may have been more complex than SOM's simply "not being invited" to work on the expansion. Boyle believes that the issue relates to the way the original construction of the academy was handled in comparison to the way subsequent additions were developed.[6]

At the time of the original academy construction, each of the other service branches had its own construction agency: the navy used the Naval Facilities Engineering Command; the counterpart for the army was the Corps of Engineers. Normally the Corps of Engineers would have been called in to handle the Air Force Academy project. But since the air force did not want the army involved in planning the academy, it sought and received special permission from Congress to form the Air Force Academy Construction Agency. Congress authorized the formation of that agency with the understanding that it would remain intact through the original construction phase, which ended with the completion of the academy chapel. After that, the procedure reverted to the older format, which placed any additional construction at the academy under the auspices of the Corps of Engineers. In contrast to the air force's involvement in the original project, and its interest in overseeing and designing a complete and unified environment that would function as a national monument, the participation of the Corps of Engineers was less immediate. A very bureaucratic organization, the corps saw the academy project as just one more of the myriad projects it oversaw around the world. The corps was less interested in hiring one specific firm to do the work than in simply getting the work done, and SOM may have been overlooked because it was not "shopping" the government jobsites for work at the time and did not apply for the later projects. The Corps of Engineers could not have randomly selected SOM due to legal restrictions. SOM would have needed to apply through a selection board process, but there is no indication that the

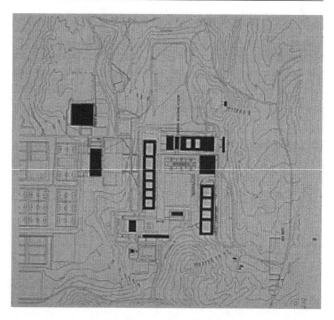

Figure 75. United States Air Force Academy Cadet Area master plan, later phases. Courtesy Skidmore, Owings, and Merrill LLP.

firm actually went through that process. In addition, the corps tended to use firms with whom it had worked in the past and had a satisfactory relationship (including Leo Daly and HD&R). Searching out specific architects or elite firms of the architectural world for its projects was not its priority.

In 1985, SOM was asked to contribute a master plan for future academy expansion projects. This was largely due to the fact that an addition to the Cadet Area had been proposed in the early 1980s. The new structure was to be a leadership building in the very center of the Cadet Area quadrangle.[7] This addition, obviously, would have completely destroyed the intent and effect of the original design. There were, however, no guidelines to bar such a development. As a result of the controversy that the intended addition elicited, SOM was rehired, originally on a two-year contract, to deal with that particular project. As a consequence of that contract, SOM became involved in creating a new master plan. That master plan was initially based on academy space requirements as they compared to the requirements of other universities, including the University of Colorado and the University of California, which often resulted in a rearrangement of functions rather than in the construction of additional buildings. SOM continues to provide those guidelines in the new millennium. As a result, there is a plan to build an addition to the west side of the cadet physical education building to balance the exterior elevation of a previously constructed east wing addition that disturbed the proportions of the original SOM building. The new addition, however, will have to be privately funded.

The attempt to bring the academy design closer to SOM's initial intent also applies to the landscape. Daniel Kiley's Air Gardens were shut down and filled in during the 1970s. The fountains have been restored since that time, but to restore the reflecting pools would cost $1.5 million—a project that seems unlikely to be undertaken unless there is private funding or funding from historic preservation grants. A project is already planned to replace the trees, originally aligned to Netsch's seven-foot grid, and to put in a new irrigation system to ensure their longevity. That phase of the renovation project is now being completed.

Even the furnishings of the cadet rooms have returned to a style that approximates the original furnishings. The original Teague-designed furniture was replaced during the 1970s with a plastic laminated particle board substitute, which was found to be unsatisfactory. In the early 1990s, Duane Boyle and the Civil Engineering Department designed new furnishings based on the older Teague designs but updated to accommodate new technologies. Both cadet quarters now have the new furnishings. The new design has proven so successful and the materials so durable that Annapolis is currently considering adopting similar furnishings for its cadet quarters.

As a result of the September 11, 2001, attacks on New York's World Trade Center and on the Pentagon, the academy has initiated several projects to protect the cadets from any possible terrorist attacks. Protective fences and barriers have been erected, particularly in the Cadet Area, with the intent that they blend as much as possible into the original design. With an area as large as the academy, the military has realized it would be difficult to secure the entire site. Since the Cadet Area seems to be the area most likely to be attacked, efforts have been concentrated on that site, with SOM consultants providing a series of proposals that are being initiated. A surrounding chain-link fence (coated in black vinyl so as to be unobtrusive) is a short-term solution. Eventually it will be replaced by architectural-style fences that match SOM's original railing designs and by granite walls that will blend into SOM's original series of monumental retaining walls. It is a solution that will still allow pedestrian access into one of Colorado's most popular tourist attractions—the Court of Honor area—while limiting vehicular access onto the site. Unfortunately, the addition of these twenty-foot-high walls will complete a process of enclosure that Sijan Hall began. In addition, parking ar-

eas surrounding the Cadet Area will be drastically reduced. Ironically, this will more accurately reflect Kiley's original landscaping intent for the areas immediately adjacent to the Cadet Area. In fact, Kiley's original landscape drawings have been consulted as a guide to this phase of the project. The historic importance of the United States Air Force Academy Cadet Area is underscored by the fact that its designation as a National Historic Landmark is imminent.

That the academy exists today is evidence of SOM's persuasive power in convincing Congress and the public that its modernist design was appropriate for the project. To the millions of visitors who arrive each year to view the site and the architecture, the technological metaphors and associative myths that were employed in defending its design continue to be a potent part of its existence. In a 1998 article in *Wallpaper* magazine, for example, Tim Rohan described the academy as "a modernist acropolis," with the chapel serving as its main symbol—"seventeen aluminum tetrahedrons set on end to resemble both a small Gothic cathedral and a squadron of fighter planes ready to zoom into the stratosphere." It is, he states, "the perfect fusion of the spiritual and the technological, the modernist dream come true."[8] Several years earlier, Elizabeth Gill Lui underscored the project's mythic associations, juxtaposing text and image in describing the academy. Included in her book was this comment by Ronald Reagan: "Where would we be if the brave men and women who built the West let the unknowns and dangers overwhelm them? Where would we be if our aviation pioneers let the difficulties and uncertainties sway them?"[9] These questions, placed opposite an exquisite color photograph of the academy planetarium, make it explicit that the frontier myth extends not only to aviation, but to the academy's designers. Her photographs emphasize the geometric order of the architecture, underscoring the formal qualities that defined modernism since the 1932 MoMA exhibition and were consciously evoked by SOM.

That the myths are potent is undeniable, but they are not incontestable. Behind the academy's sleek facades lie the debates that shaped the American architectural environment during the cold war era. The myths that attended the original academy project were intended to elicit a response that would facilitate its construction. Their validity within the context of publicity and marketing, however, should not allow their authority to remain unchallenged within the critical context of history.

Appendix One

APPLICANTS FOR THE USAFA COMPETITION

The only list of the academy competition applicants that I have located is dated June 4, 1954, and is stored at the National Archives at the Federal Center in Denver, Colorado.[1] Since the deadline for applicants was June 15, 1954, the list is incomplete, but it provides insight into the array of firms that applied for the commission.[2] The firms' names are given below in the order in which they were listed and as they were worded, with any abbreviations, on the June 4 document. By the June 15 deadline, some of the firms listed had combined to form larger joint ventures.[3] Others, such as AFAP Architects and Engineers, were initially comprised of several firms.[4]

AFAP Architects and Engineers; Chicago
Airform International Construction Corp.; New York
Albany Architects and Engineers; Albany
Allied Architects & Engineers of Indianapolis, Inc.; Indianapolis
Abenco; Los Angeles
Warren H. Ashley; West Hartford
Associated Research Design; Albuquerque
Bail, Horton & Associates; Fort Myers
Michael Baker, Jr., Incorporated; Rochester (Pennsylvania)
William F. R. Ballard; New York
Ballinger Company; Philadelphia
Welton Becket & Associates; Los Angeles
Robert A. Berne; Denver
H. R. Beister Corporation; Washington, D.C.
Blanchard & Maher; San Francisco
Thomas E. Bourne Associates, Incorporated; Washington, D.C.
Bowe, Albertson & Associates; New York
A. J. Boynton & Co.; Chicago
Buckler, Fenhagen, Meyer & Ayers; Baltimore
T. H. Buell & Company; Denver
William Emmett Burk, Jr.; Albuquerque
Burns and McDonnell; Kansas City

The Butler-Kimmel Company, Davis and Foster; Lubbock

Caudill, Rowlett, Scott & Associates; Bryan (Texas)

Chapman, Evans and Delehanty; New York

Charlotte Engineers, Inc.; Charlotte (North Carolina)

Childs & Smith; Chicago

Consoer, Townsend & Associates; Chicago

J. B. Converse & Company; Mobile

Dale S. Cooper & Associates; Houston

Bennett Crain; Washington, D.C.

Albert Criz & Associates; Los Angeles

George B. Cunningham; Wheeling (West Virginia)

Curtin & Riley; Boston

Cutler Designs; Boston

Leo A. Daly Company; Omaha

Daniel, Mann, Johnson & Mendenhall; Los Angeles

Deleuw, Cather & Company; Chicago

Deseret Architects & Engineers; Salt Lake City

De Stasio & Van Buren; Washington, D.C.

Devenco, Incorporated; Washington, D.C.

Edwards, Kelcey & Beck; Newark

Eggers and Higgins; New York

Frank L. Ehasz & Associates; New York

A. Epstein & Sons; Chicago

Ewin Engineer Corporation; Mobile

George M. Ewing Co.; Philadelphia

Howard T. Fischer & Associates, Incorporated; Chicago

Fisher, Nes, Campbell & Associates; Baltimore

Fordyce, Hamby, Strobel & Panero; New York

Foster & Caferelly; New York

Fugard, Burt, Wilkinson & Orth; Chicago

Furno & Harrison; New York

Gannett, Fleming, Gorddry and Carpenter, Inc.; Harrisburg (Pennsylvania)

Erwin Gerber; Newark

Gibbs & Hill, Inc.; New York

Giffells & Vallet, Incorporated; Detroit

Gilboy & O'Malley; Washington, D.C.

Harrison Gill & Associates; Chattanooga

Frank Grad & Sons; Newark

Graham, Anderson, Probst & White; Chicago

Groll, Beach & Associates; Washington, D.C.

Gugler, Kimball & Husted; New York

Lester C. Haas; Shreveport

Stratton O. & Neal O. Hammon; Louisville

Harbeson, Hough, Livingston & Larson; Philadelphia

Harley, Ellington & Day, Incorporated; Detroit

Frederic H. Harris, Incorporated; New York

Harrison & Abramovitz; New York

Hart, Jarman & Associates; New York

John J. Harte Company; Atlanta

Charles C. Hartmann; Greensboro (North Carolina)

Hasie & Green—Haynes & Kirby; Lubbock

Robert K. Hattis; Chicago

Hayes, Seay, Mattern & Matter [*sic*]; Roanoke

Wyatt C. Hedrick; Fort Worth

Higgins and Ferebee; Charlotte (North Carolina)

Holabird, Root & Burgee; Chicago

Holmes & Marver, Incorporated; Los Angeles

Hudgins, Thompson & Ball; Oklahoma City

Hugill, Blatharwick and Fritzel; Sioux Falls

Alfred Hopkins & Associates; New York

Albert Hunter, Jr.; Berkeley

James M. Hunter; Boulder (Colorado)

Hurt, Trudell & Berger; San Francisco

E. T. Hutchings; Louisville

Office of Louis K. Jallade; New York

Jamieson, Spharl, Hammond & Grolock; St. Louis

Johnson and Botesch; Everett (Washington)

Joseph & Joseph; Louisville

Albert Kahn; Detroit

Kahn & Jacobs; New York

Kenney & Adams; Bakersfield

Robert Keally and Howard S. Patterson; New York

Kelly & Gruzen; New York

Engineering Office of Clyde C. Kennedy; San Francisco

Louis C. Kingscott & Associates, Inc.; Kalamazoo

A. M. Kinney Incorporated; Cincinnati

Kinster, Wright & Wright; Los Angeles

Vincent G. Kling; Philadelphia

Knappen, Tipetts, Abbett, McCarthy; New York

Carl Koch & Associates; Cambridge

Koch & Fowler; Dallas

C. J. Kray; Boston

The Kuljian Corporation; Philadelphia

Lacy, Atherton & Davis; Wilkes-Barre (Pennsylvania)

Roy W. Leibele; Houston

Mark Lemmon; Dallas

William Lescaze; New York

George Stephens Lewis & Associates; Boston

Lippincott & Margulies, Incorporated; New York

Lockwood & Andrews; Houston

Lockwood Greene Engineers, Inc.; Spartanburg (South Carolina)

Lyles, Bissett, Carlisle & Wolff; Columbia (South Carolina)

McGaughan & Johnson; Washington, D.C.

McLeod & Ferrara; Washington, D.C.

Martens and Son; Welch (West Virginia)

James C. Mackenzie; New York

Chas. T. Main, Inc.; Boston

Albert C. Martin and Associates; Los Angeles

Harrison A. Martin; New York

Mills, Pitticord & Mills; Washington, D.C.

Naess & Murphy; Chicago

Leo J. Noker, Jr.; Indiana (Pennsylvania)

Naramore, Bain, Brady & Johanson; Seattle

Richard J. Neutra & Robert E. Alexander; Los Angeles

Odell, Hewlitt & Luckenback, Harry M. Demyes, Jr.; Birmingham
  (Michigan)

The Osborn Engineering Company; Cleveland

Parsons, Brinkerhoff, Hall & MacDonald; New York

Ralph M. Parsons Company; Los Angeles

J. N. Pease & Company; Charlotte (North Carolina)

Pereira & Luckman; Los Angeles

Perkins & Will; Chicago

Perry, Shaw and Hepburn, Kehoe and Dean; Boston

Alfred Easton Poor; New York

Porter, Urquhart & Bevin; Newark

Milton J. Prassas; Washington, D.C.

Rader Engineering Co.; Miami

John Lyon Reid & Partners; San Francisco

Reinhard, Hofmeister & Walquist; New York

Reisner & Urbahn; New York

Ricciuti and Associates; New Orleans

Roberts & Company Associates; Atlanta

Rogers and Taliaferro; Annapolis

Clifton E. Rodgers; Beaver Falls (Pennsylvania)

Rosenthal, Kessels, Jones; New Orleans

Damon Runyan; Denver

Russell, Mullgardt, Schwarz, Van Hoefen; St. Louis

Eero Saarinen & Associates; Bloomfield Hills

Lewis J. Sarvis; Battle Creek

Schmidt, Garden & Erikson; Chicago

Shepley, Bulfinch, Richardson & Abbott; Boston

Skidmore, Owings & Merrill; Chicago

Smith, Hinchman & Grylls, Incorporated; Detroit

J. E. Stanton & Wm. F. Stockwell; Los Angeles

Jack Steele & Company; Philadelphia

Office of A. Carl Stelling; New York

Stevens & Thompson Engineers; Portland

Stiles Clements; Los Angeles

George Wellington Stoddard & Associates; Seattle

Charles Dunwoody Strong; Denver

Harold Stuart; Washington, D.C.

W. Stuart Thompson & Phelps Barnum; New York

Andrew A. Toth; South Bend

The Vitro Corporation of America; New York

Vogt, Ivers, Seaman and Associates; Cincinnati

Eric von Hausswolff Associates; Radnor (Pennsylvania)

Voorhees, Walker, Foley & Smith; New York

Ward & Bolles; San Francisco

Warren, Knight & Davis; Birmingham

Warren & Van Praag, Inc.; Decatur

Wilbur Watson Associates; Cleveland

Weed, Russell, Johnson Associates; Miami

Weihe, Frick & Kruse; San Francisco

J. J. White; Washington, D.C.

Whitman, Requart & Associates; Baltimore

Robert Wiley; New Canaan (Connecticut)

Clyde E. Williams Associates; South Bend

Williams & Woodard; Denver

Adrian Wilson—Paul R. Williams; Los Angeles

Wilson & Co.; Denver

Eric Fisher Wood & Associates; Bedford (Pennsylvania)

William N. Woodbury; Birmingham

H. L. Yoh Company Incorporated; Philadelphia

York & Sawyer, Kiff, Colean, Voss & Souder; New York

C. Daniel J. Zimmerman, Inc.; Indianapolis

Air Force Academy Associated Architects and Engineers;
  New York

Appendix Two

OTHER FINALISTS IN THE USAFA COMPETITION

Pereira and Luckman, Architects and Engineers, in association with Giffels and Vallet, Inc., L. Rossetti

William Pereira's experience was varied and fascinating. Trained in the Chicago offices of Holabird and Root, he resigned from the firm to specialize in theater design. His interest in theater extended into the motion picture industry as well; he won an Oscar for his photographic work in the film *Reap the Wild Wind* and produced the films *Johnny Angel* and *From This Day Forward.* His Lake County Tuberculosis Sanatorium in Waukeegan, Illinois, completed in 1939 in association with William A. Ganster, was included in the Museum of Modern Art's publication *Built in U.S.A.—1932–1944.* The institution's functional requirements—providing the patients with sunny rooms—determined a design incorporating long walls of glass, thus fitting within a broad definition of modernist design. The same year, Pereira designed the Armour and Company Building at the San Francisco World's Fair. Most of Pereira's architectural commissions during the early 1950s were in association with the engineer Charles Luckman. Many were in the Los Angeles area, and included CBS-TV City, a clinic and shopping center in the Beverly Hills area, a bank in Phoenix, and a barracks and a mess facility at Camp Pendleton, California. The firm's choice of materials reflected an interest in textural effects rather than technological innovations. The materials were sometimes used to impart a regional flavor to the designs. The bank in Phoenix, for example, employed reinforced steel and concrete construction, allowing for large areas of glass on the exterior. The interior combined rough-sawn wood and a random-laid stone floor to give the whole a more rustic flavor. The Beverly Hills clinic exterior was concrete block whose outer face had been ground to reveal the red texture of the volcanic cinder aggregate. At the time of the Air Force Academy competition, the firm of Pereira and Luckman was working on a design for the Oceanarium in Palos Verde, California. Although the firm failed to receive the academy commission, within a year it had completed a government commission in the state, designing the National Bureau of Standards in Boulder, Colorado. For that industrial laboratory, the architects used porous form-scarred concrete to create a massive, foreboding presence, which seemed to reflect the influence of Le Corbusier's work of the same period.[1]

After applying for the academy commission, the firm was notified by Colonel Eckert (on May 14, 1954) that preference would be given to joint venture applicants. By the end of June, Pereira and Luckman had associated with the Detroit firm of Giffels and Vallet, Inc., L. Rossetti, a firm whose specialty was industrial design. Ray Giffels and Victor Vallet trained in the office of Albert Kahn as structural engineers, where the majority of their work was for Ford. They separated from Kahn and asked the Italian-born Rossetti to join them when they received a commission for the Detroit airport. During World War II, the firm flourished, garnering commissions from both the private and federal sectors. Its work included defense plants and projects for the Atomic Energy Commission and the National Aeronautic Advisory Commission.[2]

Harrison and Abramovitz, in association with Gugler, Kimball, and Husted; Harbeson, Hough, Livingston, and Larson; Praeger and Cavanagh; and Ammann and Whitney

The firm of Harrison and Abramovitz, in association with a host of other firms, had both the reputation and the political clout to be considered a serious contender for the academy commission. Wallace K. Harrison had been a recognized force in the architectural world since his work on the Rockefeller Center in the 1930s with the firm of Corbett, Harrison, and MacMurray. Harrison trained at the Ecole des Beaux-Arts in Paris. In partnership with J. Andre Fouilhoux, he designed the famous Trylon and Hemisphere, along with other buildings, at the 1939 New York World's Fair. In association with Max Abramovitz he did his most distinguished work, including that as director of planning for the United Nations Permanent Headquarters (Harrison himself appointed three other American architects as consultants, including Louis Skidmore of SOM). The firm's commissions during the war included work for the navy. Following the war, the firm designed such diverse projects as embassies, hospitals, housing projects, offices, and educational buildings. For its corporate commissions during the early 1950s, the firm often employed materials in innovative fashions as a form of visual advertising. The Alcoa administration building in Davenport, Iowa, for example, used aluminum as a

building material, leading the way for an even more innovative application of the material in the Alcoa Building in Pittsburgh, which employed thin stamped aluminum panels on the exterior. The Corning Glass Center, in Corning, New York, which included a museum, library, and demonstration area, was built on a marble plinth and used sheets of photosensitive glass in one section of the facade (with a pattern printed from film), glass sheets in another, and glass block in yet another, with a connecting bridge made of bent Pyrex tubing. The firm used a modernist vocabulary in its postwar government work, in such commissions as the United Nations Secretariat Building and the embassies in Havana and Rio de Janeiro.[3] Although Harrison's joint venture team did not receive the Air Force Academy commission, he was appointed as one of the original three consultants to the project.

The firm of Gugler, Kimball, and Husted of New York had associated with Harbeson, Hough, Livingston, and Larson of Philadelphia in 1953, when Secretary of the Air Force Talbott requested that Husted prepare preliminary sketches, an "ideal layout" for an undetermined site, and a scale model of an air academy.[4] The Husted firm also rendered the earliest plans of the Air Force Academy, in 1947–48, at the request of Secretary of the Air Force Symington. Husted had worked in the office of James Gamble Rogers and as a junior partner he assisted in the design of such projects as the Columbia Medical Center in New York. In 1945, he became a partner in the firm of Gugler, Kimball, and Husted. He did consulting for various government agencies, such as the Federal Civil Defense Administration, and generated interest in national architecture magazines during the cold war with his "blast resistant buildings."[5] Husted served as a consultant to the Air Force Academy Construction Agency after the architect selection process for the academy was completed. The June 1955 issue of *Progressive Architecture* noted that Husted was "Special Consultant to the Air Force on sites and master plans of air bases."[6]

The firm of Harbeson, Hough, Livingston, and Larson was the successor to the firm of Paul Philippe Cret. Cret was one of the most successful and influential federal architects. He had been appointed architectural consultant by General Pershing to the American Battle Monuments Commission in 1923. When he died in 1945, the firm of Harbeson, Hough, Livingston, and Larson replaced him as consultants. The successor firm was perhaps best known for its hospital designs. Its United States Naval Hospital in Beaufort, South Carolina, constructed in 1950, was axial in plan and had a red face-brick facade with limestone and greenstone trim. Roy Larson was later appointed as a fourth consultant on the academy project.[7]

Ammann and Whitney worked with Gugler, Kimball, and Husted in preparing cost estimates for the proposed air academy in 1954.[8] The work of O. H. Ammann, an engineer, was considered important enough to be included in MoMA's *Built in U.S.A.—1932–1944*.

York and Sawyer; Kiff, Colean, Voss, and Souder; in association with Anderson and Beckwith; Masten and Hurd; Huber and Knapik; Adache and Case; and Fay, Spofford, and Thorndike

The firm of York and Sawyer, a New York company that used a classical vocabulary comprised of both Roman and Italian Renaissance elements, continued work into the postwar era with architects Kiff, Colean, Voss, and Souder. York and Sawyer was most noted for its hospital designs, which employed Beaux-Arts axiality in the plans. Its United States Naval Hospital in St. Albans, New York, constructed in 1950, is an example. Nathaniel Owings's first job as an architect was with the firm of York and Sawyer.[9]

Anderson and Beckwith were both teachers at the Massachusetts Institute of Technology. After winning the Paris Prize in Architecture and studying in Paris for three years, Anderson joined the faculty at MIT in 1933 and became head of the architecture section of the School of Architecture and Planning in 1944. Beckwith had been on the MIT faculty since 1926. Anderson and Beckwith's design for MIT's swimming pool was included in MoMA's *Built in U.S.A.—1932–1944*. Their adoption of a modernist architectural vocabulary reflected the transition MIT was making during the war (with the hiring of William Wilson Wurster as MIT's dean of the School of Architecture and Planning in 1944, the school shifted its design emphasis from the Beaux-Arts to modernism). In 1954, the year of the Air Force Academy competition, Anderson and Beckwith were designing the MIT Laboratory. The fenestration for that building, not surprisingly, is echoed in that of Air Force Academy cadet area structures, since the SOM designers Bunshaft and Netsch both acknowledged the influence of their MIT professors.[10]

Eero Saarinen and Associates, in association with Smith, Hinchman, and Grylls, Inc., Architects and Engineers; and Knappen, Tippetts, Abbett, and McCarthy

Eero Saarinen's career was entwined with that of his father. Upon Eliel Saarinen's death in 1950, the firm reorganized as Eero Saarinen and Associates. The younger Saarinen had gained national recognition as a result of several competitions

of 1938 and 1939, winning second prize (in association with his father) in the Goucher College competition, first prize (in association with Ralph Rapson and Frederic James) in the College of William and Mary competition, and first prize (in association with his father and Robert Swanson) in the competition for the Smithsonian Art Gallery. During the war he worked for the Office of Strategic Services in Washington, D.C. In 1948, the Saarinens separately entered the competition for the design of the Jefferson Westward Expansion Memorial in St. Louis, and Eero won. His design, which included plans for a monumental gateway arch, was finally realized in the 1960s. The firm of Saarinen, Saarinen, and Associates collaborated with Smith, Hinchman, and Grylls, Inc., Architects and Engineers, on the General Motors Technical Center (1948–56), one of the largest commissions of its time. The buildings at that center were minimalist steel structures, employing vast areas of glass and glazed ceramic sand-molded brick in tones of orange and blue, that reflected in an adjoining pool. The General Motors complex was included in MoMA's publication *Built in U.S.A.: Post-War Architecture*. At the time of the academy project, Eero Saarinen and Associates was engaged in the completion of the United States Embassy in Oslo, Norway, for which it employed a modernist vocabulary.[11] Although Saarinen's joint venture team did not receive the academy commission, he was appointed as one of the original three consultants to the project. Knappen, Tippetts, Abbett, and McCarthy was an engineering firm best known for works on foreign ports, bridges, dams, and highways.[12]

Kittyhawk Associates (supervised by M. G. Probst, president of Graham, Anderson, Probst and White, and consisting of: Mitchell and Ritchey; E. J. Kump of Kump and Falk, Architects—Engineers; Richard Hawley Cutting and Associates; Harold Bush-Brown of Bush-Brown, Gailey, and Heffernan, Architects; Robert and Company Associates, Architects and Engineers; Burns and Roe, Inc.; George B. Cunningham; and R. J. Tipton)

In 1937 Marvin Probst had become head of the restructured firm of Graham, Anderson, Probst, and White, the successor to the firm of Burnham and Root. Graham, Anderson's early work was steeped in historicism and Beaux-Arts planning. Although the firm continued to design works in idioms ranging from Art Deco to modernist, its work from 1937 until the time of the academy competition appeared in none of the leading architectural magazines in this country.[13]

Mitchell and Ritchey was a Pittsburgh firm headed by James A. Mitchell, who had won a Gold Medal Award of the Beaux-Arts Institute of Design in the early 1930s. The firm finished third in the 1939 Smithsonian Institution competition (won by the Saarinens) and was, at the time of the academy competition, finishing its project for the Lower Hill Civic Auditorium Cultural Center in Pittsburgh. Mitchell and Ritchey had also associated with Harrison and Abramovitz on the Alcoa project in Pittsburgh.[14]

Ernest J. Kump, of Kump and Falk Associates, Architects, in San Francisco, was Harvard educated and had gained recognition for his school designs. He had also designed, with Kump and Falk, Architects–Engineers, the San Francisco Optical and Ordnance Building in 1948. In an article published in *Architectural Forum* in October 1953, Kump compared two schools he had designed in the same school district in San Jose, California. One was an elementary school, constructed of redwood and employing a shed roof; the other was a high school of modernist design using brick, steel, and glass. He stated that "as children mature, the architecture around them can also mature. . . . This regionalism is less geographic than mental. Or more specifically it is the 'regionalism of age groups.'" Elsewhere in the article he referred to the high school design as "more monumental" and suited in its design for older children "torn from the womb of natural architecture . . . to enter the cool, formal world of sophisticated modern structure."[15] Kump's other designs reinforced these views. His design for a technical high school in San Jose was an austere steel-and-glass structure, and his dormitory design for the Carnegie Institute of Technology in Pittsburgh was concrete slab and glass. Kump's San Jose High School was reproduced in MoMA's *Built in U.S.A.: Post-War Architecture,* while Fresno City Hall, designed by Franklin and Kump and Associates in 1941, had been reproduced in the museum's earlier text, *Built in U.S.A.: 1932–1944.*[16]

Richard Hawley Cutting and Associates of Cleveland had worked on a number of housing projects and had served as consultants to the air force for air fields in England and France. The firm's work during this period does not appear in any of the major architectural journals.

Harold Bush-Brown, of Bush-Brown, Gailey, and Heffernan, Architects, was director of the Department of Architecture at the Georgia Institute of Technology. The firm was best known for its work on college campuses, such as the engineering building and library it designed at GIT in 1950. The engineering building employed a minimalist language of modernism, expressed through the use of concrete slab and glass construction.[17]

The Atlanta firm of Robert and Company had designed a variety of projects, including hospitals, offices, and museums. Its projects of the 1950s included plans for the Stone Mountain Museum and Administration Building in Georgia, with its sculptural exterior, and an office building in Fort Mill, South Carolina, the exterior of which resembles Wright's Johnson Wax Building in Racine. After losing the Air Force Academy competition to SOM, Robert and Company was added to SOM's joint venture team as water specialists.[18]

T. H. Buell and Company

Temple Hoyne Buell was a Denver architect and land investor. His designs in the Denver area include several theaters, schools, and hospitals, many built in the 1930s. His Paramount Theater design in Denver (1930) employed an Art Deco architectural vocabulary. The exterior was concrete block sheathed in white terracotta with black marble trimming. For the Leslie Savage Library (1939), Buell employed a Spanish colonial revival architectural vocabulary, while his designs for Fruita Junior High School (1936) and Berthoud Hall (1937) used brick for the exterior facades. The former was described as "WPA Moderne," while the latter was lavishly trimmed in terracotta. Virtually nothing appeared in any of the leading architectural magazines of the time regarding Buell's work.[19]

Voorhees, Walker, Foley, and Smith, in association with Gibbs and Hill, Inc.

The New York firm of Voorhees, Walker, Foley, and Smith was a prominent national firm. Walker served as a planner for the 1933 Chicago World's Fair, and his firm designed numerous buildings for the 1939 New York Fair. During the early 1950s, the firm designed numerous office buildings, churches, memorials, hospitals, and school structures, including the library at MIT and the cyclotron building at Columbia. The firm's laboratory and research center designs employed a "flexible-modular concept." Highly efficient in terms of function, the buildings were conservative in their materials and construction techniques. The firm's corporate commissions included work for Bell Telephone, IBM, GE, Ford, DuPont, and Westinghouse. Its federal projects included army bases in Trinidad, airfields in British Guiana and Antigua, and the Argonne National Laboratory for the Atomic Energy Commission, near Chicago.[20]

Notes

Unpublished sources cited as references in the footnotes include the following:

Air Force Academy Construction Agency documents located in the National Archives at the Denver Federal Records Center, cited as NA, followed by the box number and folder title (all of these documents are included in record group 461, Records of the Air Force Academy Construction Agency).

Air Force Academy records located in the Special Collections Branch of the Air Force Academy Library in Colorado Springs, cited as AFA, followed by the record group number (RG) and series number.

Skidmore, Owings, and Merrill LLP archives in Chicago, cited as SOM, followed by the drawer or box number and (if relevant) file number (differentiation has been made between interdepartmental memos and outgoing letters).

Introduction

1. Janowitz, *Sociology and the Military Establishment,* p. 17.

2. Owings, *Spaces in Between,* pp. 155–56.

3. Craig, *Federal Presence,* pp. 227–31. Histories of the other two service academies are provided in the following texts: Crackel, *West Point;* and Sweetman, *The U.S. Naval Academy.*

4. SOM, Miscellaneous Design file, "Competition for West Point, 1944, Explanatory Text."

5. Slotkin, *Fatal Environment,* p. 23.

6. See Jencks, *Modern Movements in Architecture,* p. 202.

7. Hitchcock, "The Architecture of Bureaucracy," p. 4.

8. For a discussion of Taylorism and modernism, see T. Smith, *Making the Modern.* Comments on the organization of Kahn's firm are also to be found in the same book, pp. 57–92. The Bauhaus architect Walter Gropius was also aware of Ford's implementation of Taylor's management techniques and felt the techniques had implications for design. Gropius wrote Ford asking for funding of the first full-scale exhibition of Bauhaus work in 1923, which ran from August 15 to September 30, 1923. Whitford, *Bauhaus,* pp. 136–50. Robert Bruegmann, in his discussion of the Chicago architectural firm Holabird and Roche, summarized the pragmatics of adopting such a corporate organizational system, noting, "another problem sprang directly from the nature of commercial architecture. Commercial architects, like all architects, functioned in part as artists . . . But if they wanted to stay in business they also functioned as businessmen." Bruegmann, *The Architects and the City,* xiv.

9. For example, Carol Krinsky's text on Gordon Bunshaft does not discuss Bunshaft's contributions to the Air Force Academy project. See Krinsky, *Gordon Bunshaft.*

10. Sheri Olson, "Skidmore, Owings and Merrill: Early History," in Bruegmann, *Modernism at Mid-Century,* p. 27. Information regarding the San Francisco office is contained in Bush-Brown, *Skidmore, Owings, and Merrill,* p. 29. In the introduction to that text, Albert Bush-Brown noted that it was Edward Bassett who was responsible for the firm's most distinguished designs in that city, after moving to SOM from Saarinen's office in 1955. For information regarding the Portland office, see Clausen, *Pietro Belluschi,* pp. 192–94.

11. SOM's project files are located in Chicago, while the Air Force Academy Construction Agency documents are in the National Archives, Denver Federal Records Center.

Chapter 1: Background to the Academy

1. Landis, *The Story of the U.S. Air Force Academy,* pp. 23–26.

2. Fagan, *The Air Force Academy,* pp. 6–7.

3. Landis, *The Story of the U.S. Air Force Academy,* p. 30.

4. Bilstein, *Flight in America 1900–1983,* pp. 128–29. Bilstein provides a detailed account of the rise of both military air power and the aviation industry in the United States from 1930 until the end of World War II on pp. 83–165.

5. Fagan, *The Air Force Academy,* p. 15.

6. Emme, *The Impact of Air Power,* pp. 615–23.

7. Cannon and Fellerman, *Quest for an Air Force Academy,* pp. 104–9; Fagan, *The Air Force Academy,* pp. 16–17. Established by the War Department in 1946 to deal with air force education, the Air University was formally dedicated on September 9, 1946, at Maxwell Air Force Base. The first commander of the university was General Fairchild. Information on the history of the Air University may be found on the Maxwell Air Force Base/Air University Web site: ‹http://www.au.af.mil›.

8. For additional information on this legislative process, see Fagan, *The Air Force Academy,* pp. 15–25, and Cannon and Fellerman, *Quest for an Air Force Academy,* pp. 89–127. The other board members were Dr. James P. Baxter III, President, Williams College; Dr. Frederick A. Middlebush, President, University of Missouri; Dr. George D. Stoddard, President, University of Illinois; Dr. Edward L. Moreland, Executive Vice President, Massachusetts Institute of Technology; Major General Bryant E. Moore, Superintendent, United States Military Academy; Rear Admiral James L. Holloway, formerly Superintendent, United States Naval Academy; and General David M. Schlatter, United States Air Force (Cannon and Fellerman, *Quest for an Air Force Academy,* pp. 113–14). Moreland may have resigned soon after his appointment, since his name is not included in a memo from the committee to Forrestal dated April 4, 1949 (AFA, RG 120, ser. 17).

9. The tedious legislative process is recounted in Cannon, Holt, and Allen, *History of the United States Air Force Academy,* pp. 24–140.

10. The chronology of the secretaries of the air force during this time is as follows: W. Stuart Symington, September 1947 to April 1950; Thomas K. Finletter, April 1950 to January 1953; and Harold E. Talbott, February 1953 to August 1955.

11. Emme, *The Impact of Air Power,* p. 226. Emme's introduction (pp. 226–36) precedes Spaatz's essay, "Strategic Air Power in the European War," written in April 1946.

12. Fagan, *The Air Force Academy,* p. 27. In addition to Harmon and Spaatz, the board was comprised of Brigadier General Howard L. Clark and Dr. Bruce Hopper of Harvard University.

13. Cannon and Fellerman, *Quest for an Air Force Academy,* p. 136.

14. AFA, RG 103, ser. 1, memo from Erler to Logistics Plans Group, May 11, 1948.

15. NA, box 78, Construction Project Study Files 1947–71, "8 Preliminary Sites, Holabird and Root and Burgee." The western sites included the two Colorado sites, two Texas sites, and a California site. The eastern sites included two in North Carolina and one in Indiana. No record exists of what criteria were applied in selecting those sites. One of the North Carolina sites was soon dropped from the list. Of the original two Colorado Springs locations, one was to the south, near the Broadmoor Hotel, and one was to the north. The potential northern site was later relocated near the Pike's Peak area. Cannon, Holt, and Allen, *History of the United States Air Force Academy,* pp. 145–47.

16. Cannon and Fellerman, *Quest for an Air Force Academy,* p. 213.

17. NA, box 78, Construction Project Study Files, 1947–71, "Memorandum for General Nugent."

18. It was claimed that a sealed memorandum recommending one of the Colorado Springs site was placed in the files of the secretary of the air force by Harmon, who in 1954 showed it to Secretary of the Air Force Talbott (Fagan, *The Air Force Academy,* p. 28), but no such document has been found.

19. Public Law 325, 83d Cong., 2d Sess., Chapter 127, H.R. 5337.

20. Cannon and Fellerman, *Quest for an Air Force Academy,* p. 219.

21. U.S. Congress, House, Subcommittee of the Committee on Appropriations, July 19, 1955, p. 2.

22. Fagan, *The Air Force Academy,* p. 31. An editorial Hearst Corporation published in its November 30, 1948, issue stating its support of an academy is reproduced in Cannon, Holt, and Allen, *History of the United States Air Force Academy,* p. 11.

23. Cannon, Holt, and Allen, *History of the United States Air Force Academy,* p. 130.

24. Cannon and Fellerman, *Quest for an Air Force Academy,* p. 223.

25. NA, box 78, Construction Project Study Files, Minutes—Academy committee, letter from members of the commission (signed by all five) to Talbott, June 3, 1954.

26. NA, box 78, Construction Project Study Files, Minutes—Academy committee, "Annex to the Report of the Air Force Academy Site Selection Commission: Statement of Primary Factors Considered by the Commission in Evaluating Proposed Locations," April 6 (?), 1954.

27. Cannon and Fellerman, *Quest for an Air Force Academy,* p. 227.

28. Cannon, Holt, and Allen, *History of the United States Air Force Academy,* p. 166.

29. AFA, RG 120, ser. 11, Western Union telegraph from Dan Thornton, Governor, to Honorable Harold E. Talbott, June 7, 1954.

30. AFA, RG 120, ser. 17, unsigned memo, June 19, 1954.

31. See, for example, Parmet, *Eisenhower and the American Crusades,* pp. 247–67.

32. AFA, RG 120, ser. 11, letter to Talbott from David T. Clapp, President, Madison Chamber of Commerce, July 14, 1954.

33. Parmet, *Eisenhower and the American Crusades,* pp. 80–82, 107–8.

34. Ibid., p. 329; Rovere, *The Eisenhower Years,* pp. 307–19.

35. On the resistance mounted by the Geneva and Alton communities, see Fagan, *The Air Force Academy,* pp. 33–37. There are also letters in the files of the Air Force Academy that refer to these issues, including letters from the Principia Corporation voicing opposition to the Alton site. See AFA, RG. 120, ser. 11.

36. Cannon, Holt, and Allen, *History of the United States Air Force Academy,* p. 168.

37. Western Union message, May 17, 1954, AFA, RG 122.

38. Cannon, Holt, and Allen, *History of the United States Air Force Academy,* p. 168.

39. G. Nash, *American West Transformed,* pp. 17–36. For additional discussion regarding the development of the West during the postwar era, see the following: G. Nash, *The American West in the Twentieth Century;* Abbott, *The New Urban America* and *The Metropolitan Frontier;* and Wiley and Gottlieb, *Empires in the Sun.*

40. Berge, *Economic Freedom for the West,* pp. 1–12. Several years later, Garnsey outlined economic possibilities for the West in *America's New Frontier.*

41. G. Nash, *American West Transformed,* pp. 35–36.

42. Wiley and Gottlieb, *Empires in the Sun,* pp. 34–38.

43. G. Nash, *American West Transformed,* pp. 17–18.

44. Cannon, Holt, and Allen, *History of the United States Air Force Academy,* p. 11.

45. Ubbelohde, Benson, and Smith, *A Colorado History,* p. 324.

46. One such corporation was Martin Marietta Aerospace Corporation, the contractor for Titan missiles, which located in a suburb of Denver in 1956. Abbott, *The New Urban America,* p. 40.

47. Dorsett, *The Queen City,* p. 261.

48. Wiley and Gottlieb, *Empires in the Sun,* p. 124.

49. G. Nash, *American West Transformed,* p. 10. For the economic benefits to Denver resulting from the presence of military personnel, see Dorsett, *The Queen City,* pp. 238–39.

50. AFA, RG 103, ser. 1, "Suggested Architectural Treatment for the Air Force Academy," attachment to a memo from J. Gordon Trumbull, Inc., to Brigadier General James B. Newman Jr., Air Force Academy Planning Board, January 5, 1949.

51. NA, box 78, Construction Project Study Files 1947–1971, Budget and Operating Costs and Correspondence, memo from the Air Force Academy Planning Board to General Nugent, February 28, 1949.

52. Lee, *Architects to the Nation,* pp. 281–83.

53. For the entire text of H.R. 4754, the "Federal Property and Administration Services Act of 1949," see U.S. Congress, House, June 21, 1949, pp. 8048–56. The quotation is from p. 8048.

54. Lee, *Architects to the Nation,* p. 286.

55. "Branch Post Office, Denver, Colorado," p. 152.

56. See "Air Force Buildings," pp. 95 (first two quotes), 96 (third quote), 97 (fourth quote).

57. AFA, RG 103, ser. 1, "Memorandum for Record," from Lieutenant Colonel Thomas Sheldrake, March 27, 1953, indicated that James Wise, Assistant Deputy for Installations, brought in Husted on March 27, 1953, for consultation. Wise acted upon advice by Talbott who, in turn, had the full support of Eisenhower in making his decision. Also see AFA, RG 103, ser. 1, "Memorandum for Special Assistant for Air Force Academy Matters," from Brigadier General E. W. Ehrgott, January 8, 1954, and "Mr. Talbott's Plan," memorandum, April 28, 1953. The Husted contract was questioned by Harmon, who thought Talbott had acted prematurely in hiring the firms. See AFA, RG 103, ser. 1, "Memorandum for Colonel Boudreau from Thomas Sheldrake," June 16, 1953.

58. AFA, RG 103, ser. 1, "Cost Data Analysis Sheets and Diagrammatic Drawings for Preliminary Estimate" and "Study of Proposed Air Force Academy, Hypothetical Site."

59. AFA, RG 103, ser. 1, memorandum from Harmon to Colonel Person, November 18, 1953. Harmon stated that Gugler, in a meeting two days earlier in the firm's New York office, asked that the firm be allowed to reduce the size of the proposed 7' × 10' model for easier transport and display.

60. For an analysis of Rogers's college designs, see Betsky, *James Gamble Rogers,* pp. 139–210 (no reference to Husted is made in Betsky's

publication). For Cret's work, see Grossman, *The Civic Architecture of Paul Cret.*

61. Turner, *Campus,* p. 191.

62. For the Cret design, see Turner, *Campus,* pp. 208–9. For comments on the similarities between the Husted design and Saarinen's campus, see Bruegmann, *Modernism at Mid-Century,* p. 99.

63. AFA, RG 103, ser. 1, memorandum from Husted to Harmon and Person of a conference in Harmon's office, November 27, 1953.

64. See Craig, *Federal Presence,* pp. 280–337. Craig calls the style "Starved Classicism."

65. Betsky, *James Gamble Rogers,* pp. 40–44.

66. AFA, RG 103, ser. 1, letter from Colonel Dale O. Smith to Colonel A. E. Boudreau, May 25, 1953.

67. AFA, RG 103, ser. 1, "Request for Clearance for Flight to Mexico," May 25, 1953. In conjunction with this trip, Bruegmann noted the popularity that Latin American architecture enjoyed in the 1950s. Bruegmann, *Modernism at Mid-Century,* p. 99.

68. The University of Mexico project was overseen by the architect Carlos Lazo from plans by Enrique del Moral and Mario Pani. See Cetto, *Modern Architecture in Mexico,* pp. 66–93.

69. AFA, RG 103, ser. 1, "Trip Report, Colonel G. B. Dany," to Deputy Chief of Staff, July 6, 1953.

70. AFA, RG 103, ser. 1, "Report of Group Visit to University City, Mexico City, Mexico, 9–12 June 1953," to the Commander of Headquarters Air University at Maxwell Air Force Base in Alabama, July 9, 1953.

71. Cannon, Holt, and Allen, *History of the United States Air Force Academy,* pp. 90–92.

72. Ibid., p. 108.

73. Ibid., pp. 111, 135. Washbourne's testimony was on February 18 and 19, 1954. The Husted estimate ($145,719,400) is reported in AFA, RG 103, ser. 1, Gugler, Kimball, and Husted, and Harbeson, Hough, Livingston, and Larson Associated Architects, "Preliminary Estimate Breakdown," February 1, 1954.

74. AFA, RG 103, ser. 1, memo from Harmon to Myer, August 28, 1951, and memo from Myer to Harmon, September 13, 1951.

75. AFA, RG 103, ser. 1, memo from Harmon to Kuter, March 1, 1954.

76. NA, box 119, Construction Project Study Files, 1947–1971, Master Planning 1954–55, memo commenting on Harmon's design from Colonel Albert Stolz, Director of the Air Force Academy Construction Agency, to Harmon, April 28, 1955.

77. John Burchard, "Recollections of Gordon Bunshaft," in Bruegmann, *Modernism at Mid-Century,* p. 188 (no date is given for Bunshaft's recollections). Perhaps in recommending Spanish colonial architecture Harmon had in mind Randolph Air Force Base, where that style was employed.

78. Parmet, *Eisenhower and the American Crusades,* pp. 170–71.

79. Mills, *The Power Elite,* pp. 287–88.

80. Ibid., p. 238.

81. Ibid., p. 296.

82. AFA, RG 103, ser. 1, memo from General Myer's office, May 17, 1950.

83. NA, box 80, Construction of the Air Force Academy; file includes a typed transcription of the section of the AIA brochure entitled "Planning." Unless noted otherwise, quotes in the next paragraph are from the same source.

84. NA, box 168, Air Academy Construction Agency, A-E [Architect-Engineer] Selection Board, memo headed "Architectural Competition for Planning the Air Academy," from Person to Washbourne, January 29, 1954.

85. NA, box 168, Air Academy Construction Agency, A-E [Architect-Engineer] Selection Board, memo from Washbourne to Person, February 1, 1954.

86. Later that month, for example, Washbourne replied to Joseph Burgee, in response to an inquiry regarding the academy commission on behalf of the firm of Holabird, Root, and Burgee: "Since the section of the country in which the Academy is ultimately located will have a great bearing on the selection of the architect-engineering firm, I am sure Mr. Talbott feels it is premature to begin the evaluation of the qualifications of the architect-engineer firm. " AFA, RG 103, ser. 1, letter from Washbourne to Burgee, February 11, 1954.

87. AFA, RG 103, ser. 1, letter from William Delano to "Sonny" Whitney, March 28, 1949.

88. SOM, dwr. 51, file 01, memo from Rodgers to All Partners, San Francisco Associate Partners and Participating Associates, December 22, 1953.

89. Between World Wars I and II, Erler headed Erler Construction Company. During World War II, he supervised building and ground installations in the Far East. See "Air Force Names Aides to Help Plan Air Academy," *Architectural Forum* 101, no. 4 (October 1954): 42.

90. Owings later stated that the reason the architect Alfred Philip Shaw was not considered for the academy commission was because his firm was working on the Spanish bases. Owings, *Spaces in Between,* p. 151.

91. SOM, dwr. 51, file 01, memo from Rodgers to All Partners, San Francisco Associate Partners and Participating Associates, January 7, 1954. The memo states, "He, Nat Owings, knew Jim Douglas personally, as did Walt Severinghaus." Severinghaus was a partner in the New York office. Owings cited his friendship with Douglas as a major factor in SOM's receiving the commission in his autobiography. Owings, *Spaces in Between,* p. 151.

92. SOM, dwr. 51, file 01, memo from Rodgers to All Partners, February 5, 1954. The two Texas locations were not specifically named. The California sites were Monterey and Camp Beale, while the Missouri site was in Sedalia.

93. SOM, dwr. 51, file 01, letter from Owings to the Honorable Harold E. Talbott, March 9, 1954.

94. NA, box 168, Air Academy Construction Agency, A-E Selection Board.

95. NA., box 118, Reading File, "Memorandum for Secretary of the Air Force," March 25, 1954. Washbourne assigned four of his staff to temporarily man the project office: Lieutenant Colonel C. A. Eckert, Lieutenant Colonel J. R. White, Mr. Richard Rio, and Mr. John Huebsch.

96. SOM, dwr. 51, file 01, memo from Rodgers to Owings, March 16, 1954.

97. SOM, dwr. 51, file 01, memo from Hartmann to Owings, April 2, 1954. Hartmann was a partner in the Chicago office.

98. SOM, dwr. 51, file 01, letter from Douglas to Owings, March 17, 1954, in response to a letter from Owings to Douglas dated March 15, 1954, asking for his assistance in introducing Skidmore and Owings to Talbott.

99. NA, box 168, Air Academy Construction Agency, A-E Selection Board, memo for Chief of Staff from Office of the Secretary, Department of the Air Force, April 2(?), 1954.

100. Clausen, *Pietro Belluschi,* p. 194.

101. Loeffler, *Architecture of Diplomacy,* pp. 123–25.

102. NA, box 168, Air Academy Construction Agency, A-E Selection Board, memo from Schuyler to Air Force Academy Project Office, April 6, 1954.

103. Also included in Schuyler's original list were: G. Holmes Perkins, dean of the School of Fine Arts at the University of Pennsylvania; Douglas William Orr, past president of the AIA and a member of the Commission on Renovation of the White House; and Harold Bush-Brown, director of the School of Architecture at the Georgia Institute of Technology.

104. NA, box 168, memo from Eckert to Talbott, April 6, 1954.

105. NA, box 168, "Memorandum for the Secretary of the Air Force," April 9, 1954. Sanford was deputy chief, Architectural Branch, assistant chief of staff, Installations; Rio was deputy chief, Master Plans Branch, assistant chief of staff, Installations; and Ferry was special assistant for Installations.

106. SOM, dwr. 51, file 01, letter from Owings to Douglas, April 9, 1954.

107. NA, box 168, Air Academy Construction Agency, A-E Selection Board, memo from John Ferry to General Thomas D. White, May 26, 1954.

108. SOM, dwr. 51, file 01, letter from Owings to Hennessy, April 9, 1954.

109. SOM, dwr. 51, file 01, letter from Hennessy to Owings, April 14, 1954.

110. SOM, dwr. 51, file 01, letter from Owings to Erler, April 13, 1954.

111. SOM, dwr. 51, file 01, letter from Erler to Owings, April 19, 1954.

112. SOM, dwr. 51, file 01, letter from Owings to Erler, April 23, 1954.

113. SOM, dwr. 51, file 01, letter from Hennessy to Owings, April 26, 1954.

114. SOM, dwr. 51, file 01, letter to applicants signed by Colonel E. V. N. Schuyler, Chief, Engineering Division, Director of Construction, Assistant Chief of Staff, Installation, April 6, 1954.

115. NA, box 168, Air Academy Construction Agency, A-E Selection Board, letter from Ferry to Secretary, American Institute of Architects, April 16(?), 1954.

116. SOM, dwr. 51, file 01, letter from Owings to the Assistant Chief of Staff, Installations Headquarters, Washington, D.C., June 7, 1954.

117. SOM, dwr. 51, file 01, memo from Weese to Cutler, May 27, 1954.

118. NA, box 13, REL 2-3-2, "Fact Sheet: Air Force Academy Construction Agency," March 15, 1955.

119. SOM, dwr. 51, file 01, letter from Erler to SOM, June 25, 1954.

120. SOM, dwr. 51, file 01, memo from James Hammond (an associate partner with SOM in the Chicago office), "Re: Air Academy—Telephone call to Colonel Erler by John Weese on June 29, 1954."

121. SOM, dwr. 51, file 01, memo from Hammond to Hartmann, "Re: Telephone call to John Rodgers concerning Colonel Lutz," June 30, 1954.

122. SOM, dwr. 51, file 01, memo from Hammond to Hartmann, June 30, 1954.

123. SOM, dwr. 51, file 01, memo from Skidmore to Owings, July 1, 1954.

124. NA, box 118, Reading File, and box 13, REL 1-2, Congressional Inquiries, May 1, 1954–September 15, 1954.

125. SOM, dwr. 51, file 01, memo from Hammond to Hartmann, July 1, 1954.

126. SOM, dwr. 51, file 01, letter from Erler to SOM, June 30, 1954.

127. NA, 118, Reading File, letter from Eckert to Pereira, May 14, 1954.

128. "Air Academy Design Brawl," p. 9. This is contradictory to Owings's claim that it was Shaw's firm that was eliminated due to its involvement with the Spanish bases. See Owings, *Spaces in Between,* p. 151.

129. AFA, RG 103, ser. 1, memo for record by Lieutenant Colonel William B. Taylor, January 9, 1954.

130. Information regarding the firms comprising Kittyhawk Associates is contained in a two-page description the group sent to the air force (NA, box 13, REL 1-2, Congressional Inquiries, May 1, 1954–September 15, 1954).

131. For more information on Wright's activities, see Johnson, *Frank Lloyd Wright versus America.*

132. "Air Academy Design Brawl," p. 9.

133. NA, box 28, REL 1, Congressional Liaison 1956, letter from Congressman Glenn Davis to Major General Joe W. Kelly, dated 9/4/56; response by Noonan for the Office of Legislative Liaison, September 13, 1956; response to Davis from office of General Kelly, September 21, 1956.

134. NA, box 13, REL 1-2, Congressional Inquiries, May 1, 1954–September 15, 1954.

135. Information on Buell is nearly nonexistent. See the following: Leon-

ard and Noel, *Denver;* Noel, *Buildings of Colorado;* and "A \$25 Million Gift," *Time,* November 18, 1966, p. 98.

136. NA, box 13, REL 1-2, Congressional Inquiries, May 1, 1954–September 15, 1954.

137. Owings, *Spaces in Between,* p. 151.

138. SOM, dwr. 51, file 01, "A Proposal to Furnish Architect-Engineer Services for: **THE UNITED STATES AIR FORCE ACADEMY**."

139. "Low Cost Houses under Construction at Highland Park, Illinois," *Architectural Record* 79, no. 5 (May 1936): 404 (the firm was still called Skidmore and Owings at that time); "Houses for Defense," *Architectural Forum* 75, no. 5 (November 1941): 321–26.

140. The history of the Oak Ridge project was described shortly after its realization. See Robinson, *The Oak Ridge Story.* It was also discussed in the following articles: "Atom City," *Architectural Forum* 83, no. 4 (October 1945): 103–16; "America's No. 1 Defense Community: Oak Ridge, Tennessee," *Progressive Architecture* 32, no. 6 (June 1951): 63–84. At the height of the construction phase of that project, SOM employed over 450 persons. The Reception Building for the Great Lakes Naval Training Station was included in the MoMA's bulletin; see Mock, *Built in U.S.A.—1932–1944,* pp. 80–81. For other SOM work at the complex see "Welfare Building," *Architectural Forum* 78, no. 3 (March 1943): 55–60. In the 1950s, the firm was asked to design another building, a gunners' school, for the complex. See "The Navy's New Architecture," *Architectural Forum* 103, no. 1 (July 1955): 148–53.

141. SOM, dwr. 51, file 01, "A Proposal to Furnish Architect-Engineer Services for: **THE UNITED STATES AIR FORCE ACADEMY**," memo from Rodgers to Netsch, April 23, 1954.

142. SOM, dwr. 51, file 01, letter from Robert Johnston, of Moran, Proctor, Mueser, and Rutledge, to Hammond of SOM, April 21, 1954.

143. SOM, dwr. 51, file 01, letter from John Hennessy of Syska and Hennessy to Hammond of SOM, April 21, 1954.

144. SOM dwr. 51, file 01, SOM proposal for the academy commission. The ten partners at the time were: Louis Skidmore, who oversaw the firm's New York office; Nathaniel Owings, who headed the firm's Chicago and San Francisco offices; John O. Merrill, who had directed the projects at Oak Ridge and Okinawa; Gordon Bunshaft, who was in charge of architectural design in the New York office; William Brown, an expert on prefabricated housing and an office administrator in the New York office, who had directed projects that included the Connecticut General Life Insurance Company in Bloomfield and the Lever Brothers building in Manhattan; Robert Cutler, a specialist in hospital design in the New York office; Walter Severinghaus, a housing specialist who worked in the New York office and was formerly director of the Joint Venture for the Air Force Bases in French Morocco and the Azores; John Rodgers, who worked in the San Francisco office and had assisted Merrill in Okinawa and Japan; William Hartmann, a specialist in research laboratories and administrative facilities; and Elliott Brown, who worked in San Francisco and had been in charge of the firm's Portland office.

145. "Academy Challenge to Architectural Firm," *Colorado Gazette Telegraph,* August 31, 1958, p. 11.

146. "Group Practice," pp. 145–51. Later articles also addressed the firm's organizational structure: "\$2 Billion Worth of Design by Conference," was first published in the December 4, 1954, issue of *Business Week* and was reproduced in condensed fashion in the February 1955 issue of *Architectural Forum;* "Production Practice" appeared in the March 1955 issue of *Progressive Architecture;* "The Architects from 'Skid's Row'" was in the January 1958 issue of *Fortune;* and "Designers for a Busy World" was published in

the May 4, 1959, issue of *Newsweek.* Worth noting is that the entire April 1957 issue of *Bauen and Wohnen* was devoted to SOM, with articles by three firm members, Hartmann, Netsch, and Graham, as well as an introductory article by Sigfried Giedion.

147. Owings, *Spaces in Between,* p. 75.

148. Ibid., p. 68. At the time of this commission, the firm was still identified as Skidmore and Owings. Owings's reference to "American brewery style" probably referred to the use of brick as an exterior facing material. See "Little Traverse Hospital, Petosky, Michigan," *Architectural Forum* 71, no. 6 (November 1939): 384–87. In discussing the design, Bunshaft was less kind. He described the Owings-designed main brick section as "nonarchitecture. It was nothing." Krinsky, *Gordon Bunshaft,* p. 10. Bunshaft's wing, inspired by Le Corbusier, was limestone-faced and raised on stilts, with horizontal windows.

149. Regarding his education at MIT between 1928 and 1935, Bunshaft recalled that the favored design approach was "close to the French stripped classicism of Auguste Perret's work in the 1920's and akin to the sober pavilions of the 1925 Exposition des Arts Décoratifs." Krinsky, *Gordon Bunshaft,* p. 4.

150. Bunshaft recalled that since little was written in English about the German architect Mies van der Rohe's work at the time, Mies's work was not a great influence while Bunshaft was at MIT. Ibid., pp. 11–12.

151. Ibid., p. 9.

152. Ibid., p. 117. Ieoh M. Pei also graduated from MIT.

153. Lever House was one of the featured works (in model form, since it had not yet been constructed) in the MoMA exhibition of SOM's work, on view from September 26 to November 5, 1950. At the time of its construction, Lever House was discussed on a regular basis by the leading architectural magazines in this country. *Architectural Forum* carried articles on the structure in its June 1950 (pp. 84–89) and June 1952 (pp. 101–11) issues, and *Architectural Record* in its June 1950 (p. 12), June 1952 (pp. 130–35), and April 1953 (pp. 179–83) issues. One aspect of the design that fascinated observers was the very conscious attempt to advertise Lever Brothers as a soap producer by employing window washers who constantly cleaned the windows. *Architectural Forum* carried a photograph of the washers in its June 1952 issue. The promotional aspect was not unlike the projects for Alcoa aluminum or Corning glass by Harrison and Abramovitz, in which innovative construction techniques underscored the client's product—an aspect that would also inform the discussion of the Air Force Academy. The Manufacturers' Hanover Trust Company building was a modernist glass box with a steel frame and aluminum window mullions, sheathed with the largest sheets of glass ever used in an edifice. The work was discussed in several issues of *Architectural Forum* (September 1953, pp. 134–37, and December 1954, pp. 104–11) and in the November 1954 issue of *Architectural Record* (pp. 149–56). Horace Flannigan, board chairman of the bank, wrote a letter to Talbott during the academy competition supporting SOM's appointment. SOM, dwr. 51, file 01, letter from Flannigan to Talbott, June 4, 1954 (signed "Hap" and addressed to "Harold"). The Connecticut General Life Insurance building in Bloomfield, Connecticut, was featured in the September 1954 issue of *Architectural Forum* (pp. 212–13).

154. SOM, dwr. 51, file 01, SOM proposal for the academy commission. Bunshaft, who was eleven years older than Netsch and had served as a visiting critic at MIT while Netsch was a student, recalled that his role in the academy project was as "the old master designer overlooking and guiding, as best I could, the young Netsch." See Burchard, "Recollections of Gordon Bunshaft," p. 187.

155. William Wurster served as the dean of MIT's School of Architecture and Planning during that period. Among his faculty appointments was Gyorgy Kepes, former head of the Light and Color Department at the Bauhaus in Dessau. After moving to the United States, Kepes was in charge of drawing and color at the Light Workshop at the Institute of Design in Chicago (founded in 1937 by Moholy-Nagy and originally named the New Bauhaus). In addition to Kepes, MIT faculty members Richard Filipowski and Ralph Rapson also been at the Institute of Design—Filipowski as a student, and Rapson as the head of its Architecture Department. Carl Koch, who had studied with Gropius and Breuer, was also on the MIT faculty. Shillaber, *Massachusetts Institute of Technology,* pp. 88–90.

156. For Netsch's background and work for SOM until the academy project, see SOM, box 46, Jack Train files, ASBCA No. 5593, pp. 2–11. Netsch also recounted his background in testimony before the Air Force Academy Contract Appeals Panel on January 13, 1960. See SOM, dwr. 46 (no file no.), pp. 31–41.

157. See "The Navy's Graduate Engineering School," *Architectural Record* 117, no. 4 (April 1955): 159–71.

158. "Programming the U.S. Naval Postgraduate School of Engineering," *Architectural Record* 115, no. 6 (June 1955): 150–57.

159. Netsch was pulled from the Inland Steel Building project when SOM won the academy competition. The work was completed by Bruce Graham. Netsch's exact contribution to the building design is a subject of debate. See Bruce Graham, *Bruce Graham of SOM* (New York: Rizzoli, 1989).

160. SOM, dwr. 51, file 01, letter to F. E. Harrold, Chicago Manager of Henning and Cheadle, Inc., July 26, 1954, and letter from Walter Netsch to Morley Baer, July 26, 1954.

161. Owings, *Spaces in Between,* p. 152.

162. Kristen Schaffer, "Creating a National Monument," in Bruegmann, *Modernism at Mid-Century,* p. 62.

163. Owings, *Spaces in Between,* p. 152

164. Burchard, "Recollections of Gordon Bunshaft," pp. 186–87.

165. NA, box 168, Air Academy Construction Agency, A-E Selection Board, "Statement to be made to architects being considered for Air Academy Commission" [on the dates of the interviews, July 8–9, 1954].

166. Three days later Owings received a telegraph message from the firm of Pereira and Luckman congratulating the firm upon its selection. SOM, dwr. 51, file 01, Western Union Telegraph from Bill Pereira and Chuck Luckman to Nat Oweings [*sic*], July 26, 1954.

167. SOM, dwr. 55, file 61.4, "AF-SOM Meetings."

168. SOM, dwr. 50, file 11, Contract No. AF 33 (600)-28303, 8/4/54, Contract No. AF 33 (600)-26116, August 12, 1954.

169. NA, box 13, REL 1-2, Congressional Inquiries, May 1, 1954–September 15, 1954, three separate letters to Harrison, Becket, and Saarinen, respectively, from Ferry, July 26, 1954.

170. AFA, RG 120, ser. 22, memo for the Administrative Assistant from James Douglas, February 13, 1956.

171. See Newhouse, *Wallace K. Harrison,* and Bleecker, *Politics of Architecture.*

172. Both *Arts and Architecture Magazine* (April 1949, pp. 43–50; May 1949, pp. 42–46) and *Architect and Engineer Magazine* (March 1949, pp. 14–20; June 1949, pp. 16–21) carried articles on these buildings, as did *Architectural Forum* 90, no. 5 (May 1949): 83–92.

173. For background on the firm of Welton Becket and Associates, including commissions and design philosophy, see Hunt's *Total Design.* Information on the shopping-center designs was carried by leading architectural magazines, and included the following articles: "Bullock's Palm Springs Store, California," *Architectural Review* 103, no. 4 (April 1948): 123–27; "40 Stores," *Architectural Forum* 88, no. 5 (May 1948): 102–5; "Stonestown Shopping Center, San Francisco," *Architectural Review* 100, no. 3 (March 1951): 132–36; and "New Shopper Magnets," *Architectural Forum* 98, no. 3 (March 1953): 143–45.

174. For a discussion of the Lever Brothers building, see "Industrial Buildings," *Progressive Architecture* 32, no. 11 (November 1951): 83–89; for the laboratory, see "Small Laboratory for Oil-Well Research," *Architectural Record* 111, no. 6 (June 1952): 168–69; for the bank, see "Small Buildings," *Architectural Forum* 100, no. 1 (January 1954): 152–54; and for the Air Base project, see "P/A Progress Preview," *Progressive Architecture* 35, no. 10 (October 1954): 9–10. Sheri Olson also provided a background to the firm in "The Architectural Consultants," in Bruegmann, *Modernism at Mid-Century,* pp. 31–32.

175. Burchard, "Recollections of Gordon Bunshaft," p. 187.

176. AFA, RG 120, ser. 17, letter from Beardwood to Willis, March 29, 1954.

177. AFA, RG 120, ser. 17, letter from Willis to Talbott, Marcy 31, 1954.

178. AFA, RG 120, ser. 17, letter from Talbott to Beardwood, April 6, 1954.

179. AFA, RG 120, ser. 17, letter from Mr. Rabb to Colonel Draper, June 30, 1954. Additional information on Rabb and Hobby may be found in Parmet's *Eisenhower and the American Crusades.*

180. AFA, RG 120, ser. 17, letter from Beardwood to Adams, July 13, 1954. Adams, governor of New Hampshire, was renowned for his tyrannical bearing. He often mediated in matters of personnel policy. Parmet, *Eisenhower and the American Crusades,* pp. 177–83.

181. AFA, RG 120, ser. 17, letter from Beardwood to Willis, July 14, 1954.

182. AFA, RG 120, ser. 17, letter from Beardwood to Willis, July 27, 1954.

Chapter 2: On the Wings of Modernism

This chapter and the section in chapter 5 headed "The Construction of the Academy" expand substantially upon an essay that I contributed to *Modernism at Mid-Century,* edited by Robert Bruegmann.

1. The term "perfect city" seems appropriate, referring to the manner in which James Gilbert described the 1893 World's Columbian Exposition in his book *Perfect Cities: Chicago's Utopias of 1893* (Chicago: University of Chicago Press, 1991). In similar fashion, the Air Force Academy provided SOM a unique opportunity to design an entire community at once.

2. Skidmore had met Hood and Cret in Europe while on a Rotch Fellowship from MIT.

3. For the firm's work on the Chicago and New York World's Fairs, see Krinsky, *Gordon Bunshaft,* pp. 6–9, and Owings, *Spaces in Between,* pp. 34–60 and 77–78.

4. *Official Guide,* p. 11.

5. Skidmore, "Planning the Exhibition Displays," p. 345.

6. Skidmore, "Planning and Planners," p. 31. Cret had a decisive role in determining the fair's master plan.

7. *Official Guide,* p. 22.

8. Skidmore, "Planning the Exposition Displays," pp. 345–46.

9. Owings, "Amusement Features of the Exposition," p. 355.

10. Owings, *Spaces in Between,* p. 52.

11. Skidmore, "The Hall of Science," pp. 361–66.

12. The architects of the Administration Building were Holabird and Root, and Hubert Burnham and Edward Bennett. *Official Guide,* p. 25.

13. Ibid., pp. 18, 22.

14. Nye, *American Technological Sublime,* p. 153. Nye is referring to such

treatises as Edmund Burke's *Philosophical Inquiry into the Origin of Our Ideas of the Sublime and Beautiful* (1757) and Immanuel Kant's *Observations on the Feeling of the Beautiful and the Sublime* (1763).

15. *Official Guide,* p. 119.

16. Corn discussed how these fairs projected literary utopian visions in *Imagining Tomorrow,* pp. 97–118.

17. *Official Guide,* p. 20. Architecture as scenographic design has a long tradition. Christopher Mead, in his discussion of Garnier's Paris Opera, recounted the history of scenographic composition from the Renaissance to the Beaux-Arts approaches of the nineteenth century. See Christopher Curtis Mead, *Charles Garnier's Paris Opera* (Cambridge, Mass.: MIT Press, 1991), pp. 120–27.

18. Owings, *Spaces in Between,* pp. 61 and 57.

19. Photographs and discussions of the work of Skidmore and Owings are in Zim, Lerner, and Rolfes, *World of Tomorrow.*

20. Terry Smith discussed the 1939 New York Fair in terms of creating an image of modernity, in "Funfair Futurama: A Consuming Spectacle," in *Making the Modern,* pp. 405–21.

21. Haskell, "To-morrow and the World's Fair," p. 72.

22. Corn, *Imagining Tomorrow,* pp. 102–03.

23. Meikle, *Twentieth-Century Limited,* p. 197. The chapter entitled "A Microcosm of the Machine-Age World" (pp. 189–210) deals with the 1939 New York World's Fair.

24. Schwartz, for example, addressed the issue of exhibition pavilions as advertising within the context of the German Werkbund, in *The Werkbund,* pp. 181–91.

25. Haskell, "To-morrow and the World's Fair," pp. 65–72.

26. Meikle, *Twentieth-Century Limited,* p. 198.

27. Nye, *American Technological Sublime,* p. 200.

28. Haskell, "To-morrow and the World's Fair," p. 68.

29. Nye, *American Technological Sublime,* p. 218. Geddes thought of his Futurama, built in association with Eero Saarinen, as an actual blueprint for constructing a national highway system, and he presented his ideas to General Motors and President Roosevelt. Geddes was labeled a "creative artist" and was awarded a contract to design playground equipment instead. Geddes's fatal mistake, according to his detractors, was that he mistook imagination for pragmatics. Meikle, *Twentieth-Century Limited,* pp. 208–9.

30. Although he didn't connect the firm of SOM to these events, Terry Smith noted the intersection of world's fairs of the 1930s and the agenda of MoMA, specifically mentioning the 1932 "Modern Architecture" exhibition. T. Smith, *Making the Modern,* pp. 385–404.

31. Colomina, *Privacy and Publicity,* pp. 201–12.

32. Hitchcock, *Modern Architecture.* In that text, Hitchcock castigated the eclectic "picturesque" or "sublime" approach of the Romantics of the nineteenth century. In particular, he noted the influence of Le Corbusier, entitling one of his chapters "Towards a New Architecture" (the title of the 1931 English edition of Le Corbusier's *Vers une architecture*).

33. In *The International Style: Architecture since 1922,* the book that resulted from the exhibition, Hitchcock and Johnson outlined those principles as follows: "There is, first, a new conception of architecture as volume rather than mass. Secondly, regularity rather than axial symmetry serves as the chief means of organizing design. These two principles, with a third proscribing arbitrary applied decoration, mark the productions of the international style." Hitchcock and Johnson, *International Style,* p. 20.

34. Alfred H. Barr Jr., "Foreword," *Modern Architecture: International Exhibition* (New York: Arno Press, for the Museum of Modern Art, 1932), p. 11.

35. Riley, *International Style,* p. 220. Riley wrote this catalogue to accompany the recreation of the original exhibition at the Columbia University architecture galleries in 1992.

36. Ibid., p. 219.

37. Colomina, *Privacy and Publicity,* p. 207.

38. Riley, *International Style,* p. 24. Barr later stated that the exhibition's cost was $68,000, although Riley believes it was not that expensive (p. 203 n. 18).

39. Ibid., p. 221.

40. Ibid., pp. 79, 208.

41. The United States was not the only country in which modern architecture was being promoted through exhibitions and images. The first full-scale exhibition of Bauhaus work, which ran from August 15 to September 30, 1923, also included photographs, plans, and models of other works to illustrate the theme of "modern architecture." See Whitford, *Bauhaus,* pp. 136–50. Another interesting parallel is the role that exhibitions played in Italy between 1932 and 1942, where Fascism provided the philosophical underpinnings to a modernist discourse. For a discussion of those exhibitions, see Ghirardo, "Architects, Exhibitions," pp. 67–75.

42. For a discussion of this transition in the policy of the photography department of the Museum of Modern Art, see Christopher Phillips "The Judgment Seat of Photography," *October 22* (Fall 1982): 27–63.

43. Herbert Bayer, "Fundamentals of Exhibition Design," *PM* [Production Manager], December/January 1939/40, p. 17. In 1940, Bayer was teaching a design class in New York that was sponsored by the American Advertising Guild. Gwen Chanzit, curator of the Bayer Achives at the Denver Art Museum, discusses Bayer's exhibition design techniques in her book *Herbert Bayer and Modernist Design in America,* pp. 111–50.

44. Meikle, *Twentieth-Century Limited,* p. 209.

45. Phillips, "Judgment Seat of Photography," p. 46.

46. It was Paepke who rescued the New Bauhaus in Chicago from bankruptcy and changed its name to the Chicago Institute of Design. Paepke had also visited Aspen, Colorado, in 1945 and immediately envisioned it as a planned community that rivaled communities such as Salzburg in combining recreational and intellectual opportunities. He persuaded Bayer to move to Aspen to help realize that vision, and in 1950 the Aspen Institute of Humanistic Studies was officially inaugurated. Bayer did much of the architectural, sculptural, and graphic work for the institute during the 1950s and 1960s. For more on Paepke, Bayer, and the Aspen Institute, see Sloan, *Romance of Commerce and Culture.*

47. Edgar J. Kaufmann Jr., a Fellow at Wright's Taliesen Foundation in the 1930s, was the force behind this program.

48. A source of information for this series of exhibitions is provided by Riley and Eigen in "Between the Museum and the Marketplace," pp. 151–79.

49. Ibid., p. 167. Although this alliance of commercial design and museum exhibition was relatively new to the America, it had well-known precedents in Europe. An example was the German Werkbund. For the Werkbund, the discussion of industrially designed products involved a critique of the role of the artist and architect in society, presented within a context of nationalism and stylistic determinism. With the Werkbund's support, Karl Ernst Osthaus had founded the German Museum for Art in Trade and Industry at the turn of the century, and by 1912 it was functioning primarily as a museum of advertising. Traveling exhibitions were organized by the museum, which functioned as a go-between for artists and industry. For a discussion of the Werkbund's collusion with mass culture, see Schwartz, *The Werkbund.*

50. Museum of Modern Art, "Skidmore, Owings, and Merrill," p. 5. In the title on the cover of the publication, the museum used a lowercase typeface developed by the Bauhaus designer Herbert Bayer.

51. Ibid., p. 5.

52. Ibid., p. 8.

53. Frederic Schwartz traced the development of trademarks to the Werkbund, noting that trademarks drawn and admired by Werkbund members exhibited "an extreme reduction of means . . . a highly schematized image . . . anonymous and unspecified . . . stripped of ornament, abstracted to what contemporaries called a 'type'." Schwartz, *The Werkbund*, p. 137.

54. SOM, dwr. 55, file 61.4, "AF-SOM Meetings," minutes from the December 15, 1954, meeting. In addition, John Kirkpatrick and Albert Lockett of SOM, General N. F. Twining (Chief of Staff), and Colonel Jones attended.

55. Ibid., pp. 1–2.

56. Ibid., p. 29.

57. Ibid., p. 30.

58. Ibid., p. 35.

59. Ibid., pp. 35–36.

60. Ibid., p. 32.

61. Ibid., p. 52.

62. Ibid.

63. Ibid., p. 53.

64. Ibid., p. 54.

65. SOM, dwr. 55, file 61.4, "AF-SOM Meetings," minutes from the January 4, 1955, meeting. Generals White and Hipps, Colonel Price, Mr. Huebsch (deputy director of the Air Force Academy Construction Agency), and Robert and A. G. Stanford of Robert and Company Associates also attended.

66. Ibid., pp. 10–12. The Air Force Academy Foundation had been established that year in order to provide the academy, through private funding, with goods and services beyond those made available through air force allocated funds. The Air Defense Command was one of three combat commands with overseas extensions.

67. Ibid., pp. 13–14.

68. SOM, dwr. 51, file 02.1a, "Publicity—Exhibits, Graphic Arts."

69. SOM, dwr. 55, file 61.4, "AF-SOM Meetings," minutes from the January 4, 1955, meeting, p. 16.

70. SOM, dwr. 51, file 02.1, "Publicity—Photography," memo from Owings, Merrill, Bunshaft, and Hartmann to All A.F.A. Personnel, January 5, 1955.

71. SOM, dwr 51, file 02.1a, "Publicity—Exhibits, Graphic Arts," letter from Stoltz to J. Merrill, December 30, 1954. Colonel Stoltz informed John Merrill that the Public Information Office had been established. As outlined in a previous memo by Edward Merrill, the office was formed in part to avoid giving unfair advantages to contractors or manufacturers who might receive information prior to its release to the general public. See SOM, dwr. 51, file 02.1, "Publicity—Photography," memo to All Personnel from E. A. Merrill, December 18, 1954.

72. AFA, RG 20, ser. 22, letter from Boyd to Harmon, January 24, 1955.

73. *Time,* March 28, 1955, p. 70.

74. SOM, dwr. 35, file 61.1a, "Presentations—Air Force," letter from Byrnes to Owings, March 14, 1955.

75. SOM, dwr. 35, file 61.1a, letter from Owings to Talbott, March 17, 1955.

76. SOM, dwr. 35, file 61.1a, letter from Talbott to Byrnes, March 25, 1955.

77. SOM, dwr. 35, file 61.1a, "Draft: May Presentation," March 24, 1955.

78. SOM, dwr. 35, file 61.1a, memo from Owings to C. L. Tyler, April 1, 1955. Captain Carroll L. Tyler had been named to his position by SOM in January. He had previously been manager (1947–54) of the Atomic Energy Commission's Santa Fe office, where he was in charge of all technical and administrative aspects of the atomic weapons program at installations in the United States and the Pacific. Those duties included the creation and management of the city of Los Alamos, New Mexico. After his retirement from that position, he had served as a consultant in Spain for air base projects. He was hired by SOM after meeting Owings, in December 1954, to ensure the academy design progressed as closely as possible to schedule. He was, in other words, not responsible for any of the design work but oversaw the administration of the contract between SOM and the air force. Tyler gave this background information in testimony before the Air Force Contract Appeals Panel on June 8, 1959 (ASBCA No. 5426). A transcript of that testimony is in SOM, box 47. The information given above, pertaining to Tyler's background, is contained on pp. 16–21 of that document.

79. NA, box 165, REL 6—Presentations, Memorandum for the Assistant Chief of Staff, Installations, from John Ferry, March 29, 1955. Ferry identified the special account by the budget line item "481 funds."

80. SOM, dwr. 35, file 61.1a, "Presentations—Air Force," letter from Ferry to Owings, April 8, 1955.

81. SOM, dwr. 35, file 61.1a, letter from Tyler to Bayer, March 30, 1955.

82. SOM, dwr. 35, file 61.1a, memo from Netsch to Tyler, April 4, 1955. Conrad's and Rudolph's previous work for SOM had been pictured in such architecture magazines as *Architectural Forum* and *Architectural Record*.

83. SOM, dwr. 35, file 61.1a, letter from Richard Rush to Netsch, April 8, 1955.

84. SOM, dwr. 35, file 61.1a. An itemized statement, sent to the Air Force Academy Construction Agency on May 24, 1955, records $52,995.94 for the cost of the models out of a total of $97,142.42. Included in the cost for the models were fees to Conrad, to Rush Studio, and to Model Builders, Inc. Part of the high cost for the model work, according to one of the Rush Studio invoices, was that time constraints forced eighteen-hour work days, seven days a week. Fees for the other involved parties were obtained from the same document.

85. SOM, dwr. 35, file 61.1a, memo from Stoltz to Merrill, April 13, 1955.

86. SOM, dwr. 35, file 61.1a, memo from Owings to Bayer, Bunshaft, and Netsch, April 13, 1955.

87. SOM, dwr. 35, file 61.1a, letter from "herbert bayer" to "mr. gordon bunshaft," April 23, 1955.

88. "Lever House Complete," *Architectural Forum* 96, no. 6 (June 1952): 101–11, and "Manufacturers Trust Company Builds Conversation Piece on Fifth Avenue," *Architectural Record* 116, no. 5 (November 1954): 149–56. Other Stoller photographs of SOM's work appearing in those magazines included those of the Lever House model, the Manhattan House in New York, the Pittsburgh Heinz Building, and the Inland Steel Building.

89. Sibyl Moholy-Nagy, "Victories and Defeats of Modern Architecture," *Progressive Architecture* 34, no. 4 (April 1953): 18. The subsequent catalogue for the exhibition was entitled *Built in U.S.A.: Post-War Architecture* (New York: Museum of Modern Art, 1952). It contained articles by Philip Johnson, Henry-Russell Hitchcock, and Arthur Drexler.

90. Several months after the exhibition, Adams wrote a letter to Owings applauding the design. SOM, dwr. 35, file 61.1a, "Presentations—Air Force," letter from Adams to Nat Owings, July 16, 1955. Adams was frequently a guest of the Owingses, performing on their family harpsichord. See Owings, *Spaces in Between*, p. 192.

91. J. Alinder and Szarkowski, *Ansel Adams,* p. 15.

92. Adams and M. Alinder, *Ansel Adams,* p. 203.

93. J. Alinder and Szarkowski, *Ansel Adams,* p. 15. For Adams's Kodak commissions, see Spaulding, *Ansel Adams and the American Landscape,* pp. 229–30.

94. J. Alinder and Szarkowski, *Ansel Adams,* p. 6. The quotation is from the book's introduction by Szarkowski.

95. Adams had also contributed to the founding of *Aperture* magazine in 1952. That magazine was the direct outcome of the 1951 Aspen Conference on Photography, held at the Aspen Institute for Humanities—the very institute with which Bayer was involved. Ibid., pp. 19–20, 268–69.

96. As a founder of Group f/64, Adams's photographic output can be associated with the West Coast Precisionists, whose members included Imogen Cunningham and Edward Weston. For an explanation of Adams's Zone System, a type of visualization that employed the technologies inherent in photography to control image contrast and tone, see Jonathan Green, *American Photography: A Critical History, 1945 to Present* (New York: Abrams, 1984), pp. 27–35.

97. Charles Hagan, "Land and Landscape," *Aperture,* Summer 1990, p. 16.

98. Ansel Adams and Nancy Newhall, *This Is the American Earth* (San Francisco: Sierra Club, 1960).

99. Kennecott Copper Corporation subsequently used the photographs for advertisements that appeared in magazines such as *Time, Newsweek, Business Week,* and *Saturday Evening Post.* Adams's association with Pacific Gas and Electric Company extended over several decades. In 1939 he photographed the corporate heads of the company for a *Fortune* magazine commission. In 1946, he used his San Francisco Art Institute students to complete a commission from the corporation, and in 1954 his photographs were used in its annual report. See the following: M. Alinder, *Ansel Adams: A Biography,* pp. 156, 208, 265, and 289–93; and Spaulding, *Ansel Adams and the American Landscape,* pp. 212 and 264–65.

100. SOM, dwr. 35, file 61.1a, "Presentations—Air Force," letters from Ansel Adams to Nat Owings, April 16, 1955, and from Owings to Personnel—Air Academy Exhibit, April 18, 1955.

101. Lax, "William A. Garnett," p. 50.

102. Natalie Canavor, "William Garnett: Flying a 37-Year Mission," *Popular Photography,* December 1982, p. 133, and Lax, "William A. Garnett," pp. 50–60. The academy exhibition was one of a series of collaborations involving Owings, Bayer, Adams, and Garnett: in 1957, Bayer designed the *Nation of Nations* exhibition, which opened in West Berlin and integrated Adams's photographs and Whitman's poetry (Spaulding, *Ansel Adams and the American Landscape,* pp. 302–03); in 1969, Garnett collaborated with Owings on *The American Aesthetic;* and in 1982 Ansel Adams contributed a foreword to Garnett's book of photographs entitled *The Extraordinary Landscape* (Boston: Little, Brown).

103. SOM, dwr. 35, file 61.1a, "Presentations—Air Force"; letter from Adams to Tyler, April 24, 1955.

104. SOM, dwr. 35, file 61.1a, letter from Garnett to SOM, April 28, 1955. Both Adams's and Garnett's letters went to the newly established SOM office in Colorado Springs. Garnett confirmed this series of events in telephone interviews with the author, March 18 and June 3, 1993.

105. SOM, dwr. 35, file 61.1a, letter from Bayer to Adams, June 1, 1955.

106. SOM, dwr. 35, file 61.1a, list entitled "Mr. Talbott's Master Guest List for Reservations and Acceptances" and "Press Reservations." An interesting detail is that on May 2, the office of SOM ordered forty-four box lunches for the press at a total cost of $17.60. It gives a sense of the relative cost of the exhibition (SOM, dwr. 35, file 61.1a, "Presentations—Air Force," letter from Marion Howden, Secretary to Owings, to Lieutenant Kay Guthrie, May 2, 1955).

107. SOM, dwr. 35, file 61.1a, letters from SOM Office Manager Katherine E. Grant to the Federal Storage and Moving Company, May 6, 1955, and to T. F. Flavin (SOM office in Colorado Springs), May 7, 1955. The May 15, 1955, issue of the *Colorado Springs Gazette Telegraph* (p. B1) reported that this was simply to avoid traffic and not for the purpose of secrecy.

108. SOM, dwr. 35, file 61.1a, Air Force Academy Press Release, May 3, 1955.

109. Bainbridge Bunting, *John Gaw Meem* (Albuquerque: University of New Mexico Press, 1983), pp. 152–53. Coincidentally, Meem had employed Adams on several occasions to photograph his architecture.

110. See the *Colorado Springs Free Press,* May 15, 1955, p. 19, and SOM, dwr. 35, file 61.1a, "Presentations—Air Force," letter from Hammond (of SOM) to Byrnes, April 21, 1955.

111. SOM, dwr. 35, file 61.1a, "Presentations—Air Force," letter from Bayer to Hofgesang, April 21, 1955.

112. SOM, dwr. 35, file 61.1a, letter from Bayer to Bunshaft, April 23, 1955.

113. Ibid. This information is based on a series of snapshots and diagrams recovered at SOM's warehouse in Chicago; it is supplemented by letters from Bayer describing his design ideas for the exhibition to staff members at SOM.

114. George Cooper Rudolph provided this information in a telephone interview with the author, June 22, 1993.

115. Owings, *Spaces in Between,* p. 156.

116. A comparison may be drawn between the employment of ramps in the academy design and in the 1939 New York Fair. Discussing their application at the fair, Douglas Haskell wrote, "Yet the greatest discovery in New York was the discovery of the crowd, both as actor and decoration of great power. . . . At General Motors the crowd was decoratively the making of the building, giving life, brilliant color, and motion to the snaked ramps against the cliff-like walls." Haskell, "To-Morrow and the World's Fair," p. 67.

117. Netsch recalled Stoller photographing the model in Chicago. Interview with the author, May 20, 1993.

118. SOM, dwr. 35, file 61.1a, "Presentations—Air Force." This is also the source of the quotations in the next paragraph. This speech was delivered at 9:00 A.M. on Saturday, May 14, 1955, to members of Congress and special guests, and at 10:30 A.M. the same day to the news media. A tour of the exhibition was then conducted by members of SOM and the air force, including Owings, Harmon, Washbourne, and Stoltz. Owings entitled his speech "Introductory Comments to Secretary Talbott, Members of Congress, and Distinguished Guests at the Colorado Springs Fine Arts Center Prior to the Review of Exhibit Presenting the Architectural Concepts of the United States Air Force Academy."

119. Le Corbusier, *Towards a New Architecture,* pp. 109–27.

120. For a discussion of notions of flight and utopia in America, see Corn, *Winged Gospel.*

121. As a member of the Site Selection Commission, it was Lindbergh who had flown over the Colorado Springs site to prove to other Commission members that the site's altitude would not be a factor in flight training. Cannon, Holt, and Allen, *History of the United States Air Force Academy,* p. 163. Even as the academy was being constructed, Lindbergh's transatlantic crossing was immortalized in Billy Wilder's 1957 film *The Spirit of St. Louis.*

122. Geddes, *Horizons.* Geddes's thesis, presented in his first chapter, "Towards Design" (pp. 3–23), was illustrated with photographs by Imogen

Cunningham, Margaret Bourke-White, and Edward Steichen to underscore his precisionist approach to design. In addition to his discussion of aircraft design (pp. 110–21), Geddes wrote about applications of streamlining to automobile and railway design (pp. 44–78).

123. Teague, *Design This Day.* See, for example, chapter 10, "Rhythm of Proportion " (pp. 141–61), in which Teague presented his argument by juxtaposing the text with images of the Parthenon and Chartres and photographs by Margaret Bourke-White of aircraft.

124. Corn, *Imagining Tomorrow,* pp. 97–118.

125. Ibid., pp. 103–6. The General Motors Building itself was designed by Albert Kahn, Inc., while the United States Steel Building was designed by York and Sawyer. Both firms later applied for the academy project. Dreyfuss adopted his decentralized city plan from Ebenezer Howard's Garden City concept, while Geddes was inspired by Le Corbusier's utopian city plans. Meikle, *Twentieth-Century Limited,* pp. 192, 208.

126. Pilots themselves wrote of assuming the omnipotent power and vantage point of God. Recounting his own experiences of flight, Lindbergh stated, "I began to feel that I had lived on a higher plane than the skeptics on the ground. In flying, I tasted a wine of the gods of which they could know nothing." Stiehm, *Bring Me Men, and Women,* p. 52.

127. Zim, Lerner, and Rolfes, *World of Tomorrow,* p. 109.

128. Corn, "'An Airplane in Every Garage?': The Gospel's Most Pervasive Promise," in *The Winged Gospel,* pp. 91–111.

129. Frank Lloyd Wright, *The Living City* (New York: Mentor Books, 1963), pp. 85–87 (the illustration appears on pp. 198–99).

130. Corn, *Winged Gospel,* pp. 129–31. Corn commented that this type of teaching reduced language to minimal communication skills that served a function only within the marketplace, ultimately ignoring cultural specificities.

131. SOM, dwr. 35, file 61.1a, "Presentations—Air Force," memo from Netsch to Boyd, March 20, 1955.

132. SOM, dwr. 35, file 61.1a, "Presentations—Air Force," letter from Ferry to Owings, April 8, 1955. Reporting on the initial exhibition in its June 1955 issue, *Architectural Forum* also employed Netsch's analogy. See "The United States Air Force Academy" (*Architectural Forum*), p. 102.

133. AFA, RG 103, ser. 1, "Suggested Architectural Treatment for the Air Force Academy," January 5, 1949.

134. C. Bright, *Jet Makers,* pp. 119–20. In his autobiography, Owings stated that this analogy between architectural efficiency and aircraft was also used during the architect selection process. During that process, someone had asked him if SOM would construct the academy buildings of sandstone (which Wright had supposedly recommended). In response, Owings supposedly stated, "General, would you build an airplane of sandstone?" Owings, *Spaces in Between,* p. 152.

135. Skidmore, "Planning and Planners," pp. 29–32.

136. Gropius, *Scope of Total Architecture,* pp. 74 and 80.

137. Gropius, "Gropius Appraises Today's Architect," and idem, "Eight Steps toward a Solid Architecture."

138. SOM, dwr. 55, folder 61.4, "AF-SOM Meetings," minutes from the December 15, 1954, meeting.

139. SOM, dwr. 55, file 61.2, "SOM meetings and comments," letter from Stoltz to Merrill, 4/4/55.

140. SOM, dwr. 55, folder 61.4, "AF-SOM Meetings," minutes from the October 4, 1954, meeting, pp. 23–25.

141. SOM, dwr. 55, folder 61.4, "AF-SOM Meetings," minutes from the January 4, 1954, meeting, p. 19.

142. NA, box 78, Minutes—Academy Committee, Construction Project Study Files 1947–71, "Annex to the Report of the Air Force Academy Site Selection Commission, Statement of Primary Factors Considered by the Commission in Evaluating Proposed Locations," April 6(?), 1954.

143. R. Nash, *Wilderness and the American Mind,* p. 4.

144. J. Taylor, *America as Art.* Of particular interest within the context of this discussion is the chapter entitled "The Virtue of American Nature" (pp. 95–131), and John G. Cawelti's contribution, "The Frontier and the Native American" (pp. 134–83). The notion that wilderness could also be conceived in aesthetic terms had been articulated during the prior century by authors such as Edmund Burke and Immanuel Kant.

145. R. Nash, *Wilderness and the American Mind,* pp. 141–60. Yellowstone was established as the first national park, in 1872. The Boy Scouts, founded in 1907, became the country's largest youth organization. Sales of the Boy Scouts' 1938 *Handbook* were exceeded only by those of the Bible.

146. The debates ultimately resulted in the establishment of the National Wilderness Preservation System in 1964. Ibid., pp. 200–236.

147. Limerick, *The Legacy of Conquest,* p. 20. Turner based his argument on 1890 census figures, noting that a minimum population density of two people per square mile had been reached. His perception of the frontier was rooted in the concept of Manifest Destiny. According to that concept, defined by John O'Sullivan and others in the 1840s, the United States had a national destiny mandated by God to expand across the continent. See Merk, *Manifest Destiny and Mission.* Numerous historians of the West have commented on Turner's thesis. Gerald Nash, for example, believes that Turner's thesis has perhaps been more rigidly interpreted than intended, while Patricia Limerick has criticized it in light of its cultural assumptions—its unifying, ethnocentric concept of the frontier. Within the context of this discussion, the importance of Turner's thesis is how it conditioned notions of the American frontier, which were applied by SOM in addressing the public. See G. Nash, *Creating the West,* and Limerick, *The Legacy of Conquest.*

148. R. Nash, *Wilderness and the American Mind,* p. 146.

149. Miller and Nowak, *The Fifties,* p. 9.

150. Compare Marx, *Machine in the Garden,* pp. 113–14 ("middle landscape"), and Slotkin, *Fatal Environment,* p. 39 ("frontier community"). Henry Nash Smith wrote of the similarities between the two types: "Jefferson's agrarian ideal proves to be virtually identical with the frontier democracy that Turner believed he had discovered in the West." Smith, *Virgin Land,* p. 255.

151. Basing his study on popular literature, Smith analyzed the development and evolution of the Western hero, from the mountain man—a symbol of anarchic freedom—to the romantic figure of dime novels. H. Smith, *Virgin Land,* pp. 81–111.

152. Smith noted that Erastus Beadle, for example, sold over five million copies of his novels (actually, short stories) between 1860 and 1865. Ibid., pp. 90–91.

153. As quoted by G. Nash in *Creating the West,* p. 231. Fishwick's comments appeared in *Western Folklore 11* (1951–52).

154. Halberstam, *The Fifties,* p. 505.

155. Quoted by D. Bright, "The Public Landscape of Postwar America," p. 337.

156. G. Nash, *Creating the West,* p. 225.

157. John Burchard, "A Conversation about the U.S. Air Force Academy between Walter Netsch and John Burchard," in Bruegmann, *Modernism at*

Mid-Century, p. 184. Charles Klauder's university (the University of Colorado) is actually located in Boulder.

158. Le Corbusier, *Towards a New Architecture,* p. 71. The grid also relates to the United States one-mile-square grid—initiated by Jefferson and indebted to Classical theory—superimposed over much of the Western part of the country. J. B. Jackson noted that the landscape grid is characterized not only by its vast scale, but by "a disregard for local landscape features . . . and . . . a persistent emphasis on military and commercial functions." John Brinkerhoff Jackson, *Discovering the Vernacular Landscape* (New Haven: Yale University Press, 1984), p. 23.

159. Zim, Lerner, and Rolfes, *World of Tomorrow,* p. 110.

160. See Sanderson, "P/A News Report: Air Academy."

161. "United States Air Force Academy" (*Architectural Record*), insert following p. 172.

162. "The United States Air Force Academy" (*Architectural Forum*), pp. 100–109; the quotation is from p. 102.

163. "Air Academy Design 'Heavenly, Timeless,'" *Sunday Denver Post,* May 15, 1955, p. 17A. That issue of the paper featured a George Rudolph rendering of the design on its front page, while the "Sunday Post Picture Page" included a page of Rudolph's and Stoller's photographs of the model.

164. Hebert's and Short's comments were reported, respectively, in "Modernistic Design Highlights Air Academy Architecture," *Colorado Springs Free Press,* May 15, 1955, and "Air Academy Design 'Heavenly, Timeless.'" Both newspaper articles carried photographs of the models and reproductions of Rudolph's renderings.

165. "Chapel for Academy 'Insult to Religion' Governor Says," *Colorado Springs Gazette Telegraph,* May 17, 1955, p. 1. In his autobiography, Owings incorrectly attributed the remark to the chairman of the Appropriations Committee. See Owings, *Spaces in Between,* pp. 156–57.

166. These and other letters of criticism are to be found in SOM, dwr. 51, file 02.4, and NA, box 166, Congressional 1955–57, folder 4. Bennett was on the House Committee of the Armed Services, while Welker, Stennis, and Ervin were on the Senate Committee of the Armed Services.

167. SOM, dwr. 51, file 02.1, letter from Arthur Drexler, Curator of the Department of Architecture and Design at the Museum of Modern Art, to Hartmann of SOM, June 27, 1955. The exhibition was to take place "in galleries on the Museum's ground floor, adjacent to our Sculptural Garden."

168. SOM, dwr. 51, file 02.1, letter from Ferry to Hartmann, August 12, 1955.

169. SOM, dwr. 55, file 61.1, letter from Tyler to Byrnes, May 27, 1955.

170. SOM, dwr. 35, file 61.1a, "Presentations—Air Force," letter from Stoltz to SOM, June 6, 1955.

171. SOM, dwr. 35, file 61.1a, letter from Tyler to Mills, Acting Director of the Colorado Springs Fine Arts Center, June 7, 1955.

Chapter 3: The Design Debate

1. The exact amount of Congress's allocation was $15,338,000. See General Washbourne's testimony, U.S. Congress, House, Subcommittee of the Committee on Appropriations, June 30, 1955, p. 196.

2. Fogarty's entire speech was recorded in the *Congressional Record,* June 20, 1955, pp. 8781–83.

3. Fogarty supported his argument by a comparing the $10,000 cost of cleaning the stone National Press Building in Washington, D.C., to the $250,000 cost of installing scaffolding equipment to clean SOM's Lever Brothers building.

4. J. Taylor, *America as Art,* p. 17.

5. Craig, *Federal Presence,* p. 214.

6. Lee, *Architects to the Nation,* p. 190.

7. Ibid., p. 260.

8. The *Federal Architect* was edited by Edwin Bateman Morris. Throughout his tenure at the magazine (1930–46), Morris opposed modernist architecture. A student of Paul Cret, Morris championed "the Moderne traditionalized, the Traditional modernized." Ibid., pp. 298–99.

9. Louis A. Simon, "Federal Triangle," the *Federal Architect* 6 (October 1935): 16. The project, including the quotation, is described by Lee, *Architects to the Nation,* pp. 241–46.

10. Alex Scobie has documented the complex associations that Hitler made between his political ideology and a classical architectural vocabulary in the projects, both realized and unrealized, of Albert Speer. See Scobie, *Hitler's State Architecture.* Related issues are addressed in R. Taylor's *The Word in Stone,* and by Lane in "Nazi Architecture," in her *Architecture and Politics in Germany,* pp. 185–216.

11. Frampton, *Modern Architecture,* pp. 167–77, 213–14.

12. Mock, *Built in U.S.A.: 1932–1944,* p. 25.

13. For issues of architectural modernism and Fascism, see "Progressive Architects and Fascist Politics," in Doordan, *Building Modern Italy,* pp. 129–41. For a discussion of Terragni and his use of monumental forms as a bridge between progressive and traditional architectural vocabularies, see Curtis, "Modern Architecture, Monumentality and the Meaning of Institutions," pp. 68–69.

14. Mock concluded her discussion of monumentality by stating, "The monumental possibilities for the city square, for example, have scarcely yet been considered in modern terms." Mock, *Built in U.S.A.: 1932–1944,* p. 25.

15. The essay was reprinted by Giedion in *Architecture You and Me,* pp. 25–39; the quotation is from p. 39.

16. Ibid., pp. 48–51; the quotation is from pp. 50–51. This article was also in collaboration with Léger and Sert.

17. Riefenstahl's film was a documentary of the Nazi Party Convention at Nürnberg.

18. "In Search of a New Monumentality," pp. 117–27. At the time, Hitchcock was professor of architectural history at Wesleyan University and a lecturer at MIT; Gropius was professor of architecture at Harvard University; Roth was an architect and author and editor of *Werk;* Paulsson was professor of the history and theory of art at the University of Uppsala; and Giedion was professor of art at the University of Zurich. Besides the persons mentioned, the other contributors were William Holford, professor of town planning at the University of London, and Lucio Costa, an architect.

19. Ibid., pp. 123–24.

20. Ibid., pp. 127–28.

21. U.S. Congress, House, Subcommittee of the Committee on Appropriations, June 30, 1955, pp. 196–224.

22. Ibid., p. 200.

23. Ibid.

24. Ibid., p. 204

25. Ibid., p. 205.

26. Ibid.

27. Ibid., p. 209.

28. Ibid., pp. 210–11.

29. Ibid., p. 211.

30. Ibid., p. 212. The Supreme Court Building was designed in 1935 by Cass Gilbert. He employed a classical style, with specific reference to the

Parthenon. West Point had achieved a coherent architectural style only after the 1903 competition, won by Cram, Goodhue, and Ferguson, who designed the new buildings in stripped-down Gothic style using local stone. Duke University was designed by the Philadelphia firm of Horace Trumbauer in the 1920s and combined Beaux-Arts principles of design with a "Collegiate Gothic" style of architecture.

31. Ibid., p. 213.

32. "General Harmon Tells All About 'The West Point of the Air,'" pp. 28–32.

33. Admiral Arthur W. Radford, "The 'New Look,'" in Emme, *The Impact of Air Power,* pp. 655–61. The address was given on December 14, 1953. The effect of Eisenhower's policy was reflected in the budget of the armed forces. In 1955, the army's budget was cut by $4 billion and the navy's by $1.5 million, while the air force's was increased by $800 million. Oakley, *God's Country,* pp. 211–12.

34. U.S. Congress, House, Subcommittee of the Committee on Appropriations, June 30, 1955, p. 224.

35. The background for the ensuing discussion of the embassy debate is provided by Loeffler, *Architecture of Diplomacy,* pp. 81–126.

36. Ibid., pp. 65 (first quote), 67 (second quote).

37. "U.S. Architecture Abroad," pp. 101–2. In her book *Architecture of Diplomacy,* Loeffler noted the bias *Architectural Forum* had in promoting modernism as part of the anticommunist cold-war rhetoric of the journal's owner, Henry Luce (p. 7). She also relates that King justified the use of a "Bauhaus idiom" in Germany because it could be interpreted as a gesture of goodwill toward the German people (p. 88).

38. Loeffler, *Architecture of Diplomacy,* pp. 114–15. The memo was dated July 7, 1953.

39. "Architecture to Represent America Abroad," p. 187. Ralph Walker was part of the firm of Voorhees, Walker, Foley, and Smith, while Henry Shepley was associated with the firm of Shepley, Bulfinch, Richardson, and Abbott. Both firms applied for the academy commission.

40. Loeffler, *Architecture of Diplomacy,* p. 94.

41. For the comments of Reed and Wright, see U.S. Congress, House, Subcommittee of the Committee on Appropriations, July 7, 1955, pp. 548–61.

42. In *The Architecture of America: A Social and Cultural History,* Burchard and Bush-Brown noted that Reed had tried to convince New York authorities that the city "would be improved by tall classic and baroque skyscrapers topped by statues of Minerva" (p. 490).

43. U.S. Congress, House, Subcommittee of the Committee on Appropriations, July 7, 1955, p. 553.

44. See "Wright Terms Academy Design 'Factory-Like,'" *Colorado Springs Free Press,* May 27, 1955, p. 1. Merrill and Owings responded to Wright's criticism several days later. See "Designer Defends Outline for Air Academy Chapel," *Colorado Springs Free Press,* May 29, 1955, p. 5.

45. For Wright's testimony, see U.S. Congress, House, Subcommittee of the Committee on Appropriations, July 7, 1955, pp. 554–61. The specific quotes given are from pp. 554 and 556 (on SOM) and p. 558 (on the consultants). For a list of Belluschi's projects, see Clausen, *Pietro Belluschi,* pp. 412–17.

46. Wright had the temerity to send a draft of a press release he wrote two days later, on July 9, to Skidmore. It was published by the *Colorado Springs Free Press* in its "Letters to the Editor" on July 14, 1955, p. 4. The front page of the issue carried the story headed "Wright Wants Students to Pick Academy Design." He handwrote the following at the top of the typed copy he sent to Skidmore:

Dear "Skid"

This is yours. There is no animosity in the thing. If things were right in the profession as they may be twenty-five years from now—I would be designing the academy and you would be executing it—fifty-fifty—but—as things are now—as they are!

Sincerely, all down the line—Frank Lloyd Wright"

The letter is contained in SOM, dwr. 51, file 02.4.

In response to Wright's attack on the design, Ansel Adams wrote a letter several days later to his friend Nat Owings. It read as follows:

Dear Nat Owings,

I have read, with considerable shock, the news about the difficulties with the Academy design. I am not an architect, and I therefore have no "authority" on which to base a useful statement of opinion. I would like to go on record as saying that I was tremendously impressed with the general concept of the Academy layout, and that the designs I saw were both moving, brilliant, and contemporary in the best sense of the term. The stupidity and arrogance of Congressional opinion in such matters is exasperating—even if expected!!!!

However, I am doubly shocked at the crude, unethical, and almost infantile statements of Wright at the committee hearings. I have always had a profound distrust of this man in every respect, and am certainly one of those who do NOT consider him God's little gift to Architecture! But in this instance I believe he really has gone out on a limb. I assume that steps will be taken to severely censure him in professional circles; he does not deserve the society of ethical, professional men.

I sincerely trust this unfortunate matter will be cleared up in the very near future and that your firm can proceed with its most worthy objectives.

With all good wishes as ever,

Ansel Adams

SOM, dwr. 35, file 61.1a, "Presentations—Air Force," letter from Adams to Nat Owings, July 16, 1955.

47. "Air Academy Design Brawl," pp. 9–13. The article also discussed the role of Merton B. Tice, commander-in-chief of the Veterans of Foreign Wars, in the ongoing debate. Tice had attacked the design as being "an insult to our American heritage and tradition" in a letter sent to Talbott and Eisenhower. The collusion between Wright and Fogarty was also carried in other magazines. See, for example, George Orick, "Off They Went into the Wild Blue," *The Reporter,* November 22, 1955, pp. 28–29.

48. For these letters and others, see NA, box 166, Congressional 1955–57, folder 3.

49. Supplemental Appropriation Bill, 1956, Senate, Subcommittee of the Committee on Appropriations, July 11, 1955, pp. 153–83.

50. Ibid., p. 181.

51. *Congressional Record,* July 14, 1955, p. 10576.

52. Supplemental Appropriation Bill, 1956, Senate, Subcommittee of the Committee on Appropriations, July 15, 1955, pp. 340–53. Among those who testified were Harry C. Plummer, chairman of the Engineering Committee of the Allied Masonry Council; John J. Murphy, secretary of the Bricklayers, Masons, and Plasterers International Union of America, AFL; Neill Boldrick, vice president of Acme Brick Co.; Charles Penn, vice president of Indiana Limestone Co.; Robert Cradock, member of the board of governors of the Building Stone Institute; and John Taheny, president of the Mason Contractors Association of America. Some of the many letters received are on file at the National Archives in Denver. See NA, box 166, Congressional 1955–57, folder 1.

53. Supplemental Appropriation Bill, 1956, Senate, Subcommittee of the Committee on Appropriations, July 13, 1955, pp. 337–40.

54. The bibliography on Wright is extensive. Frank Lloyd Wright's *An Autobiography* complements the extensive series of *Frank Lloyd Wright Collected Writings,* edited by Bruce Brooks Pfeiffer (New York: Rizzoli). Henry-Russell Hitchcock addressed Wright's work in his 1942 publication *In the Nature of Materials.*

55. The *Denver Post* ran an editorial cartoon on July 13, and the *San Francisco Chronicle* carried one on July 14.

56. See Supplemental Appropriation Bill, 1956, Senate, Subcommittee of the Committee on Appropriations, July 18, 1955, pp. 365–405. Talbott had, by this time, received letters from various members of Congress who, in light of the well-publicized debate, demanded to know what procedures had been followed in all aspects of the project. Some, such as Representative Eugene McCarthy, focused on issues of water availability, while others, such as Representative Melvin Price, of Illinois, hoped the debate would lead to a reconsideration of the entire project, including the possibility of relocating the academy to the previously considered Alton, Illinois, site. See NA, box 166, Congressional 1955–57, folder 3.

57. U.S. Congress, Senate, Subcommittee of the Committee on Appropriations, July 18, 1955, p. 390.

58. Ibid., pp. 392–93. The Department of Commerce Building, when erected in 1932, was the largest building to date financed by the federal government.

59. Ibid., p. 394.

60. Ibid., p. 395.

61. Ibid., p. 396.

62. Ibid., p. 398.

63. U.S. Congress, House, Subcommittee of the Committee on Appropriations, July 19, 1955, pp. 1–48.

64. Ibid., pp. 2–3.

65. Ibid., p. 3.

66. SOM, dwr. 51, file 02.4, memo from John Merrill to Owings, July 6, 1955. In that memo, Merrill mentions the statement and the fact that it is being forwarded to Talbott. Several days after the hearing, John Merrill sent "Ned" (Purves) a letter thanking him for his testimony. Purves replied, stating, "We look back on the part we played in the Air Force Academy matter with a good deal of pride and satisfaction. I have the feeling that in both hearings an understanding of the architect and architectural services was achieved, especially at the hearing of the House Subcommittee on Appropriations which started off in an atmosphere of misunderstanding and hostility and ended, as far as I could see, in an atmosphere of complete understanding and commendation." SOM, dwr. 51, files 02.4 and 02.5, letter from John O. Merrill to Edmund R. Purves ("Ned"), July 21, 1955, and letter from Edmund R. Purves to John O. Merrill, July 25, 1955.

67. U.S. Congress, House, Subcommittee of the Committee on Appropriations, July 19, 1955, p. 10.

68. Ibid., p. 26.

69. Ibid., p. 42. Merrill may or may not have had a specific architect in mind. An interesting comparison can be made to the nineteenth-century theorist Jean-Nicolas-Louis Durand. Durand's approach to architectural design was based upon symmetrical applications of the circle and square. His reductive view of architecture—as a series of unadorned planes that emphasized structure and geometry—created a orthodoxy of formulaic solutions to problems. Architectural richness, as he stated in his *Précis des leçons d'architecture données à l'Ecole Royale Polytechnique,* would be provided

by plants—vines and creepers. See Robin Middleton and David Watkin, *Neoclassical and Nineteenth-Century Architecture* (New York: Rizzoli, 1980), pp. 28–30.

70. SOM, dwr. 51, file 02.4. These appearances were reported in the AIA's August 1 newsletter.

71. Frank Lloyd Wright, "Redesigning the Air Force Academy," *Colorado Springs Free Press,* July 30, 1955, p. 4.

72. Hitchcock and Johnson, *International Style,* pp. 19, 33.

73. See Pommer and Otto, "Weissenhof and the Politics of the International Style," in their *Weissenhof 1927 and the Modern Movement in Architecture,* pp. 158–66.

74. Adolf Hitler, *Mein Kampf,* trans. Ralph Manheim (Boston: Houghton Mifflin, 1943), pp. 258–63. Also see Lane, *Architecture and Politics in Germany,* pp. 125–67, and R. Taylor, *The Word in Stone,* pp. 117–19.

75. The translation of Camille Mauclair's critique of modernism was part of an article entitled "Toward a New Architecture," which appeared in *Living Age,* July 1933, pp. 441–43.

76. The 1960 edition of Pevsner's text was entitled *Pioneers of Modern Design: From William Morris to Walter Gropius* (Middlesex, Eng.: Penguin Books).

77. Excerpts from the symposium discussion were later published. See Museum of Modern Art, "What Is Happening to Modern Architecture?" pp. 4–21. Barr's comment appears on p. 7.

78. Mumford's *New Yorker* article was reproduced in *The Museum of Modern Art Bulletin,* Spring 1948. That publication also contained a summary (pp. 2–21) of the symposium that was held at the museum on February 11, 1948. Mumford's call for a "new humanism" was indebted in its conceptual underpinnings to Geoffrey Scott's 1914 publication *The Architecture of Humanism,* which in turn acknowledged a debt to the writings of Theodore Lipps and Bernard Berenson. Within that context, emphasis was placed upon the users' intuitive emotional response and their response to the aesthetic object.

79. The differences between Mumford and Hitchcock as they applied to the 1948 symposium were the subject of Gail Fenske's "Lewis Mumford, Henry-Russell Hitchcock, and the Bay Region Style," in *The Education of the Architect,* ed. Martha Pollak (Cambridge, Mass.: MIT Press, 1997), pp. 37–85. In part, Fenske attributed the difference between the two men to their backgrounds, contrasting Hitchcock's formalist training at Harvard in a tradition of connoisseurship (which emphasized visual qualities over social concerns) with Mumford's informal training and the subsequent influence of writers such as Patrick Geddes (who emphasized the importance of region and place). Leo Marx also underscored the influence of Geddes on Mumford, and he analyzed Mumford's application of organic and machine analogies, pointing out the ideological biases that inform them. See Marx, "Lewis Mumford: Prophet of Organicism," in Hughes and Hughes, *Lewis Mumford,* pp. 164–80.

80. Museum of Modern Art, "What Is Happening to Modern Architecture? pp. 5–8. For Wurster's work, see Treib's *An Everyday Modernism.* The mention of Wurster has direct relevance to the academy design as well, since he served as the dean of the School of Architecture and Planning at MIT (1944–50) while Netsch was in attendance. Treib has noted the more immediate impact of Wright, Schindler, and Neutra on Wurster, in contrast to modernist design approaches imported from European sources during the 1920s. His section "Regionalism, Modernism, and Regional Modernism" also mentions the architects Meem and Belluschi (pp. 31–39).

81. Museum of Modern Art, "What Is Happening to Modern Architecture?

pp. 8–10. Hitchcock had become more convinced of Wright's importance to twentieth-century architecture while mounting the 1940 MoMA retrospective of Wright's work. That exhibition was accompanied by Hitchcock's catalogue *In the Nature of Materials: The Buildings of Frank Lloyd Wright—1887–1941*.

82. Goldhagen and Legault examine this "anxious" response by cold-war architects in their introduction to *Anxious Modernisms*, pp. 11–23.

83. Hitchcock, "The International Style," pp. 89–97.

84. Jory Johnson used this definition of humanism in his discussion of the academy landscaping in his essay "Man as Nature," in Bruegmann, *Modernism at Mid-Century*, pp. 102–19.

85. For a discussion of this aspect of regionalism, see Ksiazek, "Architectural Culture in the Fifties," p. 420.

86. Giedion, *Space, Time, and Architecture*, p. 27.

87. Ferdinand de Saussure, *Course in Linguistics* (New York: McGraw-Hill, 1959), p. 89. Saussure's *Cours de linguistique générale* was based upon lectures he gave between 1907 and 1911.

88. In light of this discussion of ivy, the February 5, 1959, cover of *Engineering News-Record* is ironic. It features a photograph of the Cadet Area, with a caption that reads: "Air Academy: No Ivy on These Walls."

Chapter 4: The Academy's Construction

1. SOM, dwr. 51, file 02.1, "Publicity," *SOM News* 18 (June 15, 1956). Also see Sheri Olson, "Skidmore, Owings and Merrill: The Project Team," in Bruegmann, *Modernism at Mid-Century*, pp. 35–36. On Netsch's promotion, see "Architects Name Two New Partners," *Colorado Springs Gazette Telegraph*, May 24, 1955, p. 6.

2. Burchard, "Recollections of Gordon Bunshaft," p. 187.

3. SOM, dwr. 51, file 02.1, "Publicity," letter from Netsch to Marion Vanderbilt (SOM, New York office) and Virginia Johnson (SOM, Chicago office), May 25, 1956. The memo was sent to provide background information for the June 15, 1956, issue of *SOM News*.

4. Schaffer, "Creating a National Monument," p. 63.

5. Belluschi, "The Meaning of Regionalism in Architecture," p. 136.

6. Clausen, *Pietro Belluschi*. For Belluschi's involvement with SOM, see pp. 192–94; for his design of the Skidmore house, see pp. 242–45 (the house combined a simple Miesian geometric form with diagonal wood paneling on the exterior); for his defense of Saarinen's work at MIT, see p. 205; on Aline Louchheim, see p. 192; for comments on Belluschi's role as an advisor on the academy project, see pp. 206 and 213. Belluschi/SOM existed as a firm from 1951 to 1956.

7. Krinsky, *Gordon Bunshaft*, pp. 150–51 (a photograph on page 151 depicts the three studying site plans together).

8. In 1962, after serving as an advisor on the academy project, Belluschi advised Becket's firm on the Boston Center Plaza Building project. Clausen, *Pietro Belluschi*, pp. 279–80, 284.

9. NA, box 13, REL 2-3-2, News Releases 1955, "Fact Sheet: Air Force Academy Construction Agency," March 15, 1955, p. 2.

10. Ibid.

11. AFA, RG 120, ser. 23, "HQ Office Instruction no. 86-3: Approval Responsibility for design of United States Air Force Academy," signed by Major General Robert W. Burns, Assistant Vice Chief of Staff, U.S. Air Force, 5/13/55. Ferry's letter is contained in NA, box 164, "Construction Project Study Files, 1947–71." Dated September 7, 1955, it was sent to SOM's Chicago office.

12. AFA, RG 120, ser. 23, letter from C. L. Tyler to Director, Air Force Academy Construction Agency, February 20, 1956. The letter was in reference to renegotiating the contract for Title I.

13. Those complaints were recorded in an undated memo from the AFACA, probably sent to Washbourne.

14. NA, box 160, CONS-1, Design and Architectural Style, "Memorandum for Major General Lee B. Washbourne," from Albert E. Stoltz, September 25, 1956.

15. NA, box 160, CONS-1, Design and Architectural Style, "Memorandum for Special Ass't for Installations from Major General Lee B. Washbourne," November 23, 1956.

16. NA, box 28, REL, Relations and Liaison, 1956, letter from Albert E. Stoltz to Major General D. T. Spivey at Culver Military Academy, October 1, 1956.

17. A site office had been opened by SOM in Colorado Springs in 1954, headed by Edward Merrill and supervised by Albert Lockett. It operated until 1959, at one point employing 250 people. Schaffer, "Creating a National Monument," p. 51.

18. NA, box 48, "Memorandum for Director," AFACA from James A. Barnett, Chief, Operations Division, headed "Performance Rating for the Architect-Engineer Firm," November 13, 1958.

19. NA, box 166, Reading File 1956, "Memorandum for Major General A. M. Minton, Director of Installations," from Albert E. Stoltz, November 16, 1958.

20. The original goals were basically achieved. The cadets moved to the permanent site at the end of August 1958, in time for the academic year, and the first class graduated the following spring.

21. SOM, dwr. 55, file 61.4, "AF-SOM Meetings," minutes from the meetings of August 2 and August 3, 1954, at Headquarters United States Air Force, Washington, D.C. (no pagination). The total enrollment figure was later boosted to 2,640.

22. SOM, dwr. 55, file 61.4 "AF-SOM Meetings," minutes from the meeting of October 4, 1954, at Headquarters United States Air Force, Washington, D.C., p. 28.

23. "Models for Air Academy Shown at Colorado Site," *New York Times*, May, 15, 1955, p. 24. For Washbourne's comment, see U.S. Congress, House, Subcommittee of the Committee on Appropriations, June 30, 1955, p. 197.

24. SOM, dwr. 55, file 61.2, "SOM Meetings," letter from Owings to Bunshaft, March 2, 1955, and letters from Owings to Saarinen, Harrison, and Becket, March 2, 1955 (Harrison resigned the following day as a consultant).

25. SOM, dwr. 55, file 61.2, letter from Owings to Bunshaft, March 2, 1955.

26. SOM, dwr. 55, file 61.2, letter from Stoltz to the SOM office in Colorado Springs, March 1, 1955.

27. NA, box 119, "Master Planning 1954–55," memorandum for record, March 16, 1955, signed by Stanley P. Steward, Chief of the Architectural Branch of the Engineering Division of the AFACA.

28. NA, box 119, "Master Planning 1954–55," letter from Stoltz to the SOM office in Colorado Springs, March 23, 1955.

29. SOM, dwr. 55, file 61.2, memo from Stoltz to SOM, General Harmon, General Washbourne, and Colonel Drittler, April 4, 1955.

30. SOM, dwr. 55, file 61.2, letter from Stoltz to the SOM office in Colorado Springs, May 2, 1955.

31. The site plan was discussed in Sanderson, "P/A News Report: Air Academy."

32. A discussion of the individual buildings and specific information regarding design materials was carried in "The United States Air Force Academy" (*Architectural Forum*), pp. 100–109.

33. Ibid., p. 106; "United States Air Force Academy" (*Architectural Record*). The latter article was in the form of an insert without pagination.

34. Also see *Cadet Area Master Plan: United States Air Force Academy Base Comprehensive Plan* (prepared for the academy by SOM in 1985). Page 7 illustrates the 1955 plan, while the following two pages discuss later alterations and additions to the original plan.

35. NA, box 119, "Master Planning 1954–55," memorandum to Academy Superintendent, April 28, 1955. Parts of this letter are nearly exact transcriptions of Netsch's letter to Stoltz, April 20, 1955.

36. Hitchcock, *Painting toward Architecture*, pp. 30–34.

37. SOM, dwr. 55, file 61.4, "AF-SOM Meetings," minutes of the meeting of October 4, 1954, p. 6.

38. Cannon, Holt, and Allen, *History of the United States Air Force Academy*, pp. 307.

39. SOM, dwr. 55, file 61.4, "AF-SOM Meetings," minutes of the meeting of October 4, 1954, p. 13.

40. See Cannon, Holt, and Allen, *History of the United States Air Force Academy*, pp. 307–13. The section contains information on costs and contractors for water systems and reservoirs, plumbing and heating, sewage systems, roads, rodent and predator control, telephone and telegraph systems, gas lines, aerial surveys, and other equipment contracts.

41. Ibid., p. 496. The section "Flight Training and the Academic Curriculum" (pp. 469–96) describes the status of flight training from 1947 to 1954.

42. SOM, dwr. 55, file 61.1a, AFA-SOM Meetings (one-page summaries). The meeting took place in Colorado Springs between SOM representatives and the consultants on June 17, 1955. Members of the AFACA were not present.

43. See *Time*, August 8, 1955, pp. 11–12. Talbott died in March 1957.

44. SOM, dwr. 55, file 61.2, "SOM Meetings," Air Force Academy Conference in Chicago, Ill., Saturday, 1 October 1955." Representatives for SOM at this Chicago meeting included Owings, J. Merrill, Netsch, Bunshaft, and Hartmann.

45. Cannon, Holt, and Allen, *History of the United States Air Force Academy*, p. 311.

46. SOM, dwr. 55, file 61.1A, "For Press Release for May 1955 Exhibition."

47. Burchard, "Recollections of Gordon Bunshaft," p. 188.

48. "Air Force Buildings," p. 118. The plans were prepared by the Architectural Services Branch, Directorate of Installations, U.S. Air Force. In discussing building types, the article stated that the normal dormitory height was three storeys, employing a concrete frame, masonry walls, and a fire-resistant design (p. 119). The discussion included an illustration of a sample dormitory type.

49. Lui, *Spirit and Flight*, p. 89. Interspersed with Lui's photographs of the academy are "Memories" written by Netsch.

50. See, for example, Sullivan's fenestration in the Carson, Pirie, Scott store of 1899–1904.

51. Wright, *An Autobiography*, pp. 218–28.

52. Le Corbusier, *Towards a New Architecture*, pp. 229–65.

53. Hitchcock and Johnson, *International Style*.

54. Gropius, *Scope of Total Architecture*, p. 51.

55. "Air Force Buildings," pp. 118–19.

56. SOM, dwr. 55, file 61.2, "SOM Meetings," SOM Inter-Office Communication from F. A. Byrne to Walter Netsch, September 30, 1955 (Subject: Cadet Quarters).

57. James S. Russell, "Learning from Industry: Architectural Technology at the U.S. Air Force Academy," in Bruegmann, *Modernism at Mid-Century*, pp. 148–55.

58. For John Merrill's defense of the use of the mockups before the Air

Force Contract Appeals Panel, see SOM, dwr. 47, "Various Items," ASBCA No. 4199, June 9–12, 1959, pp. 252–72.

59. AFA, RG 120, ser. 22. See "Tabulation of Votes," an undated document.

60. "Teague Wins U.S.A.F. Contract," *Industrial Design,* April 1956, p. 10.

61. For photographs of Teague's projects, see Zim, Lerner, and Rolfes, *World of Tomorrow*.

62. See Meikle's *Twentieth-Century Limited* for these and other Teague projects. Teague received the Boeing contract in 1957.

63. Walter Dorwin Teague, "Art of the Machine Age," *Industrial Education Magazine* 38 (November 1936): 228.

64. Walter Dorwin Teague, "Basic Principles of Body Design Arise from Universal Rules," *Society of Automotive Engineers Journal* 35 (September 1934): supp. 18.

65. Teague, *Design This Day*. An insightful reading of Teague's design approach is also provided by Terry Smith, *Making the Modern*, pp. 353–84.

66. Walter Dorwin Teague, "Designing for Machines," *Advertising Arts*, April 2, 1930, p. 19.

67. AFA, RG 120, ser. 23, memorandum from John O. Merrill to Mr. John M. Ferry, November 30, 1955.

68. AFA, RG 120, ser. 23, memorandum for the Superintendent, USAF Academy, from John M. Ferry, December 28, 1955.

69. AFA, RG 120, ser. 23, memorandum for Mr. Douglas from John M. Ferry, February 8, 1956.

70. SOM, dwr. 140, memo from Walter Netsch to N. A. Owings, June 27, 1956. Sheri Olson provided an account of Teague's academy work in "A Comprehensive Design Vision," in Bruegmann, *Modernism at Mid-Century*, pp. 140–47.

71. SOM, dwr. 140, memo from N. A. Owings to Walter Netsch, June 28, 1956.

72. NA, box 165, REL 5, Conferences, "Colorado Springs Meeting—Secretary of the Air Force and His Consultants, 16 April 1956."

73. Russell, "Learning from Industry," pp. 149–50.

74. NA, box 165, REL 5, Conferences, "Colorado Springs Meeting—Secretary of the Air Force and His Consultants, 16 April 1956."

75. For details of this presentation, see SOM, dwr. 47, "Various Items," ASBCA No. 4199, June 9–12, 1959, pp. 252–72. In an interview with the author on May 20, 1993, Netsch stated it was Bunshaft's idea to erect the "billboard" of materials.

76. Although the Colorado town of Marble produced marble for past projects, its quarries were not in operation at the time of the academy project, so the marble used in the academy buildings came from the Georgia quarry. See "Local Stone Urged for Air Academy," *Colorado Springs Free Press,* August 21, 1956, p. 1.

77. The cadet quarters were completed at a cost of approximately $15 million. For cost figures on the quarters, see U.S. Congress, House, Subcommittee of the Committee on Appropriations, July 18, 1957, pp. 144–49.

78. Russell, "Learning from Industry," p. 148. In an interview with the author on May 20, 1993, Netsch stated that the use of "Bauhaus colors" was Bunshaft's choice.

79. Lui, *Spirit and Flight*, p. 89.

80. In a letter to Congressman Rogers, who had inquired on behalf of a prospective contractor, Major General Joe Kelly (Director, Legislative Liaison for the Office of the Secretary of the Air Force) reiterated the qualities that Netsch described. In an attempt to placate Rogers, Kelly noted that 186,000 square feet of ceramic tile would be used, while only about 74,000 square feet of the tesserae would be used. See NA, box 166, Congressional 1955–

57, folder 2, letter from Major General Joe Kelly to Representative Byron Rogers, December 21, 1956.

81. Cannon, Holt, and Allen, *History of the United States Air Force Academy*, pp. 267–69.

82. Burchard, "A Conversation about the U.S. Air Force Academy between Walter Netsch and John Burchard," p. 182.

83. SOM, dwr. 55, file 61.2, "SOM Meetings," SOM Inter-Office Communication from Walter Netsch, November 11, 1955.

84. For information and photographs of the dining hall construction, see Sheri Olson, "Raising the Roof: The Dramatic Construction of Mitchell Hall," in Bruegmann, *Modernism at Mid-Century*, pp. 74–75. *Engineering News-Record* reported on the innovative technique in the article "Jacks on Columns Erect Two-Acre Roof at AF Academy," in its January 23, 1958, issue (pp. 26–27). *Architectural Forum* followed with an article entitled "New Way to Raise the Roof" in March 1958 (pp. 126–28). Additional construction information was obtained from SOM project information sheets (one-page documents on each project that include design and engineering details) supplied to the author by SOM's New York office.

85. Peterhaus quoted in Schaffer, "Creating a National Monument," p. 63.

86. The cost was reported in the February 5, 1959, issue of *Engineering News-Record*, p. 42.

87. SOM project information sheet about Fairchild Hall.

88. Cannon, Holt, and Allen, *History of the United States Air Force Academy*, p. 293. For a detailed discussion of the academic building's programmatic needs, see pp. 283–93.

89. AFA, "Interview with Lieutenant Colonel Arthur J. Larsen, Director of the Library, United States Air Force Academy, By the Command Historian, Major Edgar A. Holt, 27 September 1956," in Cannon, Holt, and Allen, *History of the United States Air Force Academy*, appendix, vol. 3, p. 10.

90. SOM, dwr. 55, file 61.2, "SOM Meetings," "Notes for File," signed C. L. Tyler, October 4, 1955.

91. For cost figures on these two buildings, see U.S. Congress, House, Subcommittee of the Committee on Appropriations, July 18, 1957, pp. 144–49. At that time, the estimates for the Social Center and Administrative Building were given as $2.3 million and $3.9 million, respectively.

92. Russell, "Learning from Industry," p. 154.

93. For publications that carried both designs, see the May 15, 1955, issue of the *New York Times*, or the May 22, 1955, issue of the *St. Louis Post-Dispatch*.

94. Danz, *Architecture of Skidmore, Owings, and Merrill*, p. 48.

95. Ibid., p. 40.

96. AFA, RG 120, ser. 23, undated memorandum on the use of aluminum in the Academy construction.

97. *Cadet Area Master Plan: United States Air Force Academy Base Comprehensive Plan*, p. 19.

98. "Mid-City Shopping Center," *Architectural Forum* 98, no. 3 (March 1953): 134.

99. Johnson, "Man as Nature," 110–11.

100. Ibid., p. 116.

101. NA, box 72, Reading File, January 1–June 30, 1958; memo from A. M. Milton, Director of Installations to Colonel S. F. Noonan, Deputy Director for the Air Force Academy Construction Agency, June 5, 1958.

102. For a discussion of Kiley's work on the Cadet Area and Court of Honor, see Johnson, "Man as Nature," pp. 110–14. The quotation appears on p. 114.

103. Ibid., p. 110.

104. Hitchcock, quoted in Danz, *Architecture of Skidmore, Owings and Merrill*, p. 11. The introduction to the text was written by Henry-Russell Hitchcock in December 1961.

Chapter 5: "In God We Trust"

1. For a summary of religion in America in the 1950s, see Miller and Nowak, "Ain't Nobody Here but Us Protestants, Catholics, and Jews," in *The Fifties*, pp. 84–105, and Carter, "Under God, By Act of Congress," in *Another Part of the Fifties*, pp. 114–40.

2. Carter, *Another Part of the Fifties*, p. 121.

3. Herberg quoted in Miller and Nowak, *The Fifties*, p. 102.

4. Turner, *Campus*, p. 188.

5. Mardges Bacon, *Ernest Flagg: Beaux-Arts Architect and Reformer* (Cambridge, Mass.: MIT Press, 1985), p. 131. The Hennebique system was patented by François Hennebique in 1892. In his system, bars of cylindrical section embedded within the concrete were hooked together, reinforcing the concrete and creating a monolithic joint that more effectively resisted stresses. Frampton, *Modern Architecture*, pp. 37–8.

6. Turner, *Campus*, p. 230. Owings later wrote that Goodhue was one of his early heroes and that he was especially inspired by Goodhue's religious architecture, which he compared in its evocative power to Chartres and Mont-Saint-Michel. Owings, *Spaces in Between*, pp. 37–38.

7. *Life*, October 28, 1940, p. 44; ibid., July 7, 1941, pp. 56–57.

8. Reinhold Niebuhr, "Religious Buildings: Tradition and Today's Ethos," *Architectural Record* 114, no. 6 (December 1953): 117–18.

9. "Can Today's Church Contribute Importantly to Today's Architecture," *Architectural Forum* 91, no. 12 (August 1949): 63. The article included a photograph of SOM's Catholic church in Amuay Bay, Venezuela, which incorporated a double cantilevered concrete shell construction in its design. It was shown on the same page as Bruce Goff's quonset-hut-inspired design for the San Lorenzo Community Church in San Lorenzo, California, although SOM's approach to architecture and Goff's approach, indebted to Wright, have little in common.

10. Bruegmann, *Modernism at Mid-Century*, pp. 93–94.

11. NA, box 701, General Correspondence Academy Chapel, memorandum for Special Assistant for Air Academy Matters [Major Witters at the Pentagon] from Major General Charles I. Carpenter, August 3, 1954. That proposal represented simply a doubling of the typical chapel type, which seated three hundred. See "Air Force Buildings," p. 123.

12. NA, box 701, General Correspondence Academy Chapel, minutes of the February 28, 1955, meeting.

13. Sheri Olson, "Lauded and Maligned: The Cadet Chapel," in Bruegmann, *Modernism at Mid-Century*, p. 166.

14. SOM, box 46, ASBCA No. 5593, p. 12. The entire history of the chapel project between June 1, 1955, and January 11, 1959, was meticulously recalled by Walter Netsch in a grueling two-day testimony before the Air Force Contract Appeals Panel. His testimony is contained in Vol. 1 and 2, Chapel, ASBCA No. 5593, January 13–14, 1960, pp. 1–208. Netsch also confirmed many of these facts in personal interviews and telephone conversations with the author over a ten-year period, 1993–2003.

15. Schaffer, "Creating a National Monument," p. 65.

16. "A Benedictine Monastery," *Architectural Forum* 101, no. 1 (July 1954): 148–55.

17. "Church Architects," *Architectural Forum* 100, no. 2 (February 1954): 39.

18. Eugène-Emmanuel Viollet-le-Duc, *The Foundations of Architecture,* trans. Kenneth D. Whitehead (New York: Braziller, 1990), pp. 229–63. The argument was meticulously developed by Viollet-le-Duc in the entry "Style," in his *Dictionnaire raisonné de l'architecture française du Xie au XVIe siècle,* written between 1854 and 1868. The entry appears in the original text in volume 8, pp. 474–97. A discussion of style also appeared in the sixth "Entretien" of Viollet-le-Duc's *Entretiens sur l'architecture,* published circa 1863. A concert hall design based on these principles was published in approximately 1867, in his twelfth "Entretien."

19. Another exaggerated example of this type was Leo von Klenze's Walhalla, near Regensburg (1831–42). His Parthenon-type temple was approached by dramatically steep staircases.

20. "Architects Cautious of Wright's Opinion," *Colorado Springs Free Press,* May 28, 1955, p. 1.

21. "Reaction to Design of Academy Mixed," *Colorado Springs Free Press,* May 16, 1955, p. 1.

22. Owings, *The Space in Between,* p. 159.

23. *Colorado Springs Free Press,* May 16, 1955, p. 3.

24. "Air Academy Design 'Heavenly, Timeless,'" *Denver Post,* May 15, 1955, p. 17A.

25. Netsch, quoted in Lui, *Spirit and Flight,* p. 29.

26. U.S. Congress, House, Subcommittee of the Committee on Appropriations, June 30, 1955, p. 205.

27. Supplemental Appropriation Bill, 1956, Senate, Subcommittee of the Committee on Appropriations, July 11, 1955, p. 181.

28. Supplemental Appropriation Bill, 1956, Senate, Subcommittee of the Committee on Appropriations, July 18, 1955, p. 373.

29. Ibid., p. 380.

30. *U.S. News and World Report,* July 22, 1955, p. 12.

31. *Engineering News-Record* 154, no. 24 (June 16, 1955): 17.

32. NA, box 160, "Design and Architectural Style," letter from Ferry to the Assistant Chief of Staff, Installations, recounting the conversation, June 24, 1955.

33. *Colorado Springs Gazette Telegraph,* July 3, 1955, p. 1. Ironically, SOM had designed the Swift Building at the 1939 New York World's Fair (see figure 16), which had been touted by Swift publicists as resembling "the good-old American hot dog." On the other hand, the fair's *Official Guide Book* described the building as "a gleaming super-airline." See Zim, Lerner, and Rolfe, *World of Tomorrow,* p. 124.

34. The new design appeared in a front-page photograph in the July 3, 1955, issue of the *Colorado Springs Gazette Telegraph* and in the July 10 issue of the *Colorado Springs Free Press.* Nevertheless, the previous design appeared on the cover of the July 10 *New York Times Magazine* and in the July 22 issue of *U.S. News and World Report* (p. 12).

35. Olson, "Lauded and Maligned," p. 159.

36. SOM, dwr. 55, file 61.2, "SOM—Consultant Meetings."

37. SOM, dwr. 55, file 61.1a, "AF—SOM Meetings."

38. Schaffer, "Creating a National Monument," p. 51. Bunshaft stated that it was also Saarinen who selected the Lehman Mesa site for the Cadet Area. See Burchard, "Recollections of Gordon Bunshaft," p. 188.

39. For Belluschi's religious projects, see Clausen, *Spiritual Space.*

40. Burchard, "A Conversation about the U.S. Air Force Academy between Walter Netsch and John Burchard," p. 185.

41. NA, box 59, INS 3-3C, Chapel—Correspondence—1955–57, memo from Albert Stoltz to Major General Lee B. Washbourne, headed "Subject: Design of the Academy Chapel," March 9, 1956.

42. SOM, dwr. 51, file 02.1a, "Publicity—Exhibits, Graphic Arts," memo from Walter Netsch to J. O. Merrill, C. L. Tyler, O. Stark, Bob Cohlmeyer, and Jim Scheeler, headed "Subject: Material for Congressional Hearings," March 2, 1956. Stark assisted in developing individual site plans for the academy, and Cohlmeyer was Netsch's Administrative Assistant on the Academy project.

43. NA, box 59, INS 3-3C, Chapel—Correspondence—1955–57, memo from Lieutenant Colonel Noonan to Major General Washbourne, headed "Subject: Design of the Academy Chapel," April 5, 1956. The magazine article was entitled "The Relation of Architecture to Worship" and appeared in *Church Management* 31, no. 1 (October 1954).

44. U.S. Congress, House, Subcommittee of the Committee on Appropriations, May 15, 1956, p. 91. No members of SOM were present at that hearing.

45. "Final Air Academy Plans Revealed by Quarles: Chapel Only Item Unsettled," *Colorado Springs Free Press,* April 24, 1956, p. 1.

46. NA, box 44, INS 1-2-10, Chapels—1958. Design Directive FY 1955, #42, USAFA, reflected the suggestions made at the February 28, 1955, design meeting. Those directives had first been proposed on July 23, 1954, by Major Witters and Chaplain Witherspoon and were issued as a memorandum (signed by Charles Carpenter, Chief of the Air Force Chaplains) to the Pentagon on August 3, 1954 (Carpenter was also present at the February 28, 1955, meeting). Minutes for the February 28, 1955, meeting are contained in NA, box 701, General Correspondence Academy Chapel.

47. Ibid., Design Directive FY 1955, #42A, USAFA.

48. NA, box 701, General Correspondence Academy Chapel, memo from Brigadier General Stillman to John Ferry, Special Assistant to the Secretary of the Air Force for Installations, 6/9/56. This is also the source for Stillman's remarks that are discussed in the next paragraph.

49. See "Air Force Buildings," p. 123.

50. Drew Pearson, "One Church for Protestant GIs?" *Washington Post,* July 14, 1957, p. E4.

51. SOM, box 46, vols. 1 and 2, Chapel, ASBCA No. 5593, p. 58, discusses Design Directive FY 1957, #6.

52. Ibid., p. 59, discusses Design Directive FY 1957, #6-B.

53. "Air Academy Chapel May Look Like a Row of Teepees After All," *Colorado Springs Free Press,* March 20, 1957, p. 8.

54. SOM, dwr. 51, file 02.1. The file includes the following documents: a letter from SOM's Robertson Ward to Arthur Drexler, Director, Department of Architecture, Museum of Modern Art, January 11, 1957, that discusses samples of materials (paving material, granite, marble, and various glass and aluminum samples) to be included in the exhibition; and a letter from SOM's Ralph Youngren to Drexler, January 15, 1957, that mentions a site plan of the academy area and a chapel elevation and section that reflects its most recent design changes.

55. SOM, dwr. 35, file 62, "SOM—Consultants Meetings," minutes from the March 12, 1957 Consultants' Meeting in Colorado Springs. The quotation is from p. 5 of that document.

56. *Colorado Springs Free Press,* March 13, 1957, p. 1.

57. Burchard, "Recollections of Gordon Bunshaft," p. 188.

58. Lui, *Spirit and Flight,* pp. 47, 117. Netsch confirmed this in discussions with the author.

59. Ibid., p. 109.

60. Walter Netsch, interview with the author, May 20, 1993.

61. Netsch's approach to spatial organization using geometric forms

would lead to projects such as the Chicago Circle Campus of the University of Illinois, constructed between 1963 and 1965, which derived its proportions from the Golden Section. Netsch further developed these notions of geometrically determined space in his "field theory," using an eight-pointed star as the basis for design. He noted that the forms were also being explored by other artists at the time, including Motherwell, Oldenburg, Siegel, Lichtenstein, Indiana, and the Geometricists. For further information on these later designs, see "Campus City, Chicago," *Architectural Forum* 123, no. 3 (September 1965): 23–29; "New Galaxies at Chicago Circle," *Architectural Forum* 133, no. 5 (November 1970): 24–33; and "A New Museum by Walter Netsch of SOM Given Order by His Field Theory," *Architectural Record* 167, no. 1 (January 1980): 111–20.

62. *Congressional Record,* August 6, 1957, p. 13790.

63. Douglas remained secretary of the air force until December 1959. In Netsch's acceptance speech for the AIA's 1996 Twenty-Five Year Award for the chapel design, he singled out Douglas and his support for the chapel stating, "I must admit there would be no Chapel without the great defense by Secretary of the Air Force Douglas" (Lui, *Spirit and Flight,* p. xxiv). Not surprisingly, Owings referred to Douglas in his autobiography as "our favorite secretary." Owings, *Spaces in Between,* p. 155.

64. SOM, dwr. 35, file 62, "SOM—Consultants Meetings," minutes from the May 15, 1957, Consultants' Meeting in Washington, D.C. Representing SOM at the meeting were Owings, J. Merrill, Bunshaft, Netsch, Tyler, and Youngren. Some of this material had been presented several weeks earlier to Quarles, at his final meeting as secretary of the air force. In a memo to other SOM members, Netsch mentioned using the materials from a University of Illinois exhibition in February for that presentation, as well as "new material being prepared on the Chapel" for an April 22 meeting. The memo was dated April 10, 1957. SOM, dwr. 51, file 02.1a, "Publicity—Exhibits, Graphic Arts."

65. SOM, dwr. 72, file P-141-000, "Academy Chapel 1955–Aug. 1959," memo from Netsch to Walter Holtkamp of Holtkamp Organ Company in Cleveland, June 5, 1957.

66. U.S. Congress, House, Subcommittee of the Committee on Appropriations, July 1, 1957, pp. 453–54.

67. U.S. Congress, House, Subcommittee of the Committee on Appropriations, July 11, 1957, p. 155.

68. U.S. Congress, Senate, Subcommittee of the Committee on Appropriations, August 9, 1957.

69. SOM, dwr. 72, file P-141-000, "Academy Chapel 1955–Aug. 1959," memo from Albert E. Stoltz, Deputy Director for the AFACA, to SOM, Chicago, July 31, 1957.

70. *Congressional Record,* August 6, 1957, pp. 13769–70.

71. Ibid., p. 13788.

72. Ibid.

73. Ibid., p. 13789. Both Scrivner's and Siemenski's remarks were repeated in an August 19, 1957, *Time* magazine article entitled "Air Force Gothic."

74. Ibid.

75. Ibid., p. 13790.

76. NA, box 72, Reading File, Jan. 1–June 30, 1957.

77. *Congressional Record,* August 6, 1957. Mahon's remark appeared on p. 13789. The vote was 102–53 to withhold funds.

78. *Congressional Record,* August 7, 1957, pp. 13926–28.

79. NA, box 59, INS 3-3C, Chapel—Correspondence—1955–57, memorandum for the Director of Installations from Capt. Harvey Wexler, September 11, 1957. Also see SOM, ASBCA No. 5593, p. 72, January 13–14, 1960.

80. SOM, dwr. 72, file P-141-000, "Academy Chapel 1955–Aug. 1959," memo from Stoltz to SOM, Colorado Springs, September 20, 1957.

81. NA, box 42, REL 2-2, Civil Liaison 1957, memorandum for Secretary of the Air Force from Col. Noonan, October 23, 1957.

82. NA, box 59, INS 3-3C, Chapel—Correspondence—1955–57, press release by the Office of Information Services, AFACA, November 6, 1957. See also NA, box 42, REL 2-2, Civil Liaison 1957, "Memorandum for Secretary of the Air Force," October 23, 1957.

83. "Academy Designed to Fit Site, Says Local Architect," *Colorado Springs Gazette Telegraph,* September 14, 1957, pp. 1, 8. The "hands in prayer" metaphor had earlier been used to describe Wright's Unitarian Church of 1947 in Shorewood Hills, Wisconsin.

84. "Air Academy Chapel: Professional Opinion," pp. 9, 266.

85. NA, box 59, INS 3-3C, Chapel—Correspondence—1955–57, press release by the Office of Information Services, AFACA, November 6, 1957. See also NA, box 42, REL 2-2, Civil Liaison 1957, "Memorandum for Secretary of the Air Force," October 23, 1957.

86. SOM, dwr. 72, file P-141-000, "Academy Chapel 1955–Aug. 1959."

87. NA, box 166, Reading File 1958, memorandum for Major General Milton, Director of Installations from Colonel Albert Stoltz, Deputy Director for the AFACA, January 20, 1958.

88. SOM, dwr. 72, file P-141-000, "Project Analysis: Academy Chapel."

89. SOM, dwr. 72, file P-141-000, memo from Netsch to the Air Force Academy Construction Agency, February 27, 1958.

90. SOM, dwr. 72, file P-141-000, "Academy Chapel 1955–Aug. 1959," memo from Wegner (of SOM) to Train, March 6, 1958.

91. "New Attack on Chapel Design Threatens Delay at Academy," *Denver Post,* April 25, 1958, p. 21.

92. SOM, dwr. 72, file P-141-000, "Academy Chapel 1955–Aug. 1959," memo from Netsch to Ferry, October 16, 1958, outlining the results of the October 14 meeting. Most of the items mentioned were minor.

93. "AF Academy Set to Invite Bids on Chapel," *Rocky Mountain News,* December 14, 1958, p. 48.

94. Olson, "Lauded and Maligned," p. 158. In an interview with the author on May 20, 1993, Netsch recalled that the criticism came from SOM's Bruce Graham and others.

95. SOM, dwr. 72, file P-141-000, "Academy Chapel 1955–Aug. 1959," memo from Netsch to Bunshaft, May 12, 1958.

96. SOM, box 46, vols. 1 and 2, Chapel, ASBCA No. 5593, p. 120.

97. SOM, dwr. 72, file P-141-000, "Academy Chapel 1955–Aug. 1959," notes from a telephone conversation between Hartmann (of SOM) and Ferry, August 6, 1959.

98. SOM, dwr. 72, file P-141-000, "Academy Chapel 1955–Aug. 1959," memo to John Ferry, Special Assistant for Installations, from Netsch, August 10, 1959.

99. The June 1963 issue of *Architectural Forum* (pp. 122–23) listed the firm of Robert E. McKee, Inc., as one of the largest building contractors in the United States.

100. Olson, "Lauded and Maligned," pp. 156–67. Also, "Air Academy Chapel Shapes up," *Architectural Forum,* May 1961, pp. 128–29.

101. Russell, "Learning from Industry," pp. 152, 154–55.

102. "Spires That Soar," *Time,* July 27, 1962, pp. 34–39. The article was illustrated with four pages of photographs.

103. Lui, *Spirit and Flight,* p. 117.

104. Olson, "Lauded and Maligned," p. 166.

105. Ibid., p. 167. For details of the chapel furnishings, also see the

United States Air Force Academy's publication *The United States Air Force Academy Cadet Chapel.*

106. "Spires That Soar," p. 39.

107. Ibid.

108. Netsch mentioned this in an interview with the author on May 20, 1993.

109. Temko, "Air Academy Chapel," pp. 75–78. Temko championed Saarinen's architectural solutions. His book *Eero Saarinen* was also published in 1962 (New York: Braziller). The chapter entitled "Search for Form: Expression and Overexpression," began with a Sigfried Giedion quotation dealing with monuments and monumentality, and then developed that theme as it related to Saarinen's work.

110. Louis Skidmore died in September 1962. John Merrill would survive until 1975, Owings until 1984, and Bunshaft until 1990. Walter Netsch continues to live and design in Chicago.

111. Robert Venturi, *Complexity and Contradiction in Architecture* (New York: The Museum of Modern Art, 1966). The book was published by the MoMA but it did not accompany an exhibition.

112. SOM, box 46, vols. 1 and 2, Chapel, ASBCA No. 5593, p. 4. Ironically, the firm of Cram, Goodhue, and Ferguson never completed its work for West Point due to a fee dispute which lasted thirty years. Cram's words of warning to future architects on government projects were prophetic: "how wise and accurate in their diagnosis were those who, when by a miracle we won the great competition, had little to say except 'Beware!'" Construction at the Naval Academy at Annapolis, begun in 1899 by Ernest Flagg, was also hampered from the start by Congress members who advocated a competition to chose the architectural firm and demanded a more careful review of the academy's functional requirements. Craig, *Federal Presence*, p. 227. Some of the more contentious issues of the Cram, Goodhue, and Ferguson design are also recounted in Crackel, *West Point*, pp. 176–79.

113. For information on this firm, see Sobiezek, *Architectural Photography of Hedrich-Blessing.*

114. Examples of Hedrich-Blessing's work for SOM included the Great Lakes Training Center, in the August 1942 and March 1943 issues of *Architectural Forum;* the Oak Ridge project, in the October 1945 issue of *Architectural Forum;* and a hospital in Waterloo, Iowa, in the August 1946 issue of *Architectural Record.*

115. This information was provided by Cloyd Brunson in a telephone interview with the author on June 3, 1993. Copies of the Stewarts prints were compiled in monthly albums beginning in July 1957 and extending through May 1965. Coil wrote Netsch that the work was done at Stewarts's expense, except for a few photographs for the Exchange National Bank of Colorado Springs. SOM, dwr. 51, file 02.1, "Publicity—Photography," letter from C. G. Coil of Stewarts to Netsch, August 20, 1959.

116. SOM, dwr. 51, file 02.1, "Publicity—Photography," memo from E. A. Merrill to Jack Train, "Subject: Supply of Photographs for Advertisers," November 21, 1958.

117. "The Air-Age Acropolis," p. 158.

118. "U.S. Air Force Academy," pp. 152–53. The title page (p. 151) also bore a Hedrich-Blessing photograph.

Epilogue

1. SOM, ASBCA No. 5593. The case was heard on January 13–14, 1960. SOM received $146,834.52.

2. NA, box 74, Memorandum for Record signed by William T. Secor, Attorney-Advisor for the AFACA, June 15, 1962. The former claim was ASBCA

6802. The latter had not yet been assigned an ASBCA docket number at the time.

3. Owings, *Spaces in Between,* p. 161.

4. The story, "Air Force May Sue Academy Designers for $2.7 Million," ran on the front page.

5. Owings, *Spaces in Between,* p. 161.

6. The following comments are excerpted and edited from an interview I conducted with Boyle on September 19, 2002, and in subsequent telephone interviews.

7. The project was never realized or well defined. It would have entailed, in part, moving the offices of the commandant from their location in the west wing of the library.

8. Tom Rohan, "Air-Conditioned Unit," *Wallpaper,* Special Edition, 1998, p. 88.

9. Lui, *Spirit and Flight,* p. 27.

Appendix 1: Applicants for the USAFA Competition

1. NA, box 118, Reading File, list signed by Leo Erler, Director, Air Force Academy Construction Agency, June 4, 1954.

2. One of the firms that submitted an application after this list was compiled was the joint venture firm of Mies van der Rohe, Philip C. Johnson and Pace Associates, Airways Engineering Corporation, and Frederic R. Harris, Incorporated. NA, box 13, REL 1-2, Congressional Inquiries, May 1, 1954–September 15, 1954, letter from Brigadier General Joe Kelly to Ernest R. Underwood, Professional Staff Member of the Committee on Appropriations of the United States Senate, July 7, 1954. Kelly responded to Underwood's letter of recommendation on behalf of the joint venture.

3. Several of the firms that eventually made the list of the eight finalists combined as joint ventures: Pereira and Luckman joined with Giffels and Vallet Incorporated; Harrison and Abramovitz joined with Gugler, Kimball and Husted and Harbeson, Hough, Livingston, and Larson; and Eero Saarinen and Associates joined with Smith, Hinchman, and Grylls, Incorporated and Knappen, Tippetts, Abbett, McCarthy. Kittyhawk Associates, another joint venture firm that reached the finalists, included the following firms: Graham, Anderson, Probst, and White; Robert and Company Associates; and George B. Cunningham.

4. AFAP Architects and Engineers, for example, was comprised of an impressive eleven firms that included: Roberts and Schaeffer (Chicago and New York); Hellmuth, Yamasaki, and Leinweber (St. Louis); Karsunky, Weller, and Gooch (Washington, D.C.); Justement, Elam, and Darby (Washington, D.C.); Kuehne, Brooks, and Barr (Austin); Page, Sutherland, and Page (Austin); Phelps, Dowees, and Simmons (San Antonio); Stone and Pitts (Austin); Carber and Burgees (Fort Worth); Linder, Hodgson, and Wright (Denver); and Horner and Shifrin (St. Louis). NA, box 13, REL 1-2, Congressional Inquiries, May 1, 1954–September 15, 1954.

Appendix 2: Other Finalists in the USAFA Competition

1. For Pereira's background, see "William the Conqueror," *Architectural Forum* 85, no. 3 (September 1946): 114–16, 122, 124, 128. For the Lake County Tuberculosis Sanatorium, see Mock, *Built in U.S.A.,* pp. 92–93. For more on Pereira's work during the 1950s, see the following: "CBS-TV City," *Architectural Forum* 98, no. 3 (March 1953): 146–49; "Hospital Cores in Doctor's Offices," *Architectural Forum* 98, no. 5 (May 1953): 128–29; "Bank Planning, Phoenix Arizona," *Progressive Architecture* 33, no. 10 (October 1952): 90–91; "Progressive Architecture for Defense," *Progressive Architecture* 33, no. 1 (January 1952): 86–87. For Pereira and Luckman's work in

Colorado at the National Bureau of Standards in Boulder, see "Industrial Laboratory," *Architectural Forum* 102, no. 3 (March 1955): 158–61.

2. For the background and work of Giffels and Vallet, Inc., L. Rossetti, see "Today's Industrial Building," *Architectural Forum* 94, no. 5 (May 1951): 144–59.

3. For information regarding Harrison, see Newhouse, *Wallace K. Harrison.* For information on the Alcoa commissions, see "Aluminum," *Architectural Forum* 112, no. 6 (June 1949): 76–80, and "Alcoa Building: Innovations in Aluminum," *Architectural Record* 112, no. 2 (August 1952): 120–27. For the Alcoa project in Pittsburgh, Harrison and Abramovitz entered into a joint venture with Mitchell and Ritchey, Associate Architects (this firm applied for the academy commission as part of Kittyhawk Associates) and used Moran, Proctor, Mueser, and Rutledge (one of the joint venture firms with SOM during the academy competition) as consultants on the foundations. For information on the Corning Center, see "Glass Center, Corning, N.Y.," *Architectural Forum* 95, no. 2 (August 1951): 125–31. For a project with a contrasting design approach, see "The Most Controversial Building in Ohio," *Architectural Forum* 100, no. 1 (January 1954): 124–29. The article dealt with the firm's design for Oberlin Auditorium, which was sculptural in nature and employed the use of limestone facing on the exterior. For the firm's embassy work, see Loeffler, *Architecture of Diplomacy.*

4. AFA, RG 103, ser. 1, memo from Brigadier General H. W. Ehrgott for Special Assistant for Air Force Academy Matters, January 8, 1954.

5. On Husted, see "Blast Resistant Buildings," *Architectural Forum* 95, no. 5 (November 1951): 158. Husted's obituary was carried in the November 1967 issue of *Progressive Architecture* (pp. 56–58).

6. See Sanderson, "P/A News Report: Air Academy."

7. For projects of Harbeson, Hough, Livingston, and Larson, see the following: "U.S. Naval Hospital, Beaufort, S.C.," *Architectural Record* 107, no. 4 (April 1950): 101–10; "Big Psychiatric Laboratory," *Architectural Forum* 95, no. 5 (November 1951): 150–53; "Neurological Building, Philadelphia General Hospital," *Architectural Record* 111, no. 2 (February 1952): 120–27. No precise date or reason has been found for the addition of Roy Larson as a consultant on the academy project. His name first appears on lists of the consultants in January 1956, along with the names of Belluschi, Saarinen, and Becket.

8. See AFA, RG 103, ser. 1, Proposal of cost estimates from Husted to Director of Installations, February 1, 1954.

9. See "St. Claire's Hospital, Schenectady N.Y.," *Architectural Record* 107, no. 2 (February 1950): 119–23; and "Navy Buildings," *Architectural Record* 112, no. 3 (September 1952): 177–80. In the former article, the firm is identified as York and Sawyer, Architects; in the latter article, the firm is identified as the Office of York and Sawyer: Architects Kiff, Colean, Voss and

Souder. In his autobiography, Owings condemned the firm's "cavalier application" of classical motifs to its architectural projects. See Owings, *Spaces in Between,* p. 36.

10. For Anderson's Paris Prize design, see "Paris Prize Awarded," *Pencil Points,* August 1930, pp. 661–64. For the firm's MIT work see Mock, *Built in U.S.A.,* pp. 82–83, and "M.I.T. Laboratory: The Building," *Progressive Architecture* 34, no. 10 (October 1953): 79–91. Also see Shillaber's history of MIT.

11. See Allan Temko, *Eero Saarinen* (New York: Braziller, 1962). For the importance of the competitions of the 1930's to modern architecture, see Kornwolf, *Modernism in America.* For Saarinen's embassy work, see Loeffler, *Architecture of Diplomacy.*

12. Knappen's obituary was carried in the May 1951 issue of *Architectural Record* (p. 258).

13. The firm of Graham, Burnham, and Company was formed after the death of Daniel Burnham in 1912 but was dissolved in 1917, after which the partnership of Graham, Anderson, Probst, and White was formed. For information on the work of the firm of Graham, Anderson, Probst, and White prior to its 1937 restructuring, see Sally A. Kitt Chappell, *Architecture and Planning of Graham, Anderson, Probst, and White, 1912–1936: Transforming Tradition* (Chicago: University of Chicago Press, 1992).

14. The firm of Mitchell and Ritchey is discussed in Kornwolf, *Modernism in America,* pp. 256, 259.

15. "Should the Design of Today's School be Domestic . . . or Institutional," *Architectural Forum* 99, no. 4 (October 1953): 166–68.

16. For more on Kump's school designs, see "For Technical Training," *Progressive Architecture* 35, no. 4 (April 1954): 88–95; "An Undergraduate Dormitory," *Arts and Architecture* 70, no. 7 (July 1953): 22.

17. For the work of Bush-Brown, Gailey, and Heffernan, Architects, see "Harrison Textile Engineering Building," *Architectural Record* 107, no. 6 (June 1950): 124–29, and "Progressive Architecture for Public Use—1952," *Progressive Architecture* 33, no. 1 (January 1952): 78–9.

18. For the work of Robert and Company, see the following: "Progressive Architecture for Public Use—1952," *Progressive Architecture* 33, no. 1 (January 1952): 84; "Bottom-Lighted Office," *Architectural Forum* 97, no. 5 (November 1952): 126–27; "Planned for Expandability Plus Economy," *Architectural Record* 112, no. 4 (October 1952): 206–13. The last article cited dealt with a hospital in Quincy, Florida—a modernist design with brick facing.

19. Brief discussions and some photographs of Buell's work appeared in Noel's *Buildings of Colorado.*

20. A source for the work of Voorhees, Walker, Foley, and Smith is Walker's autobiography, *Ralph Walker* (New York: Henahan House, 1957). Also see, "Voorhees Walker Foley & Smith," *Architectural Forum* 101, no. 11 (November 1954): 140.

Selected Bibliography

Archival Sources

National Archives, Denver Federal Records Center
  U.S. Air Force Academy Construction Agency Documents
Skidmore, Owings, and Merrill, Chicago
  Corporate Archives
U.S. Air Force Academy Library, Colorado Springs
  Special Collections Branch

Books, Journals, and Public Records

Abbott, Carl. *The Metropolitan Frontier: Cities in the American West.* Tucson:
  University of Arizona Press, 1993.
———. *The New Urban America: Growth and Politics in Sunbelt Cities.* Chapel
  Hill: University of North Carolina Press, 1981.
Adams, Ansel, and Mary Alinder. *Ansel Adams: An Autobiography.* Boston:
  Little, Brown, 1985.
———. *This Is the American Earth.* San Francisco: Sierra Club, 1960.
"Air Academy: A Better Man for a Better Plane." *Newsweek,* June 6, 1955, pp.
  59–65.
"Air Academy: U.S. Air Force Exhibits Plans at Colorado Springs." *Progres-
  sive Architecture* 36, no. 6 (June 1955): 2–5.
"Air Academy Chapel: Professional Opinion." *Architectural Record* 122, no. 6
  (December 1957): 9, 266, 272, 278.
"Air Academy Chapel Shapes Up." *Architectural Forum* 114, no. 5 (June
  1961): 128–29.
"Air Academy Design Brawl." *Architectural Forum* 103, no. 8 (August 1955):
  9–13.
"The Air-Age Acropolis." *Architectural Forum* 110, no. 6 (June 1959): 158–65.
"Air Force Buildings: Architectural Record's Building Types Study, Number
  182." *Architectural Record* 111, no. 1 (January 1952): 95–126.
"Air Force Gothic." *Time,* August 19, 1957, p. 62.
Alinder, Mary Street. *Ansel Adams: A Biography.* New York: Henry Holt,
  1996.
Alinder, James, and John Szarkowski. *Ansel Adams: Classic Images.* Boston:
  Little, Brown, 1985.
"The Architects from 'Skid's Row.'" *Fortune,* January 1958, pp. 137–40.
"Architecture to Represent America Abroad." *Architectural Record* 117, no. 5
  (May 1955): 187–92.
Belluschi, Pietro. "The Meaning of Regionalism in Architecture." *Architec-
  tural Record* 118, no. 6 (December 1955): 131–39.
Berge, Wendell. *Economic Freedom for the West.* Lincoln: University of Ne-
  braska Press, 1946.

Betsky, Aaron. *James Gamble Rogers and the Architecture of Pragmatism.* Cambridge, Mass.: MIT Press, 1994.

Bilstein, Roger. *Flight in America 1900–1983: From the Wrights to the Astronauts.* Baltimore: Johns Hopkins University Press, 1984.

Bleecker, Samuel E. *The Politics of Architecture: A Perspective on Nelson A. Rockefeller.* New York: Rutledge Press, 1981.

Boyer, Paul. *By the Bomb's Early Light: American Thought and Culture at the Dawn of the Atomic Age.* New York: Pantheon, 1985.

"Branch Post Office, Denver, Colorado." *Architectural Record* 112, no. 3 (August 1952): 152.

Bright, Charles. *The Jet Makers: The Aerospace Industry from 1945 to 1972.* Lawrence: Regents Press of Kansas, 1978.

Bright, Deborah. "The Public Landscape of Postwar America." In *Multiple Views,* edited by Daniel P. Younger, pp. 329–61. Albuquerque: University of New Mexico Press, 1991.

Bruegmann, Robert. *The Architects and the City: Holabird and Roche of Chicago, 1880–1918.* Chicago: University of Chicago Press, 1997.

——, ed. *Modernism at Mid-Century: The Architecture of the United States Air Force Academy.* Chicago: University of Chicago Press, 1994.

Burchard, John, and Albert Bush-Brown. *The Architecture of America: A Social and Cultural History.* Boston: Little, Brown, 1961.

Bush-Brown, Albert. Introduction and regional prefaces to *Skidmore, Owings, and Merrill: Architecture and Urbanism, 1973–1983.* New York: Van Nostrand Reinhold, 1984.

Byrd, Warren T., and Reuben M. Rainey. *The Work of Dan Kiley: A Dialogue of Design Theory.* Charlottesville: University of Virginia School of Architecture, 1983.

Cannon, M. Hamlin, and Henry S. Fellerman. *Quest for an Air Force Academy.* Colorado Springs: United States Air Force Academy, 1947.

Cannon, M. Hamlin, Edgar A. Holt, and Carlos R. Allen. *History of the United States Air Force Academy: 27 July 1954 to 12 June 1956.* Colorado Springs: United States Air Force Academy, 1957.

Cannon, M. Hamlin, Edgar A. Holt, and Elizabeth Wiley. *History of the United States Air Force Academy: 10 June 1957 to 11 June 1958.* Colorado Springs: United States Air Force Academy, 1960.

——. *History of the United States Air Force Academy: 10 June 1958 to 30 June 1959.* Colorado Springs: United States Air Force Academy, 1961.

Cannon, M. Hamlin, Edgar A. Holt, Victor H. Cohen, and Emory H. Dixon. *History of the United States Air Force Academy: 13 June 1956 to 9 June 1957.* Colorado Springs: United States Air Force Academy, 1958.

Carter, Paul A. *Another Part of the Fifties.* New York: Columbia University Press, 1983.

Cetto, Max L. *Modern Architecture in Mexico.* New York: Praeger, 1961.

Chanzit, Gwen Finkel. *Herbert Bayer and Modernist Design in America.* Ann Arbor: UMI Research Press, 1987.

Clausen, Meredith L. *Pietro Belluschi: Modern American Architect.* Cambridge, Mass.: MIT Press, 1994.

——. *Spiritual Space: The Religious Architecture of Pietro Belluschi.* Seattle: University of Washington Press, 1992.

Collins, Christiane, and George Collins. "Monumentality: A Critical Matter in Modern Architecture." *Harvard Architecture Review 4: Monumentality and the City* (Spring 1984): 14–35.

Collins, George, Adolf Placzek, et al. "Modern Architecture Symposium (MAS 1964): The Decade 1929–1939." *Journal of the Society of Architectural Historians* 24, no. 1 (March 1965): 3–107.

Colomina, Beatriz. *Privacy and Publicity: Modern Architecture as Mass Media.* Cambridge, Mass.: MIT Press, 1994.

"Congressional Architecture Critics Object to the Contemporary Design of US Embassies." *Architectural Forum* 100, no. 3 (March 1954): 45.

Congressional Record. House. 84th Cong., 1st Sess., vol. 101, pt. 7, June 16–June 30, 1955. Washington, D.C.: U.S. Government Printing Office, 1955.

——. House. 84th Cong., 1st Sess., vol. 101, pt. 8, July 1–July 19, 1955. Washington, D.C.: U.S. Government Printing Office, 1955.

——. House. 85th Cong., 1st Sess., vol. 101, pt. 10, July 26–August 8, 1957. Washington, D.C.: U.S. Government Printing Office, 1957.

——. Senate. 85th Cong., 2d Sess., vol. 104, pt. 1, January 7–January 30, 1958. Washington, D.C.: U.S. Government Printing Office, 1958.

——. Appendix. 85th Cong., 2d Sess., vol. 1. Washington, D.C.: U.S. Government Printing Office, 1958.

"Controversy over a Chapel." *U.S. News and World Report,* January 17, 1958, p. 14.

Corn, Joseph. *Imagining Tomorrow: History, Technology, and the American Future.* Cambridge, Mass.: MIT Press, 1986.

——. *The Winged Gospel: America's Romance with Aviation, 1900–1950.* New York: Oxford University Press, 1983.

Crackel, Theodore J. *West Point: A Bicentennial History.* Lawrence: University of Kansas Press, 2002.

Craig, Lois. *The Federal Presence: Architecture, Politics and National Design.* Cambridge, Mass.: MIT Press, 1978.

Curtis, William J. R. "Modern Architecture, Monumentality, and the Meaning of Institutions." *Harvard Architectural Review 4: Monumentality and the City* (Spring 1984): 68–69.

Danz, Ernst. *Architecture of Skidmore, Owings, and Merrill, 1950–1962.* New York: Praeger, 1963.

"Designers for a Busy World," *Newsweek,* May 4, 1959, pp. 97–100.

Doordan, Dennis P. *Building Modern Italy: Italian Architecture, 1914–1936.* Princeton: Princeton Architectural Press, 1988.

Dorsett, Lyle W. *The Queen City: A History of Denver.* Boulder: Pruett, 1977.

Drexler, Arthur, and Henry-Russell Hitchcock, eds. *Built in U.S.A.: Post-War Architecture.* New York: Museum of Modern Art, 1952.

Emme, Eugene, ed. *The Impact of Air Power: National Security and World Politics.* New York: Van Nostrand, 1959.

Fagan, George V. *The Air Force Academy: An Illustrated History.* Boulder: Johnson Books, 1988.

Frampton, Kenneth. *Modern Architecture.* New York: Oxford University Press, 1980.

Garnsey, Morris. *America's New Frontier: The Mountain West.* New York: Knopf, 1950.

Geddes, Norman Bel. *Horizons.* Boston: Little, Brown, 1932.

Gelernter, David. *1939: The Lost World of the Fair.* New York: Free Press, 1995.

"General Harmon Tells All About 'The West Point of the Air.'" *U.S. News and World Report,* May 27, 1955, pp. 28–32.

Ghirardo, Diane. "Architects, Exhibitions, and the Politics of Culture in Fascist Italy." *Journal of Architectural Education* 45, no. 2 (February 1992): 67–75.

Giedion, Sigfried. *Architecture You and Me.* Cambridge, Mass.: Harvard University Press, 1958.

——. *Space, Time, and Architecture.* Cambridge, Mass.: Harvard University Press, 1954.

Goldhagen, Sarah Williams, and Réjean Legault, eds. *Anxious Modernisms: Experimentations in Postwar Architectural Culture.* Cambridge, Mass.: MIT Press, 2000.

Gordon, Elizabeth. "The Threats to the Next America." *House Beautiful,* April 1953, pp. 126–31.

Gropius, Walter. "Eight Steps toward a Solid Architecture," *Architectural Forum* 100, no. 2 (February 1954): 156–57, 178, 182.

———. "Gropius Appraises Today's Architect." *Architectural Forum* 96, no. 5 (May 1952): 111–13.

———. *Scope of Total Architecture.* New York: Collier, 1943.

"Group Practice." *Architectural Review* 114, no. 681 (September 1953): 145–51.

Grossman, Elizabeth Greenwell. *The Civic Architecture of Paul Cret.* Cambridge: Cambridge University Press, 1996.

Halberstam, David. *The Fifties.* New York: Villard, 1993.

Haskell, Douglas. "To-morrow and the World's Fair." *Architectural Forum* 88, no. 2 (August 1940): 65–72.

Hitchcock, Henry-Russell. *Architecture: Nineteenth and Twentieth Centuries.* Middlesex, Eng.: Penguin, 1958.

———. "The Architecture of Bureaucracy and the Architecture of Genius." *Architectural Review* 101, no. 601 (April 1947): 3–6.

———. "In Search of a New Monumentality." *Architectural Review* 104, no. 621 (September 1948): 117–27.

———. "The International Style: Twenty Years After." *Architectural Record* 110, no. 2 (August 1951): 89–97.

———. *Modern Architecture: Romanticism and Reintegration.* New York: Payson and Clarke, 1929.

———. *Painting toward Architecture.* New York: Duell, Sloan, and Pearce, 1948.

Hitchcock, Henry-Russell, and Philip Johnson. *The International Style: Architecture since 1922.* New York: Norton, 1932.

Hughes, Thomas P., and Agatha C. Hughes. *Lewis Mumford: Public Intellectual.* New York: Oxford University Press, 1990.

Hunt, Dudley. *Total Design: Architecture of Welton Becket and Associates.* New York: McGraw-Hill, 1972.

"Jacks on Columns Erect Two-Acre Roof at AF Academy." *Engineering News-Record* 160, no. 4 (January 23, 1958): 26–27.

Janowitz, Morris. *Sociology and the Military Establishment.* New York: Russell Sage Foundation, 1959.

Jencks, Charles. *Modern Movements in Architecture.* New York: Anchor Press, 1973.

Johnson, Donald. *Frank Lloyd Wright versus America: The 1930's.* Cambridge, Mass.: MIT Press, 1990.

Kornwolf, James, ed. *Modernism in America, 1937–1941: A Catalogue and Exhibition of Four Architectural Competitions.* Williamsburg, Va.: Joseph and Margaret Muscarelle Museum of Art, 1985.

Krinsky, Carol. *Gordon Bunshaft of Skidmore, Owings, and Merrill.* Cambridge, Mass.: MIT Press, 1988.

Ksiazek, Sarah. "Architectural Culture in the Fifties: Louis Kahn and the National Assembly Complex in Dhaka." *Journal of the Society of Architectural Historians* 52, no. 4 (December 1993): 416–35.

Landis, Lawrence. *The Story of the U.S. Air Force Academy.* New York: Holt, Rinehart, and Winston, 1959.

Lane, Barbara. *Architecture and Politics in Germany.* Cambridge, Mass.: Harvard University Press, 1968.

Lax, Eric. "William A. Garnett." *American Photographer* 4, no. 2 (February 1980): 50–60.

Le Corbusier. *Towards a New Architecture.* Translated by Frederick Etchells. New York: Dover, 1986. (Originally published 1923 under the title *Vers une architecture.*)

Lee, Antoinette. *Architects to the Nation: The Rise and Decline of the Supervising Architect's Office.* New York: Oxford University Press, 2000.

Lemann, Nicholas. *Out of the Forties.* New York: Simon and Schuster, 1983.

Leonard, Stephen, and Thomas Noel. *Denver: Mining Town to Metropolis.* Boulder: University of Colorado Press, 1990.

Limerick, Patricia. *The Legacy of Conquest: The Unbroken Past of the American West.* New York: Norton, 1987.

Loeffler, Jane C. *The Architecture of Diplomacy: Building America's Embassies.* New York: Princeton Architectural Press, 1998.

Lui, Elizabeth Gill. *Spirit and Flight: A Photographic Salute to the United States Air Force Academy.* Colorado Springs: United States Air Force Academy, 1996.

Marx, Leo. *The Machine in the Garden: Technology and the Pastoral Ideal in America.* New York: Oxford University Press, 1964.

Meikle, Jeffrey. *Twentieth-Century Limited: Industrial Design in America, 1925–1939.* Philadelphia: Temple University Press, 1979.

Merk, Frederick. *Manifest Destiny and Mission in American History: A Reinterpretation.* New York: Vintage, 1963.

Miller, Douglas T., and Marion Nowak. *The Fifties: The Way We Really Were.* New York: Doubleday, 1977.

Mills, C. Wright. *The Power Elite.* New York: Oxford University Press, 1956.

Mock, Elizabeth, ed. *Built in U.S.A.: 1932–1944.* New York: Museum of Modern Art, 1944.

Museum of Modern Art. "Skidmore, Owings, and Merrill, Architects, U.S.A." *Museum of Modern Art Bulletin* 18, no. 1 (Fall 1950).

———. *Modern Architecture International Exhibition.* New York: Museum of Modern Art, 1932.

———. "What Is Happening to Modern Architecture?" *Museum of Modern Art Bulletin* 15, no. 3 (Spring 1948): 1–21.

Nash, Gerald. *The American West in the Twentieth Century: A Short History of an Urban Oasis.* Englewood Cliffs, N.J.: Prentice-Hall, 1973.

———. *The American West Transformed: The Impact of the Second World War.* Bloomington: Indiana University Press, 1985.

———. *Creating the West: Historical Interpretations 1890–1990.* Albuquerque: University of New Mexico Press, 1991.

Nash, Roderick. *Wilderness and the American Mind.* New Haven: Yale University Press, 1967.

Newhouse, Victoria. *Wallace K. Harrison, Architect.* New York: Rizzoli, 1989.

"New Way to Raise the Roof." *Architectural Forum* 108, no. 3 (March 1958): 126–28.

Noel, Thomas J. *Buildings of Colorado.* New York: Oxford University Press, 1997.

Nye, David. *American Technological Sublime.* Cambridge, Mass.: MIT Press, 1994.

Oakley, J. Ronald. *God's Country: America in the Fifties.* New York: Dembner Books, 1986.

Official Guide: Book of the Fair 1933. Chicago: Century of Progress Administration Building, 1933.

Owings, Nathaniel A. "Amusement Features of the Exposition." *Architectural Record* 73, no. 5 (May 1933): 354–62.

Owings, Nathaniel Alexander. *The American Aesthetic.* New York: Harper and Row, 1969.

———. *The Spaces in Between: An Architect's Journey.* Boston: Houghton Mifflin, 1973.

Parmet, Herbert S. *Eisenhower and the American Crusades.* New York: Macmillan, 1972.

Payne, Alina. "Rudolf Wittkower and Architectural Principles in the Age of Modernism." *Journal of the Society of Architectural Historians* 53, no. 3 (September 1994): 322–42.

Pevsner, Nikolaus. *Pioneers of Modern Design: From William Morris to Walter Gropius.* Middlesex, Eng.: Penguin Books, 1960 (originally published 1936 under the title *Pioneers of the Modern Movement*).

Pommer, Richard, and Christian Otto. *Weissenhof 1927 and the Modern Movement in Architecture.* Chicago: University of Chicago Press, 1991.

Powers, Richard Gid. "The Cold War in the Rockies: American Ideology and the Air Force Academy Design." *Art Journal* 33, no. 4 (Summer 1974): 304–13.

"Production Practice." *Progressive Architecture* 36, no. 3 (March 1955): 116–17.

Riley, Terence. *The International Style: Exhibition 15 and the Museum of Modern Art.* New York: Rizzoli, 1992.

Riley, Terence, and Edward Eigen. "Between the Museum and the Marketplace: Selling Good Design." In *The Museum of Modern Art at Mid-Century,* edited by Barbara Ross Geiger and Lucy O'Brien, pp. 150–79. New York: Abrams, 1994.

Robinson, George. *The Oak Ridge Story.* Kingsport, Tenn.: Southern Publishers, 1950.

Rovere, Richard. *The Eisenhower Years.* New York: Farrar, Straus, and Cudahy, 1956.

Sanderson, George A. "P/A News Report: Air Academy." *Progressive Architecture* 36, no. 6 (June 1955): 2–5.

Schwartz, Frederic J. *The Werkbund: Design Theory and Mass Culture before the First World War.* New Haven: Yale University Press, 1996.

Scobie, Alex. *Hitler's State Architecture: The Impact of Classical Antiquity.* University Park: Pennsylvania State University Press, 1990.

Shillaber, Caroline. *Massachusetts Institute of Technology School of Architecture and Planning, 1861–1961: A Hundred Year Chronicle.* Cambridge, Mass.: MIT Press, 1963.

Skidmore, Louis. "The Hall of Science: A Century of Progress Exposition." *Architectural Forum* 57, no. 4 (October 1932): 361–66.

———. "Planning and Planners." *Architectural Forum* 59, no. 7 (July 1933): 29–32.

———. "Planning the Exposition Displays." *Architectural Record* 73, no. 5 (May 1933): 345–46.

"Skirt or Wigwam?" *U.S. News and World Report,* July 22, 1955, p. 12.

Sloan, James Allen. *The Romance of Commerce and Culture: Capitalism, Modernism, and the Chicago-Aspen Crusade for Cultural Reform.* Chicago: University of Chicago Press, 1983.

Slotkin, Richard. *The Fatal Environment: The Myth of the Frontier in the Age of Industrialization.* New York: Atheneum, 1985.

Smith, Henry Nash. *Virgin Land: The American West as Symbol and Myth.* Cambridge, Mass.: Harvard University Press, 1950.

Smith, Michael, ed. *Possible Dreams.* Dearborn, Mich.: Henry Ford Museum, 1992.

Smith, Terry. *Making the Modern: Industry, Art, and Design in America.* Chicago: University of Chicago Press, 1993.

Sobieszek, Robert. *The Architectural Photography of Hedrich-Blessing.* New York: Holt, Reinhart, and Winston, 1984.

"SOM Organization." *Bauen and Wohnen* 4 (April 1957).

Spaulding, Jonathan. *Ansel Adams and the American Landscape: A Biography.* Berkeley: University of California Press, 1995.

"Spired Monstrosity?" *America,* August 24, 1957, pp. 514–15.

"Spires That Soar." *Time,* July 27, 1962, pp. 34–39.

Stiehm, Judith. *Bring Me Men, and Women.* Berkeley: University of California Press, 1981.

Sweetman, Jack. *The U.S. Naval Academy: An Illustrated History.* Annapolis: Naval Institute Press, 1984.

Taylor, Joshua, with a contribution by John G. Cawelti. *America as Art.* Washington D.C.: Smithsonian Institution Press, 1976.

Taylor, Robert. *The Word in Stone: The Role of Architecture in the National Socialist Ideology.* Berkeley: University of California Press, 1974.

Teague, Walter Dorwin. *Design This Day: The Technique of Order in the Machine Age.* New York: Harcourt, Brace, 1940.

Temko, Allan. "The Air Academy Chapel—A Critical Appraisal." *Architectural Forum* 117, no. 6 (December 1962): 75–78.

Treib, Marc. *An Everyday Modernism: The Houses of William Wurster.* Berkeley: University of California Press, 1995.

Turner, Paul Venable. *Campus: An American Planning Tradition.* Cambridge, Mass.: MIT Press, 1984.

"$2 Billion Worth of Design By Conference." *Business Week,* December 4, 1954, pp. 96–97, 100–104.

Ubbelohde, Carl, Maxine Benson, and Duane A. Smith. *A Colorado History.* Boulder: Pruett, 1965.

"The United States Air Force Academy." *Architectural Forum* 102, no. 6 (June 1955): 100–109.

"United States Air Force Academy." *Architectural Record* 117, no. 6 (June 1955): insert following p. 172.

"The U.S. Air Force Academy." *Architectural Record* 119, no. 3 (March 1956): 162a–62d.

"U.S. Air Force Academy." *Architectural Record* 125, no. 7 (June 1959): 151–62.

"U.S. Architecture Abroad." *Architectural Forum* 98, no. 3 (March 1953): 101–15.

U.S. House Subcommittee of the Committee on Appropriations. *Military Construction Appropriations for 1956.* 84th Cong., 1st Sess., 1955.

———. *Military Construction Appropriations for 1957.* 84th Cong., 2d Sess., 1956.

———. *Military Construction Appropriations for 1958.* 85th Cong., 1st Sess., 1957.

U.S. Senate Subcommittee of the Committee on Appropriations. *The Supplemental Appropriation Bill, 1956.* 84th Cong., 1st Sess., 1955.

Whitford, Frank. *Bauhaus.* London: Thames and Hudson, 1984.

Wiley, Peter, and Robert Gottlieb. *Empires in the Sun: The Rise of the New American West.* New York: Putnam, 1982.

"With Steeple." *Time,* July 18, 1955, p. 38.

Wright, Frank Lloyd. *An Autobiography.* 1932. New York: Horizon Press, 1977.

———. *Frank Lloyd Wright: Collected Writings.* Edited by Bruce Brooks Pfeiffer. New York: Rizzoli, 1992.

Zim, Larry, Mel Lerner, and Herbert Rolfes. *The World of Tomorrow: The 1939 World's Fair.* New York: Harper and Row, 1988.

Index

ON THE WINGS OF MODERNISM

The University of Illinois Press
is a founding member of the
Association of American University Presses.

———————————————————————

Composed in 9.5/13.5 Meta Normal
with Meta display
by Jim Proefrock
at the University of Illinois Press
Designed by Paula Newcomb
Manufactured by Sheridan Books, Inc.

University of Illinois Press
1325 South Oak Street
Champaign, IL 61820-6903
www.press.uillinois.edu

ROBERT ALLEN NAUMAN teaches the history of art and architecture in the Department of Art and Art History at the University of Colorado at Boulder.